MASALA

Much more than an Indian Cookery Book

Alain Vanden Abeele
Christophe Lambert
Sam Paret

Photography
Christophe Lambert
Michèle Francken

CONTENTS

- 17   Thali, tiffin and chaat
- 39   Masalas
- 57   Spices and herbs
- 83   Ginger
- 99   Rice, lentils and bread
- 121   Fruit and nuts
- 145   Chicken and eggs
- 167   Crustaceans and shellfish
- 189   Kerala fish

RECIPES

APPETIZERS

- 181   Goan crab cake
- 92   Indian meatballs
- 156   Lacquered pinchos of chicken with tamarind
- 31   Masala dosa
- 35   Pakora of chicken and vegetables
- 33   Raita of cucumber
- 201   Small balls of tuna rilette with a mayonnaise of vadouvan masala
- 128   Spiced cashew nuts
- 163   Spiced mini-clafoutis of chicken and asparagus curry
- 36   Vegetarian samosa

STARTERS

- 126   Fried duck liver with mango, pineapple and sweet curry broth
- 66   Marinated salmon with savoury spices and chilli of peas
- 174   Marinated tiger prawns in a nut and saffron sauce
- 177   Mulligatawny of mussels
- 178   Mussels au gratin with Indian herb butter
- 182   Oysters in a jelly of cucumber with chutney
- 133   Quick-fried scallops on a mango chutney with mango coconut cream
- 185   Razor shells in lime-coriander marinade
- 91   Scoubidou of sole filled with tomato and ginger compote in a Crécy soup

SOUPS

90	Crécy soup with ginger and ginger powder
78	Gazpacho carrot and pumpkin with turmeric and pomegranate
61	Rasam
51	Soup of coriander with smoked fish and whipped cream with garam masala
119	Soup of lentils, lime and turmeric

MEAT DISHES

80	Anjou pigeon with three carrot preparations with aromatic spices
106	Biryani of lamb
52	Chicken tikka masala
155	Chicken vindaloo
159	Fried spring chicken with a pachadi of beetroot
152	Indian chicken casserole Flemish style
130	Kalaan of banana with minced meat and cashew nut bread
116	Kali dahl with with preserved pig's cheeks and lomo
164	Nargisi koftas with thakkali curry
141	Pork tenderloin filled with cashew nuts, aloo masala mash croquettes and turmeric gobi
65	Ragout of venison rogan josh with rice croquettes and beetroot pachadi
62	Rogan josh

FISH DISHES

202	Avial of root vegetables with squid and salmon
186	Baingan of aubergines with tiger prawns and tomato chutney
194	Eel ras chawal
198	Molee fish curry of mackerel
197	Pollichathu of swordfish
55	Sambhar of monkfish
205	Thoran of pineapple and white cabbage with Cochin fishburgers

VEGETARIAN DISHES

32	Aloo chaat
109	Chapati
105	Lime rice pulihora
113	Naan
115	Paratha
93	Spicy curry of young green beans and ginger
160	Theeyal of Mechelen asparagus and free-range egg
110	Uttapam

DESSERTS

75	Kulfi of cardamom and nuts with a raisin-and-yoghurt filling
108	Payasam with caramelized banana
137	Pickles of sweet fruit with vadouvan masala and meringue
76	Poached saffron pears
95	Salad of fresh fruit with whipped ginger cream and chutney
72	Upama with cinnamon and vanilla with a strawberry salad

BISCUITS

97	Colonial ginger cake
96	Crunchy ginger biscuits
97	Ginger pudding
134	Muffins of banana, ginger and lime
68	Turban shapes with cinnamon and garam masala

BEVERAGES

87	Ginger lemonade
87	Ginger orangeade
88	Ginger punch
89	Ginger tea
71	Kerala masala coffee
129	Mango lassi
129	Salted lassi (chaas)

INTRODUCTION

Producing a good book is always one of the nicest challenges there are. *Masala* is no exception to this rule. This cookery book is the result of a great deal of thought, of intensive preparation, of research, of knowledge and of the creativity and inspiration of enthusiastic chefs. It is certainly not simply an opportunistic impulse while the spirit of the times is that cookery books seem to constantly appear like ripe fruits falling from the trees. No, *Masala* is an innovative cookery book. If for no other reason than the fact that *Masala* has the ambition to want to be more than the umpteenth cookery book in an endless row.

The word 'masala' means 'roasted mixture of spices'. It is a term that originates from India. For us it has acquired a much broader meaning, because masala reflects perfectly the symbiosis between the various participants in this book.

The book *Masala* is a river which has sprung from several sources. Its starting point is the friendship between Alain Vanden Abeele and the authors Christophe Lambert and Sam Paret, who write about India. They got to know each other in 2004 and since then Alain, too, has not escaped the fascination and love that India can inspire in a person. In the past five years therefore, the three of them travelled eastwards several times. Following the example of his companions, Alain became strongly intrigued by the mix of cultures, traditions and local customs, which make Gandhi's country so amazingly interesting. And he was obviously also irresistibly attracted and fascinated by the inexhaustible riches of the complex Indian kitchen. It became such a revelation that the idea of cooking Indian food would not go away. Partly by study, partly by observation, but particularly by attending many cooking sessions during his visits to Southern India, the eager-to-learn chef gradually acquired a clear view of the greatest secrets of the Indian cuisine.

From a smouldering fire grew the dream of being able to share this initially complex matter and make the Indian way of cooking accessible to those who are wary of travelling to other paths and to those who panic just at the thought of having to mix some ten spices to compose a single dish.

In nearly all temples in Tamil Nadu we see how the priests look after the gods every day. They wash their images, clothe them and see to it that there is always enough food.

The idea of a real literary masala in the form of an interesting cookery book slowly gained shape. Alain's friend, chef Biju of Malabar House in Cochin, put together a series of authentic recipes for those who were quite capable of working with a pestle and mortar and with spice mixtures.

Alain himself accepted the challenge to combine Indian elements with traditional dishes from our own regions. In addition he created a whole range of recipes which will give experienced chefs as well as occasional cooks the pleasure of being able to work with the immense wealth of Indian spices. Without any qualms, he together with Biju could compose his own basic masalas.

Apart from that, the book is also full of small dishes, sweet treats, drinks and finger foods.

Christophe and Sam complete the masala. From the many experiences they have shared on their travels during the run-up to the book, they have extracted a few relevant texts which should illustrate the experience and the inspiration of their adventure. They are light-hearted stories, sometimes anecdotal, but often also with useful background information for the reader who wants to get to know Southern India a little better.

Chef Alain Vanden Abeele has no intention whatsoever to pass himself off as an Indian chef with *Masala*. The fact that he works from his own experiences and knowledge without pretensions makes this book innovative and unique.

Christophe

MASALA, AND THE WORLD WILL BE US

What does Masala mean?
  The Oxford Dictionary, authority on British and Indian English, tells us
  1. a mixture of ground spices used in Indian cooking
  2. someone or something that comprises a varied mixture of elements
  3. someone, we, you, us...

We, Txuku and Joerg, a Basque and a German, came to Kerala on the southern tip of India 15 years ago to make our dream a reality. We built Malabar House, an eclectic boutique hotel focused on art and food, followed by creating the Malabar escapes, a circuit of highly personalized destinations and experiences. We started with our combined knowledge and learned more while connecting to the new cultural context.

Developing our own food concept from our central European and Mediterranean inheritance with its inventory of recipes and techniques was part of this learning exercise.

Very quickly something new developed, a new space beyond the limitations of a defined culture of origin. Linking our world of flavours with the Kerala cuisine not only opened doors beyond the established inherited authenticity; it created the ground for discovery and rediscovery. By identifying spices and pairing them with the fresh produce of the region we crossed cultural boundaries and developed our own cosmos of mixtures, our own Masala.

At times it was confusing; did we lose our own world of cultural origin, for most of us so close to our heart? October 2009 we queued up in the courtyard of the Royal Academy of Arts in London to see an exhibition of Anish Kapoor, the eminent British sculptor of Indian origin. Walking through Anish Kapoor's installations and objects was a soul and mind moving experience, showing the essence of inherited cultural wealth in the present –here and now – beyond the claims of a sovereign cultural territory.

The catalogue of the exhibition contains a wonderful essay by Homi Bhabwa where he trails the definition of culture and origin:

'They are instances of a translational cosmopolitanism that challenge claims to cultural sovereignty in favour of a commitment to something at once more

Txuku Iriarte
and Joerg Drechsel

conceptual and practical: the intimacy of anachronistic times; the proximity of strangers; a dialogue across uneven and unequal places.'

Yes, dialogue is the key to navigate through unequal places and cultures. This dialogue, be it in the world of visual or culinary art, opens the doors to new frontiers and experiences. The world is on a plate, and it is up to us what we do with it. Simply fusing is not enough, one of the reasons why we hate the term 'fusion cuisine'.

The new world with its new space is beyond cultural and sovereign limitations. Building on our own cultural inheritance and absorbing what enriches us we create our own mixture, our own masala.

We as humans have always been driven by our curiosity, by the aim of experience and learning. Vasco da Gama navigated around Africa 500 years ago to find the spice coast of Kerala and its wonders. Today with the global availability of virtually everything the task seems easier but more confusing. Mixing our inheritance with the new requires judgement, skill and a disciplined effort.

Playing with new mixtures becomes hard work, and hard work becomes an investigative game, welcome to the world of Masala.

We, you, us, we all are part of this dialogue with many answers, flavours and masalas.

Develop your own, enjoy it, pass it on and the world will be us...!

Txuku Iriarte and Joerg Drechsel
www.malabarescapes.com

p 14-15
Cochin is known for its centuries-old, gigantic rain trees, some of which will certainly have been there in Vasco da Gama's time. On hot days their enormous branches cast their shadow over the many stalls which are opened at dawn.

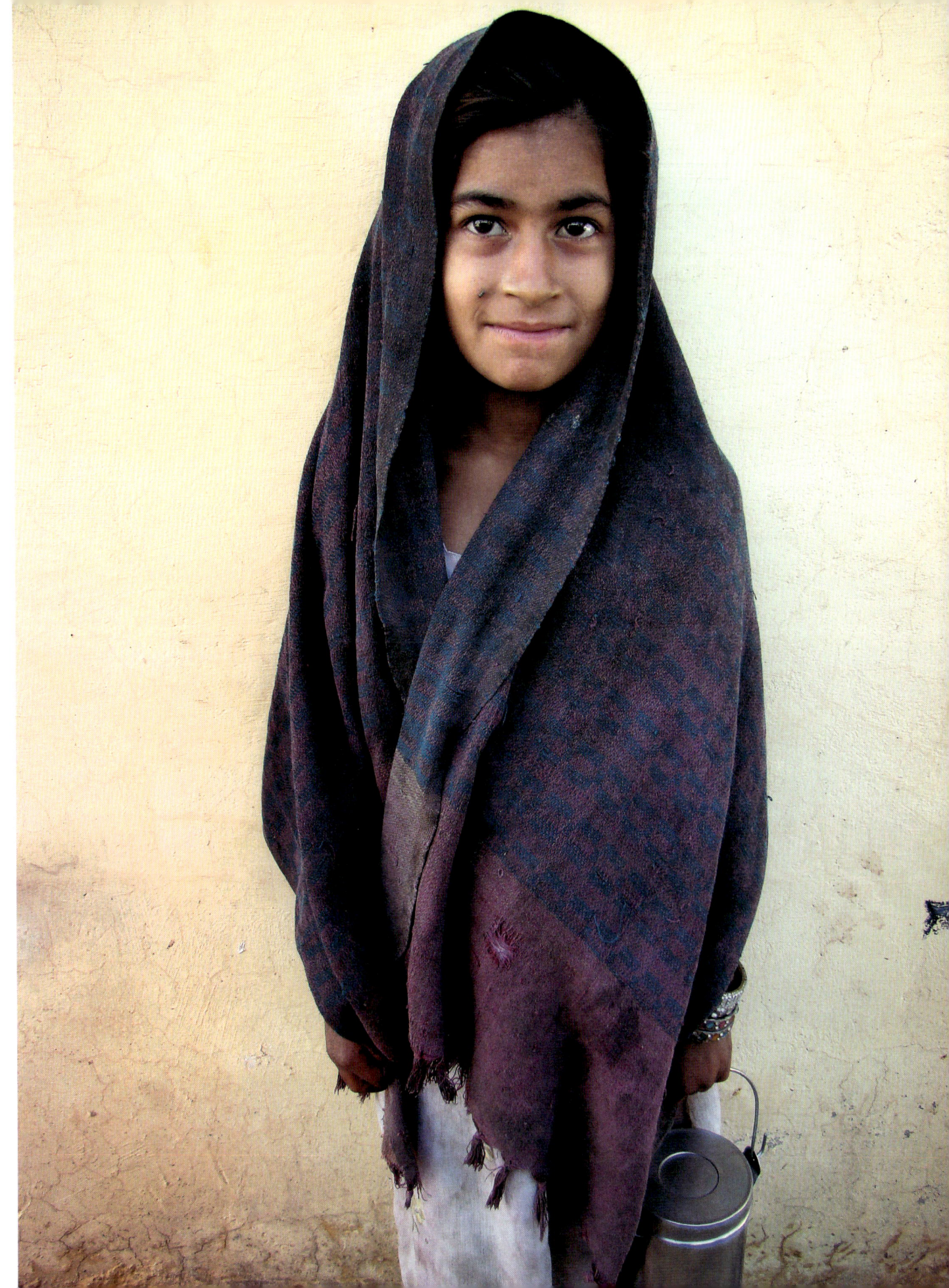

THALI, TIFFIN AND CHAAT

'WE ARE WHAT WE EAT'

In India there's nothing more entertaining than simply wandering through the streets. Round every corner a new experience may well await you. At the coffee stall the performance of the Indian Cricket team for the World Cup is being discussed in great detail. Further on women are carrying baskets full of bricks on their heads to a building site some distance away. The local eating houses gradually fill up for lunch. Indians generally prefer traditional dishes for this, such as masala dosa and thali.

    The thali is predominantly the meal to have if you want to get to know the Indian cuisine and customs better. You will find it everywhere in India, although there may be slight differences from one region to another. The Kerala thali is known as 'Sadya', which means a banquet in Malayalam. This already explains its origin to a large extent. It was originally a festive meal to celebrate a special occasion. What is even more striking is that everywhere in India people use their hands to eat their food. For this, too, there is a reason. Mr. Shamboo, manager of the Malabar Escapes Purity and Serenity, is happy to tell us more about it...

Mr. Shamboo: 'A traditional thali here consists of twenty-one items. These are served on a banana leaf following established lines. When hot food is resting on a banana leaf, this adds aromas and flavours to the food. We start below on the left with salty items. Above them you will find something sweet and a few papadams, those deep-fried crackers. More towards the middle three spicy pickles are served. The right side of the leaf is occupied by various curries, among them thoran, avial, kaalan, rasam and sambhar. Obviously there is a great deal of rice among it. The idea is that you divide this in two and eat the first portion with lentils and ghee, a kind of clarified butter. The other portion you eat with the sambhar. You then have another helping of rice. This time you use part of it with kaalan and the rest with rasam. Only then you have the sweet payasam. You may, throughout the meal, supplement the curries with the other items on your leaf. Sweet flavours you would generally combine with the spicy pickles. You finish the meal again with rice, this time mixed with curds. This helps to clean your system... It may sound a lot, but it is expected that not even a single curry leaf will be left over.

If you leave something in a traditional eating establishment, there is a good chance that the waiter will come and ask you what you didn't like and that he will slink away disillusioned. Remember too, that after the meal you should fold your banana leaf from top to bottom. This means that you will come back again for this festive meal. If you do this in reverse, you actually turn down the meal. The "banquet" to which we refer is the party menu for a wedding. It is the task of the bride's family to prepare this fixed menu for all invited guests, and we easily talk about a thousand people. The first guests to have a turn are the members of the groom's family. They show their pleasure or disappointment by folding the leaf from top to bottom or the reverse. I don't need to tell you how much tension can be seen on the faces of the bride's family.

This party meal is eaten with your hands. The Ayurveda, the knowledge of life, has influenced our eating culture in more ways than one. The slogan is that we are what we eat. Herbs and spices are selected on the basis of their medicinal properties. Nothing is done without reason, but only for the taste of it. Moreover, the Ayurveda teaches us that the hands, and certainly the finger tips, are most sensitive. Touching food with your hands stimulates the appetite. Moving your right hand to mix the food and put it in your mouth improves your circulation. It is a real part of the five senses: to hear, see, smell, taste and feel. The Ayurveda strives for a balance between our senses. So the contact with food is essential to us, whereas with Westerners this is gradually being lost. Only your cooks have the privilege of touching food. Now you know why most of them have a good appetite...

Sam

Following pages:
The Discovery, the Malabar Group's houseboat, an interpretation by its owner, Joerg Drechsel.

HE WHO LITTERS OPENS EVIL'S DOOR

பாணி பூரி... மசாலா பூரி... பேல் பூரி...

In India people get up at the crack of dawn to avoid the extreme heat later in the day. This way of life obviously also affects culinary customs. Indians eat small snacks at every hour of the day.

Everything they eat before midday is called tiffin – a name from the early days of British colonization, when 'tiffing' apparently meant 'sipping', or a small drink. Stuffed pancakes (dosas) and steamed rice cakes (idlys) are particularly popular.

Chaat – a large selection of fried savoury snacks in pastry, such as samosas (meat pasties) or pakoras – are much in demand between meals.

Main meals consist of meat with vegetables, lentils and rice. Long ago the assortment of dishes was served on a large banana leaf, but now a round tray or thali is used on which small bowls with food are placed.

Throughout the day you can buy tasty snacks in all the markets and in the many street stalls. The samosas are very popular: spiced, crisp deep-fried triangles made of dough with either a vegetarian or chicken filling, which are eaten as a snack or a bite to eat.

The chefs at work in the splendid country house escape Serenity at Kanam. A peaceful area where only the rubber plantations mark the undulating landscape.

TIP

The thali is served with a generous portion of rice, bread (roti), a sour element such as pickled onions or gherkins, and a chutney, for instance of tomato, mango or pineapple. In addition serve yoghurt curds or raita with it.

ORIGINAL THALI

CLASSIC

On the hillside of a rubber plantation in Kerala is a beautiful colonial residence which was converted into a luxurious hotel by Malabar Escape. In Hotel Serenity Chef Sinaj serves a fantastic thali with at least seven delicacies. Together with rice, they are served on a banana leaf, as prescribed by tradition. It turned out to be a culinary voyage of discovery.

A thali is a selection of Indian dishes which are served together on a round platter. The combination differs according to the region, but together with fellow-chef and friend Olivier Monbaillu of Restaurant La Tâche in Bruges a Western culinary version has been created with the following dishes:

SAMBHAR

Lentil soup with a vegetable curry which is often served with dosa, idli and vada snacks

PREPARATION

Heat a little coconut oil in a pan or karahi and crisp the mustard seeds in this. Sauté some chopped shallots and add coriander, chilli and turmeric to them.
Cut vegetables such as carrots, aubergines, courgettes, green beans, potatoes, tomatoes or okra into cubes and add them to the spicy shallots. Dowse with water and allow to simmer till done. Flavour to taste with salt, a little tamarind puree and asafoetida.

THORAN OF CABBAGE

Chopped vegetables with grated coconut

PREPARATION

Heat a little coconut oil in a pan or karahi and crisp the mustard seeds in it. Add the finely chopped ginger root, onion and white cabbage to it. Season with salt. Add grated coconut, curry leaves and a small chopped chilli pepper and moisten with water. Leave it to simmer until the cabbage is ready.

KALAN OF BANANA

PREPARATION

Braise some chopped shallot and ginger root in a little coconut oil. Add curry leaves, salt, turmeric and coconut paste. Peel a few bananas, cut them into pieces and briefly cook them in coconut milk. Add the mixture of spices and let it all simmer until the bananas are cooked.

PACHADI OF ROOT VEGETABLES

Root vegetables with a coconut paste

PREPARATION

Chop the vegetables into cubes and boil them in salted water with chopped ginger root. Strain and leave to drain.

Heat a little coconut oil in a pan or karahi and sauté a few shallots in it. Add a generous helping of grated coconut, cummin seeds and mustard seeds to the pan and mix it to a smooth paste.

Add the paste to the root vegetables and the ginger, together with a few tablespoons of yoghurt. Flavour to taste with chilli and add some curry leaves and mustard seeds as a finishing touch.

In India you usually eat with your hands. This is particularly 'handy' for mixing the various taste variations with the rice, to knead the food and then, with a firm twist of the thumb, take it to the mouth.

DHAL FRY

Thick-flowing lentil puree

PREPARATION

In a pan or karahi allow mustard and cummin seeds to colour.
Add chopped garlic, shallot and ginger root to it and flavour to taste with Kashmir chilli and turmeric.
Add cooked lentils and finely chopped tomatoes. Dilute with water to a thick flowing puree.

PAYASAM

Sweet, slightly liquid pudding of vermicelli with cardamom

PREPARATION

Break the vermicelli and fry it in a little clarified butter or ghee.
Pour some full-cream milk over it and add a generous spoonful of sugar.
Heat some butter and fry cashew nuts and raisins in it.
Add this to the milk. Add cardamom seeds to taste
The vermicelli can be replaced by rice or lentils.

KERALA FISH CURRY

This curry is the only non-vegetarian recipe in chef Sinaj's thali. That is typical for the south, where the thali is often completely vegetarian, with the exception of the occasional piece of fish.

PREPARATION

Make a marinade of Kashmir chilli, turmeric, salt, lemon juice and coconut oil.
Chop a tomato and a shallot very finely. Add them to the marinade.
Cut a firm fish, such as swordfish or monkfish, into pieces and immerse them in the marinade. Fry the fish to a golden colour with chopped garlic and ginger root. Moisten with a little coconut milk and leave it to simmer until the fish is done.

CHEF ALAIN'S THALI

ARTISTIC

A thali is a selection of Indian dishes which are served together on a round platter. The combination differs according to the region, but together with fellow-chef and friend Olivier Monbaillu of Restaurant La Tâche in Bruges a Western culinary version has been created with the following dishes:

FOR 4 PERSONS

KAALAN OF BANANA

PREPARATION

Braise 2 shallots in 2 tablespoons of coconut oil and season with salt and 2 tablespoons turmeric. Halve a coconut and remove the hard and the soft shell. Pulverize the flesh in the blender and add this paste to the shallots.
Add 2 dl coconut milk, 1 dl chicken stock, a tablespoon vadouvan masala, a piece of palm sugar, 2 tablespoons lime juice, and 3 to 4 curry leaves (or kefir leaves).
Peel two bananas and break them into pieces. Add them to the rest of the preparation and leave it all to simmer for 5 minutes on a low heat. Add some extra coconut milk if the kaalan is getting too dry.

TERRINE OF OXTAIL

PREPARATION

Peel 8 shallots, chop them fine and braise them in goose fat. Add half an oxtail to it, together with 2 bay leaves, a sprig of thyme and 3 tablespoons garam masala. Leave them to conserve for 6 hours on a low heat and add a little veal stock if the mixture gets too dry. Take the meat out of the pan and remove the bones. Return the meat to the shallots and season to taste with salt. Spoon the mixture into a terrine and leave it to rest in the refrigerator for 12 hours. Turn the terrine out onto a plate, cut it into thick slices and warm these a little just before serving.

TIP

The thali is served with a generous portion of rice, bread (roti), a sour element such as pickled onions or gherkins, and a chutney, for instance of tomato, mango or pineapple. In addition serve yoghurt curds or raita with it.

TANDOORI OF GIANT PRAWNS

PREPARATION

Make a marinade of 1 clove of garlic, a piece of ginger, a teaspoon of salt, the juice of ½ lime and 1 tablespoon of water. Leave the prawns to marinate in this mixture for 20 minutes.

Mix a tablespoon of mustard with 25 g mustard leaves and grind them fine in the blender with a little oil. Add two small green chilli peppers and ½ cm grated ginger root. Rub the prawns with this mix and bake them for 5 to 6 minutes in a hot-air oven at 220 °C.

For the dip sauce mix 3 tablespoons mustard, 150 ml coconut milk, 4 teaspoons shellfish stock, ½ teaspoon salt and a teaspoon of sushi vinegar.

MANGO PICKLES

PREPARATION

Chop 4 shallots fine and braise them. Peel a ripe mango, cut it into cubes and add it to the shallots together with a tablespoon garam masala and ½ teaspoon Kashmir chilli. Add 3 cardemom pods, 1 teaspoon cummin seeds and a little cane sugar and leave the mixture to caramelize. Deglaze with a little lime juice and leave it on a low heat until the dish thickens. If desired add a little more mango just before serving.

PAKORA WITH SOLE, FENNEL AND MARSH SAMPHIRE

PREPARATION

Clean ½ fennel, 1 onion and 1 potato and cut them into fine slices with a mandolin. Add 50 g marsh samphire. Cut 2 soles (200 g each) into very fine strips, add them to the vegetables and leave it all to marinate in a mixture of 1 teaspoon fennel seed, ½ tablespoon vadouvan masala, 1 teaspoon cummin seed, 1 teaspoon salt and two cloves of crushed garlic.

Make a batter of 150 g besan flour, 325 g mineral water, a teaspoon turmeric, ½ teaspoon chilli and a teaspoon salt. If desired, the mixture can be put into an espuma bottle to make it froth more. Roll the sole mixture into small balls and dip them into the pakora batter. Deep-fry them for 5 minutes in deep-fry oil at 175 °C.

CORIANDER RAITA

PREPARATION

Cut ½ cucumber into small cubes and scatter a teaspoon of salt over it. Leave to rest for a little, pour off any moisture that has come away, and stir the cucumber into 0.5 litre of full-cream (Greek) yoghurt. Season with chilli, lime juice, a finely chopped small green chilli pepper and ½ bundle finely chopped coriander.

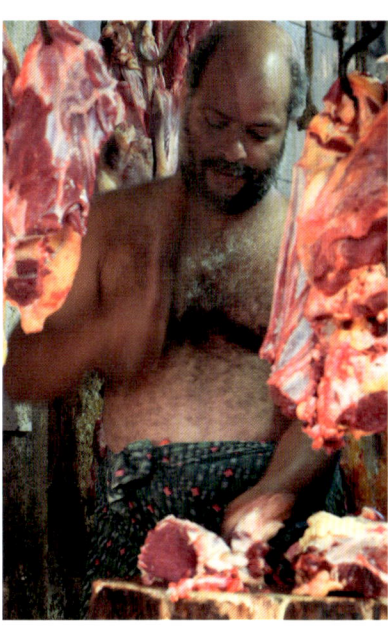

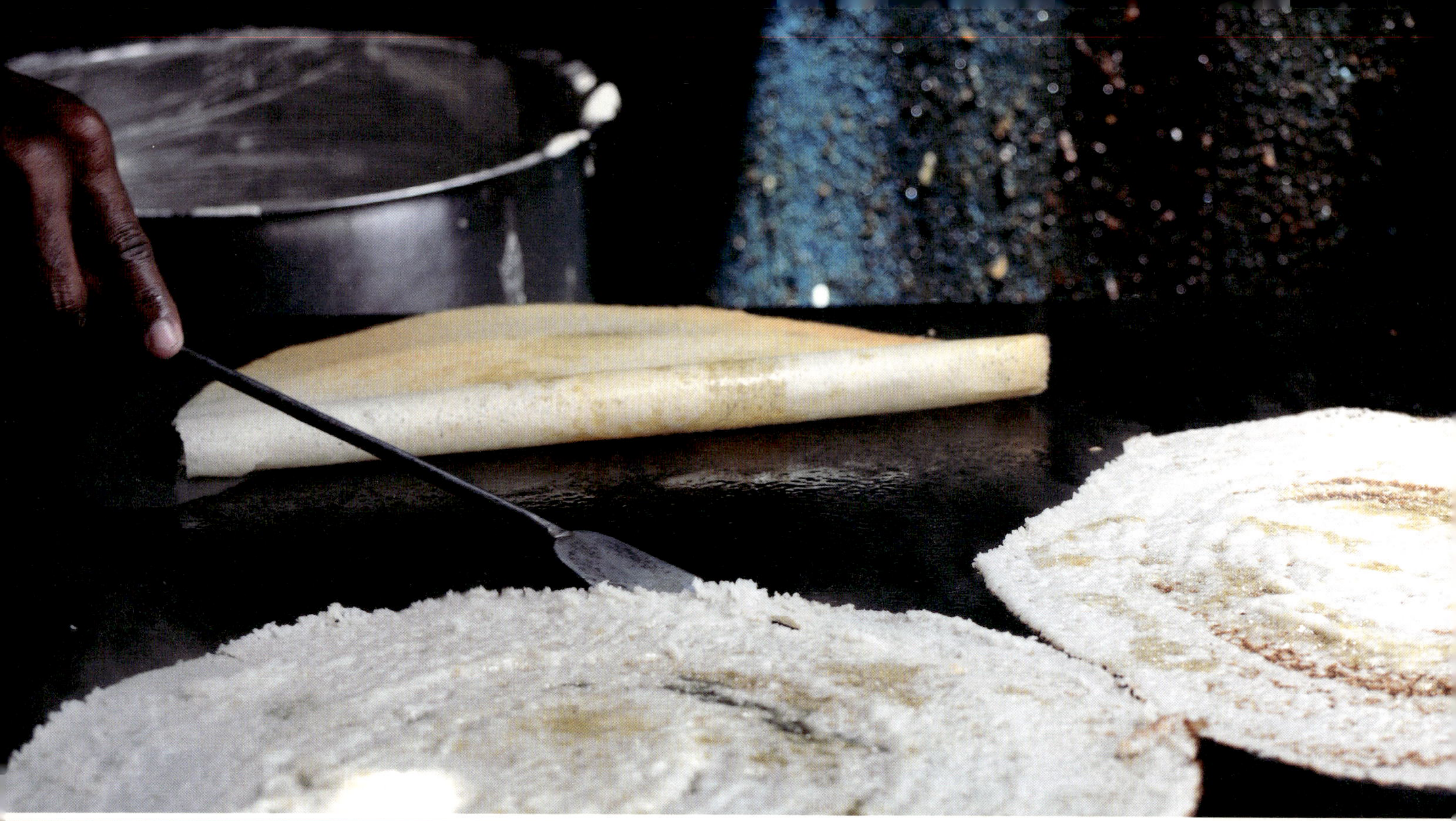
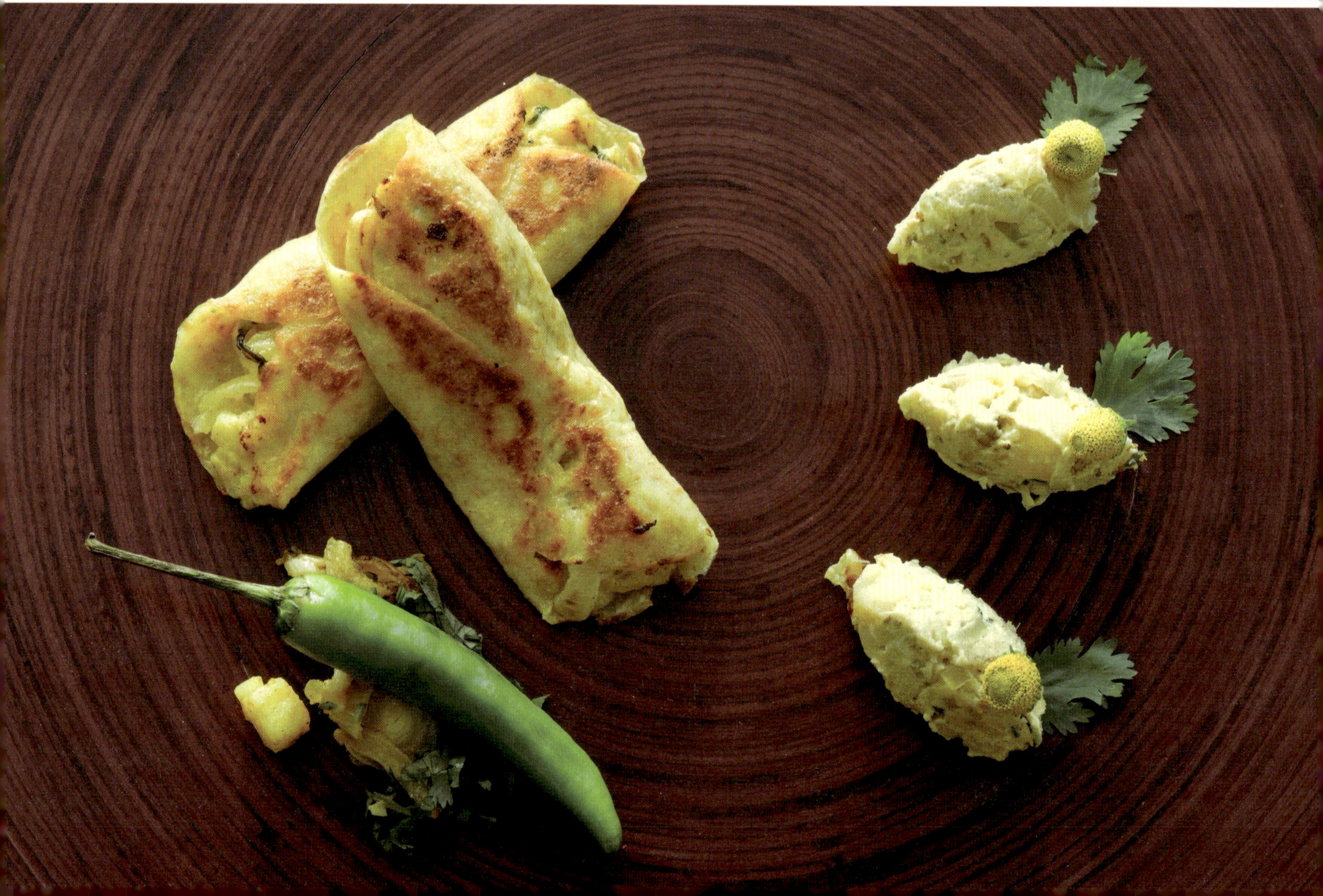

MASALA DOSA

CLASSIC

TIP

Make 12 small pancakes instead of 4 large ones, and serve them as an appetizer or a snack.

FOR 4 PEOPLE

DOUGH *125 g rice flour, 125 g wholemeal flour, 3.5 dl water, 2 tablespoons Greek yoghurt, 2 eggs, 2 teaspoons salt, 1 teaspoon vadouvan masala* – **FILLING** *2 tablespoons corn oil, 2 teaspoons vadouvan masala, 3 cloves of garlic, 250 g onion, 250 g potatoes, cooked, 1 teaspoon salt, freshly ground pepper, 50 g fresh coriander, 1 teaspoon cummin seed, 4 tablespoons Greek yoghurt – corn oil for frying*

PREPARATION

Stir the rice flour, the wholemeal flour, the water, yoghurt, eggs, salt and the vadouvan masala to a smooth batter.

For the filling, heat the oil in a pan and briefly stew the vadouvan masala in it.

Peel the garlic and the onion. Crush the garlic and cut the onion into rings. Fry them in the oil to a golden brown.

Cut the potatoes into large pieces and add them to the onion and the garlic. Fry them golden brown and season to taste with the salt and four turns of the peppermill.

Finely chop the coriander.

Mash the potatoes with a fork and add the coriander, the cummin seed and the yoghurt.

Heat a spoonful of oil in a 30cm diameter frying pan. Don't allow it to get too hot.

Bake 4 thin pancakes (dosas) from the batter.

While baking, spread ¼ of the filling onto the middle of each dosa. Fold the sides in and turn the dosa carefully round with the fold underneath.

Coat the top of the dosa with a little oil, turn it over, and do the same with the other side. Fry to a golden brown and finish off with a little extra chopped coriander. Serve with a cucumber raita (see Cucumber raita on page 33) or mango chutney (see Quick-fried scallops on mango chutney with mango-coconut cream on page 133).

ALOO CHAAT

CLASSIC

This potato dish is prepared in a masterly way in the small eating booths of Mahabalipuram. The slightly floury potatoes taste delicious as a result of the well-balanced spicing. A far cry from the insipid potato salads often served at barbecues in Europe.

Prepare the aloo chaat beforehand and keep the potatoes hot in a cooking pot or dish on the edge of the barbecue.

FOR 4 PEOPLE

6 large, dense potatoes, 2 tablespoons coconut oil,
2 tablespoons tikka masala, 1 tablespoon cummin powder,
10 shallots, 3 large tomatoes

PREPARATION

Boil the potatoes *al dente* in the skin. Peel carefully and cut them into large cubes.
Heat the coconut oil in a pan and fry the potato cubes golden brown. Mix in the tikka masala and the lightly roasted cummin powder.
Peel the shallots and cut them roughly. Cut the tomatoes into pieces.
Add the shallots and the tomatoes to the potatoes and stew them until the tomatoes fall apart. Finish off with chopped coriander if you like.

CUCUMBER RAITA

CLASSIC

TIP

A delicious appetizer on a spoon: put some raita on a spoon and finish off with bits of tomato, cucumber and a large pink prawn.

Raita is often served with spicy Indian dishes because it cools the mouth and gives the palate a rest. For this reason it is recommended to everyone who is not yet familiar with the highly seasoned cuisine.
The basic ingredient of this dish is a mild yoghurt to which spices and mustard seed oil are added. As an addition chopped raw vegetables can be mixed in.

INGREDIENTS

450 g cucumber, 1 large ripe tomato, 1 red chilli pepper, 3 dl full-cream (Greek) yoghurt, juice of ½ lime, salt, 1 teaspoon oil, 1 teaspoon mustard seed, 1 teaspoon fresh coriander, chopped

PREPARATION

Peel the cucumber, remove the pips and grate the pulp.
Make an incision across the top of the tomato, dip it into boiling water and then plunge it into cold water. Peel the tomato, remove the pips and cut it into small cubes.
Leave the tomato and the cucumber to drain in a colander.
Cut the chilly peppers along their length, remove the pips and chop them finely. Mix the yoghurt with the cucumber, the tomato and the chilli. Season to taste with a pinch of salt.
Heat the oil and crisp up the mustard seeds. Sprinkle them together with the chopped coriander over the yoghurt and leave it to rest.

33

PAKORA OF CHICKEN AND VEGETABLES CLASSIC

Pakoras are immensely popular snacks in India. They are mainly prepared as vegetarian food. The vegetables are cut into fine little strips and then dipped in a dough of besan or chickpea flour. They are fried in oil until they are nicely crisp, but still deliciously soft inside.

INGREDIENTS

150 g carrots, 150 g potatoes, 150 g leeks, 150 g onions, 2 chicken fillets, 1 tablespoon vadouvan masala (mild) or tikka masala (spicy), 2 cloves of garlic, ½ tablespoon cummin seed, salt, 150 g flour, 150 g chickpea flour (or besan), 3.5 dl water, 1 teaspoon turmeric, ½ tablespoon Kashmir chilli, oil for deep-frying

PREPARATION

Wash all vegetables and cut them into fine strips (julienne). Cut the chicken fillet into narrow little strips and add them to the vegetables. Season them with vadouvan masala for a mild preparation and with tikka masala for a more seasoned dish.

Peel the garlic and crush it. Mix it with the cummin seed and a pinch of salt. Stir this mixture into the vegetables and chicken.

Make a smooth batter of the flour, the chickpea flour and 3.5 dl water. Season with the turmeric powder, the Kashmir chilli and a pinch of salt.

Stir the vegetables and chicken into the batter.

Heat the oil to 180 °C. Using two tablespoons, shape small balls of the chicken and vegetable mixture and deep-fry the pakoras in the hot oil until crisp.

Leave the pakoras to drain on kitchen paper and serve with one of the chutneys in this book, or with raita.

TIP

This is a perfect dish to finish off leftover chicken, fish and vegetables. The pakoras will keep well in a deep-freezer. Fry them briefly in hot oil, freeze them and thaw before use. Deep-fry them golden brown and crisp just before serving.

Make small balls instead of larger pakoras. They make delicious appetizers.

TIP

These samosas have the shape of a half moon, but in India they are also often folded into small horns. Cut the circles in half and fold the straight edge double with a slight overlap. Push it together well so that it results in a small horn which can be filled. After filling it push the top edge together to close it and deep-fry the samosa in oil.

VEGETARIAN SAMOSA

CLASSIC

Samosas can be made in any taste and are an ideal food for using up leftovers. The filling is fried in spiced oil, so that it always has a delicious taste. A lovely and budget-friendly snack!

FOR 10 SAMOSAS

DOUGH 2 tablespoons oil, 450 g flour, a pinch of salt, 2 dl warm water

FILLING 400 g potatoes, 80 g peas, 4 tablespoons oil, 1 teaspoon cummin seed, 1 teaspoon coriander seed, ½ onion, a pinch of turmeric, a pinch of garam masala, 2 small green chilli peppers, 2 cm ginger root, ⅛ bundle of coriander, juice of 1 lime, salt, oil for deep-frying

PREPARATION

Rub the oil into the flour with the salt to a grainy mixture.
Little by little add warm water and knead for 5 minutes to a supple dough. Add some flour if the dough is too wet. Cover the dough and leave to rest for 2 hours.
Peel the potatoes, cook them till done and cut them into small cubes. Blanch the peas and rinse them under cold running water.
Heat 1 tablespoon of oil in a pan and roast the cummin seed and the coriander seed until they release their aromas. Crush the spices fine in a mortar.
Peel the onion, chop it finely and sauté it in the remainder of the oil. Season with the crushed spices, the turmeric and the garam masala.
Cut the chilli peppers open along their length and remove the seeds. Chop the peppers finely. Peel the ginger and grate it. Chop the coriander finely.
Add the potato cubes, peas, chilli pepper and ginger to the onion and briefly fry it together. Add the lime juice and the chopped coriander to it. Season to taste with salt.
Roll out the dough to ½ cm thickness and cut out 10 circles of about 8 cm diameter.
Put a spoonful of the filling in the middle of the circle. Dampen the edges with a little water and fold the flap of dough over. Press the edges down with a fork. Make all the samosas in this way. Heat the oil to 180 °C and deep-fry the samosas until golden brown.

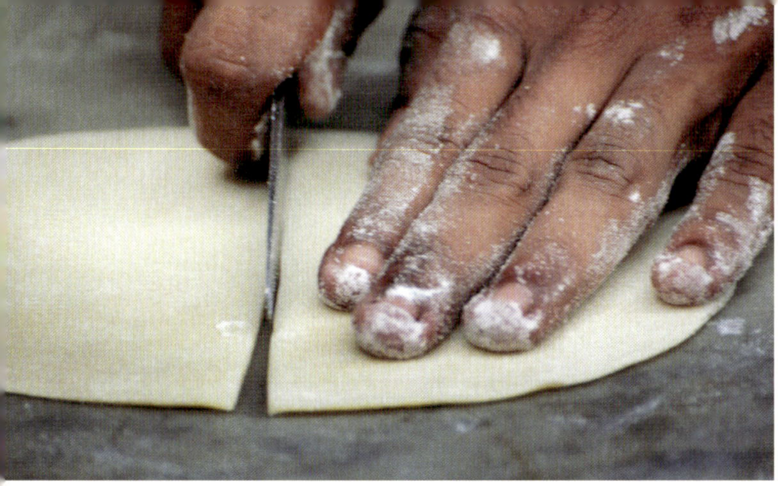
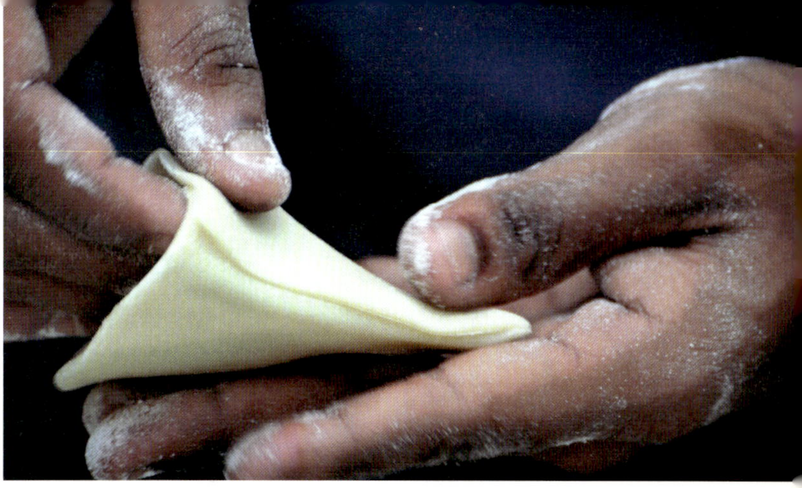
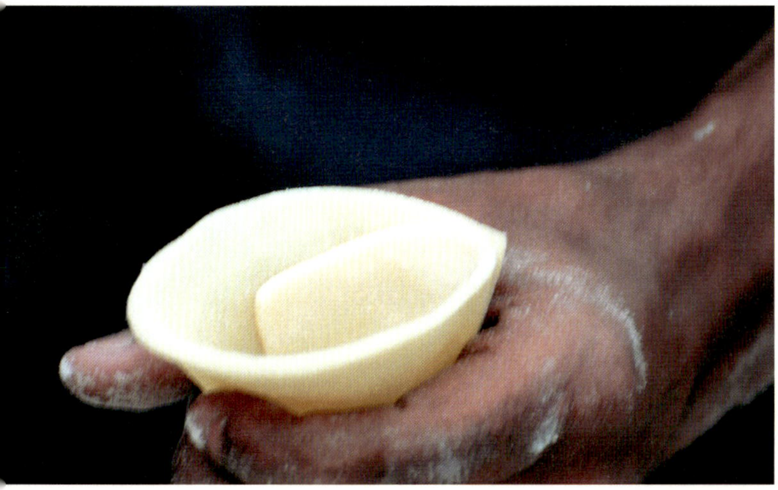
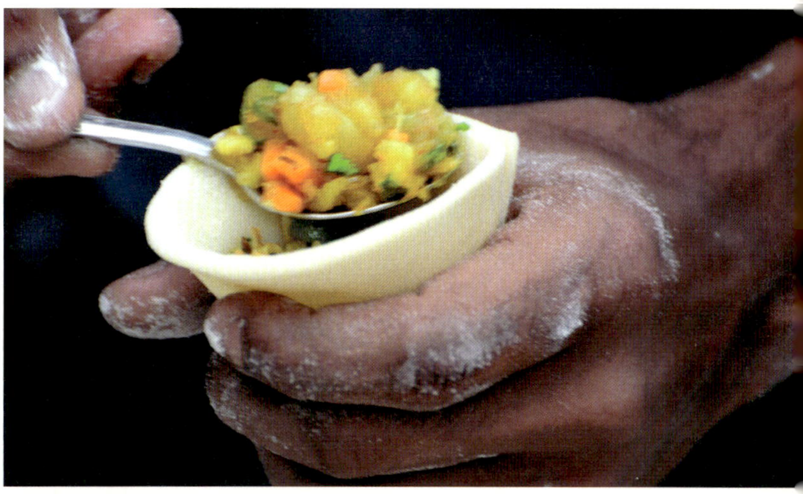
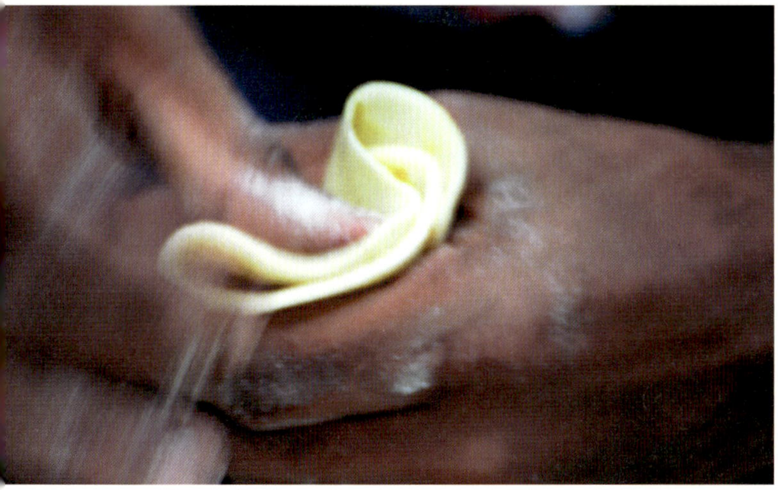
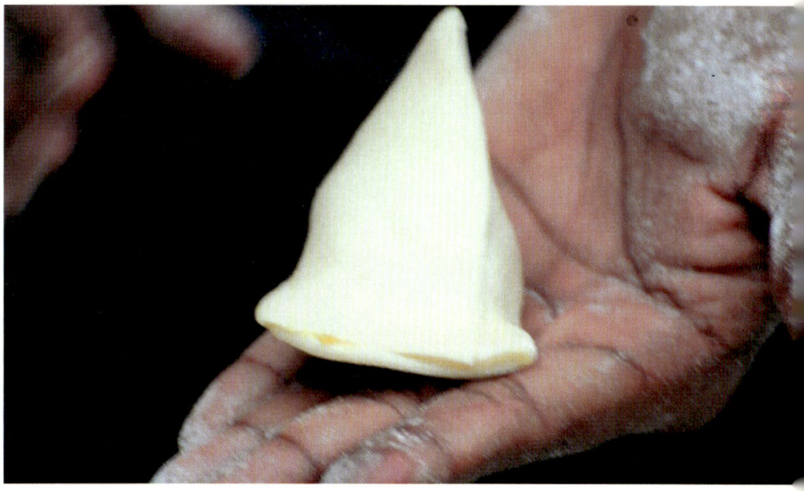
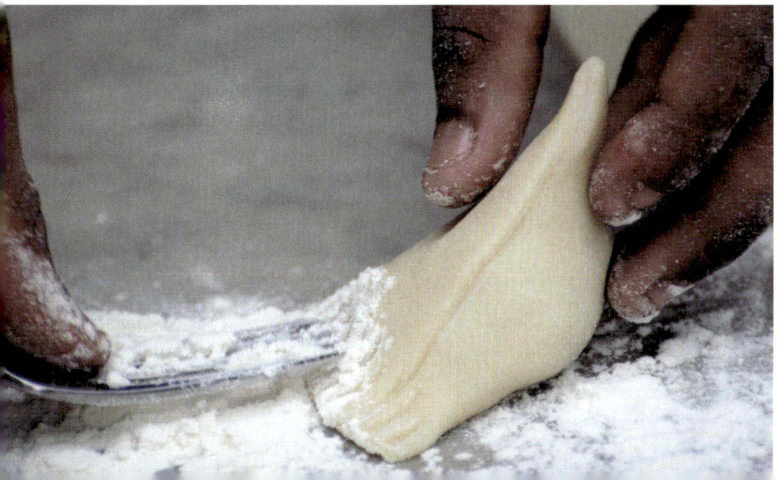
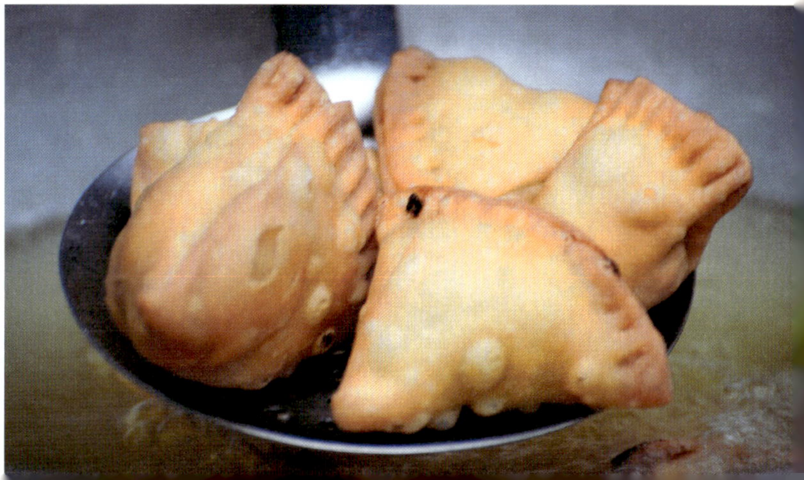

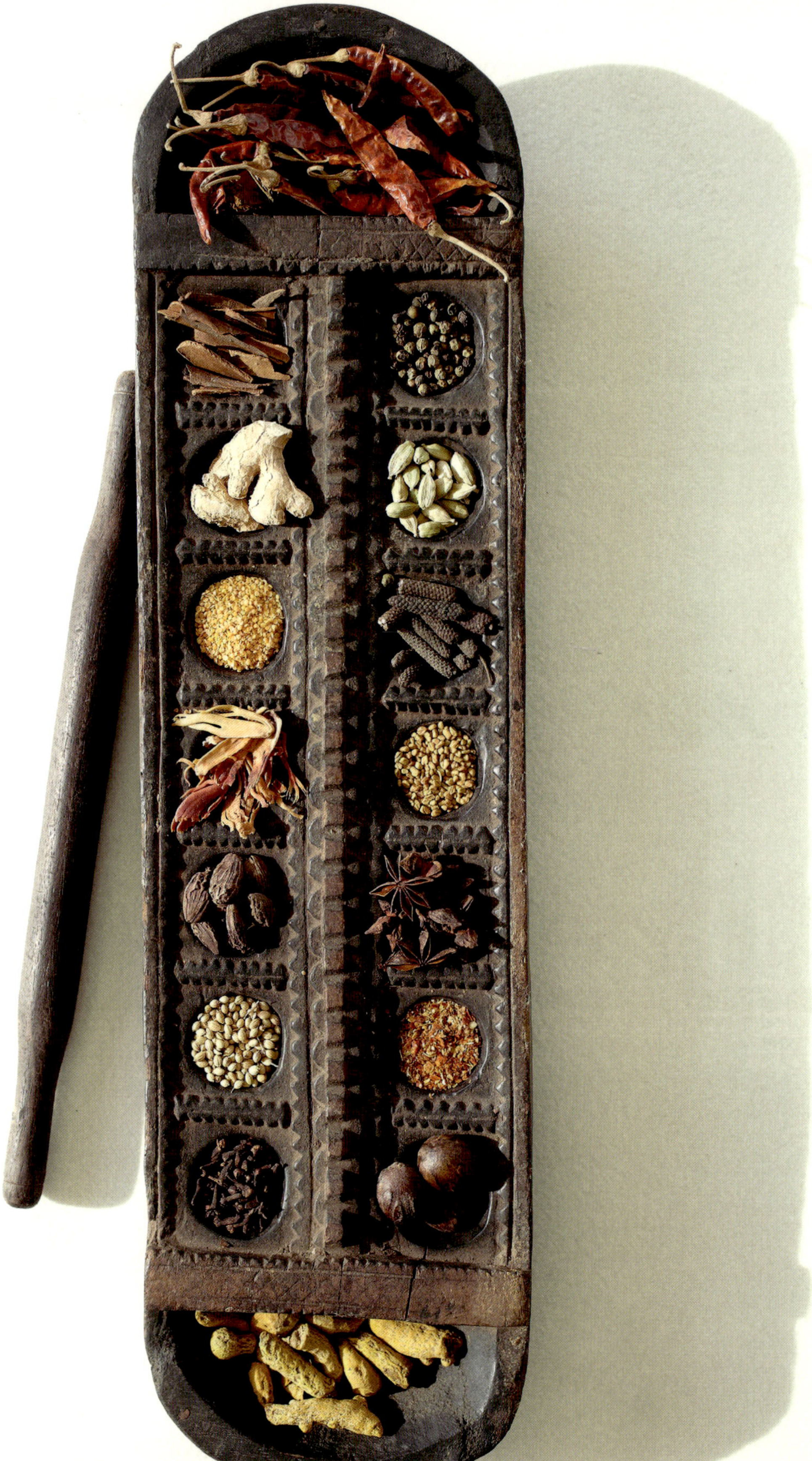

MASALAS

EXPERIMENT WITH SPICES
AND DISCOVER A NEW WORLD OF TASTES

Biju: In India every domestic kitchen has a rich arsenal of spices. For each authentic dish you need a specific mix of them. Although certain spices often reappear, these masalas are actually very complex. Every housewife takes a great deal of time, when she is cooking, to make these specific masalas herself. Here all recipes are passed on from generation to generation. So every masala can also easily differ from family to family.

Alain: To make life easier for every amateur chef, Biju and I have put together four basic spice mixtures. For those who, despite everything, still want to achieve a very authentic result, we are pleased to give the contents for every masala. With the aid of a mortar you can prepare them yourself in that way. Our four spice mixtures each have their own specific properties and you can't just use them for every dish. A fish masala is, for instance, not recommended for use when you are making a chicken dish. In the last the quantity of coriander dominates, while in the Vadouvan chilli has the upper hand.

Biju: In the composition of masalas here in Kerala we also pay attention to the medicinal properties of spices. We don't select them only for their taste. Here you find yourself in the cradle of the centuries-old Ayurveda. For everyone in Kerala this means a way of life, which is reflected in every aspect of his or her life. And not least in the kitchen. This is why you will find ginger and turmeric in most masalas. Ginger helps in the digestion of food, turmeric has several healing properties. Everyone among us here has this knowledge, whether you have had a proper schooling or not. During my training in Ernakulam I had a very special chef, from whom I have learned a great deal. For instance, I personally experienced that turmeric helps when you have cut

The word curry comes from the Tamil *kari* and means 'addition to the main course'.

yourself. That man really had a natural solution for everything. Sometimes he seemed to be a walking encyclopedia.

Alain: The same goes for asafoetida or 'devil's dung', which you will only find in the Sambhar. The particular feature of this spice, of which the root and the trunk, as well as the leaves are used, is that in the first instance it really does not smell at all nice. Forget that the powder might not encourage you to scatter it happily into your dishes. Once it heats up, however, the taste becomes pleasant and in India it is sometimes used to replace garlic.

Biju: For many of the Indian herbs and spices it is true that they get better as you cook them. That is why, after heating the oil, we first add our spices and leave them to simmer, so that they release their tastes, scents and colours freely. Only then do we put the fish or meat in the pan, so that this can feed itself thoroughly on the masala and becomes drenched by it.

Alain: That is actually very different from our cuisine; we mostly only add our spices towards the end. So we will have to teach our readers to get started on the spices first. There is an advantage in this that, when you are cooking an Indian meal, your kitchen will have a delicious smell… Besides this, we have to get rid of the one-sided view some of our people have of the Indian cuisine. For them India means highly spiced, and therefore not good. It's of course true that Indians like it, but not everyone has to.

Biju: It's true we grow up with an extensive variety of herbs and spices. What you have available in plenty, you are likely to use more easily. We know of some twentyfive different sorts of chilli peppers. Even so, I don't think it's a good idea to eat very spiced up food in a hot climate. Maybe I am an exception, but I am not in favour of it. At home with my wife we usually eat rice with some three curries, of which only one is a hot one. That is usually the fish or meat curry which we supplement with a thoran and vegetable curry. We mix them, and so you get a slightly milder taste. Or we make it with coconut milk. You must not forget either that here in India our plates are mainly filled with rice. Side dishes only have a secondary role to play, as opposed to you people who make a combination of equal quantities of fish, vegetables and rice. And usually without mixing them up with each other.

Chefs Alain and Biju in Purity: how do you make the perfect masala?

Alain: With our masalas we also want to encourage our readers to adjust their eating habits. As a tip I would very much like to encourage them to use these rich spice mixtures on a daily basis. They don't actually have to prepare the recipes in the book only when they want to cook an Indian meal. But have the courage to experiment with it and you will soon see how they could enrich our cuisine. Forget the usual nutmeg with mashed potato or chicory, and try out the somewhat richer garam masala. Or add a pinch of ginger powder to your carrots and discover new tastes for yourself. Moreover, the healing qualities of ginger will see to it that you will digest everything better and are not left with a feeling of being bloated!

Sam

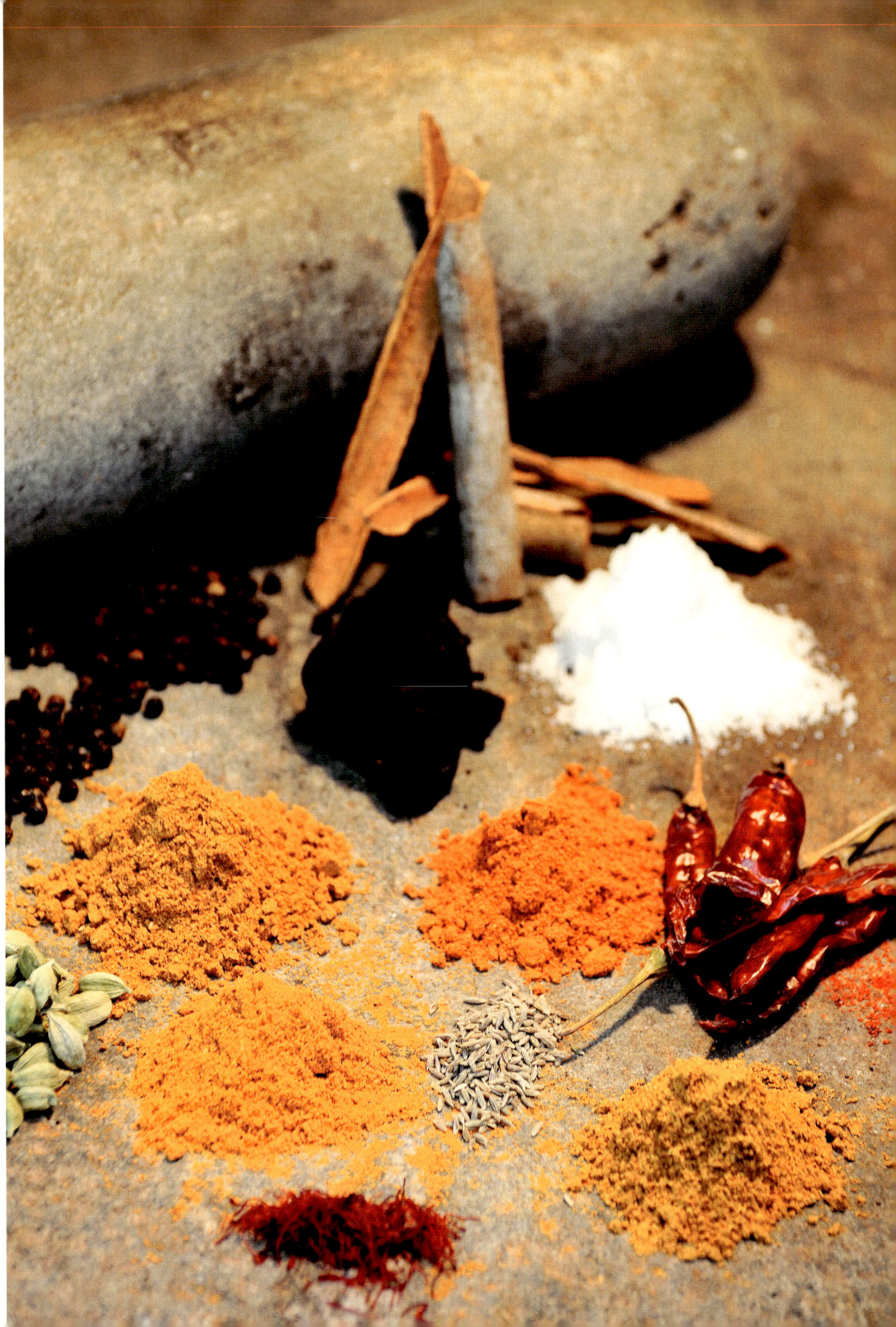

MASALA

In the kitchen of the magician shines
The magic of Kerala treasures
In the light of rows of golden pots
real Aladdins hidden in spices

Masala
Fill the air with aroma!

The southern chef begins his cooking
His steady hand full of fiery spices
With small heaps and dashes he fills his pots
In a cloud of delight, his cooker rejoices

Masala masala
Stir up some life in this feast!

A mouthful of tastes on a single plate
A cascade of Indian munificence
Refined by a mild velvet composition
Robust through a mature spicy dosage

Masala
Fiery gentle, gently fiery

Christophe

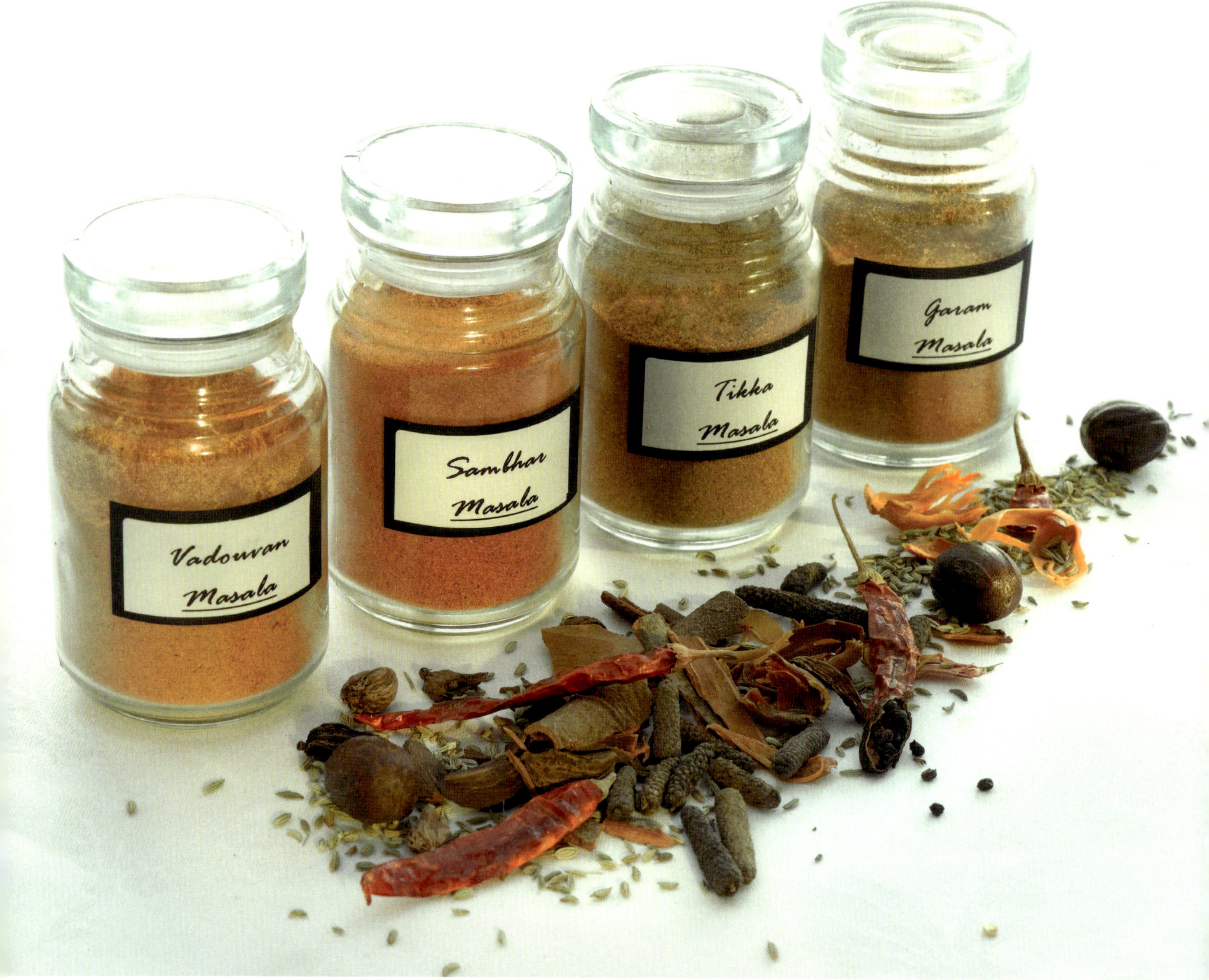
Vadouvan Masala
Sambhar Masala
Tikka Masala
Garam Masala

GARAM MASALA

The Indian cuisine is to a large extent determined by garam masala, undoubtedly the most famous spice mixture in the range. This mix, which gives extra pep to the traditional dishes from Northern India, bears the stamp of the Mogul kitchen. Meanwhile its preparation has also become established in the south, where it differs very slightly from the northern version.

Translated literally, 'garam' means 'hot' in Hindi. That has nothing to do with 'highly seasoned', but with 'heated', because all the ingredients are roasted in a pan and only then ground into a fine powder. In garam masala 'warm' spices are also used, such as cinnamon, cloves, pepper and cardamom.

For a classic garam masala all spices are mixed in equal quantities.

Cardamom pods

INGREDIENTS

cardamom pods, cinnamon, cloves, black pepper, nutmeg, cummin seed

PREPARATION

Remove the seeds from the cardamom pods.
Break the cinnamon into pieces.
Roast all ingredients for about 4 minutes in a pan to release the aromas. Allow the spices to cool and grind them in a food processor to a fine powder.

USAGE

The taste of the mildly roasted spices of garam masala livens up many dishes, but it is particularly used in those that can do with some extra taste. You can use the mixture perfectly well to replace nutmeg in recipes with chicory, in mashed potato, and in some soups.
The dish will taste milder as a result of the addition of cinnamon, cummin and cloves.

TIKKA MASALA

The best known chicken recipe from India is undoubtedly murgh tikka masala, in which tikka masala is the specific spice mixture in which the chicken is marinated. This mix is a variant of garam masala, but contains spices which are less sweet, like nutmeg, cinnamon and cloves, and it tastes rather more spicy. The Kashmir chilli is responsible for the spicy boost while ginger and turmeric enrich the offering of tastes even more. It is after all the double portion of nutmeg and the refined aroma of mace which make the tikka masala more robust and voluminous, without spoiling the delicate taste.

Equal parts of all spices are mixed, with the exception of nutmeg and turmeric which are added in double the quantity. The proportions can be adjusted to personal tastes, to make the mix spicier or less so.

INGREDIENTS

Kashmir chilli, 2 × turmeric, mace, ginger powder, cinnamon, cardemom, coriander, cummin, clovesl, 2x nutmeg, black pepper

USAGE

Because of its subtle and at the same time spicy taste tikka masala is used particularly in poultry dishes or vegetable stews, but it is also very suitable as a basis for various marinades.
Chef Biju adds this spice mixture to dishes that need to be more highly spiced than you can achieve with garam masala.

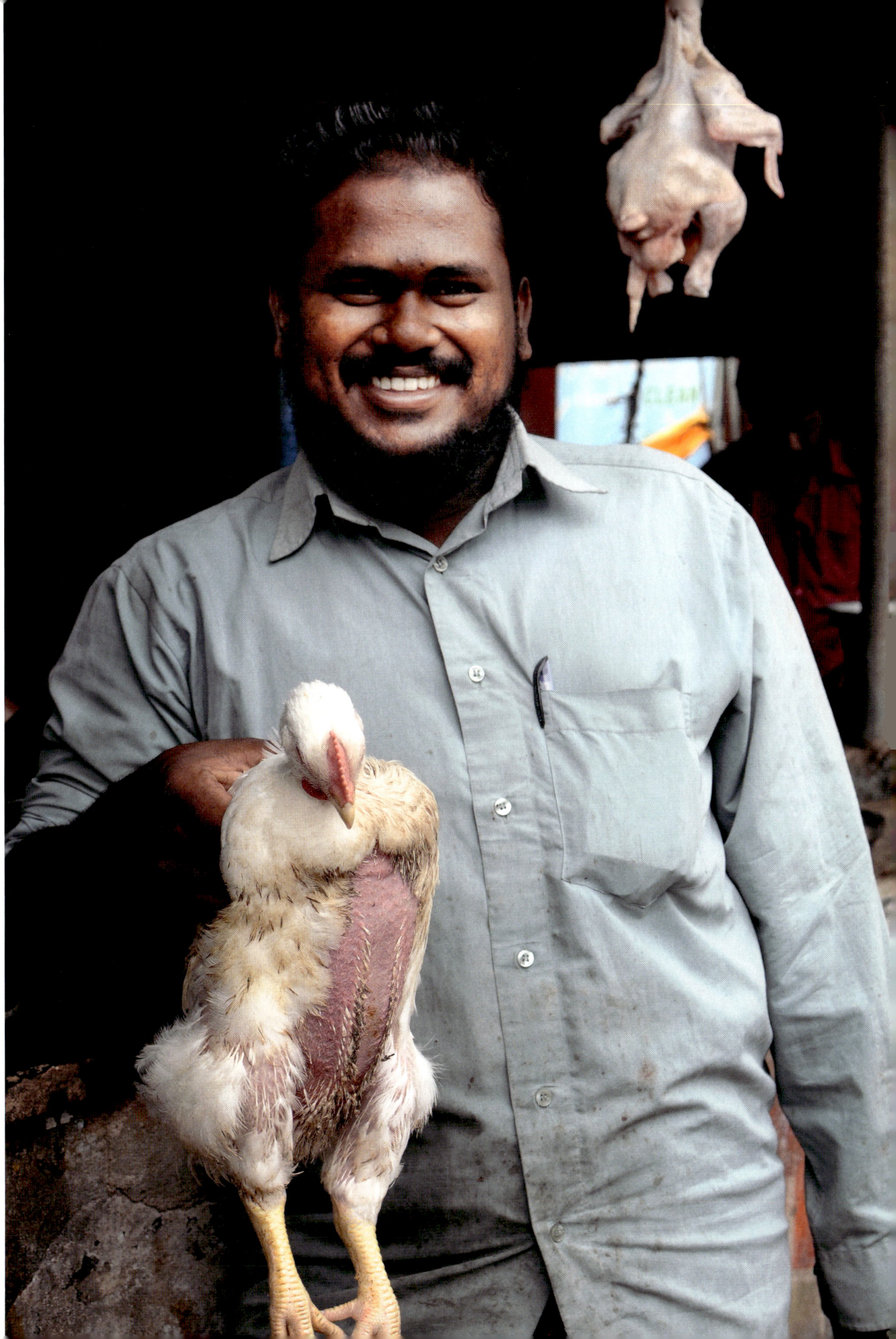

Sri Rangam, the largest temple complex in the whole of India, has no less than seven walls around it. In the outer walls this holy place houses many small shops, eating places, and stalls full of knickknacks.

VADOUVAN MASALA

The composition of vadouvan masala is determined regionally, but traditionally the mix always contains curry leaf, fenugreek, mustard seed, garlic and cummin. The taste is very distinctive, but is difficult to describe. Vadouvan is spicy, but also has a slightly sweet and smoky taste.

All spices are mixed in equal parts.

INGREDIENTS

asafoetida (a typically Indian spice with an onion and garlic taste), turmeric, fenugreek, ginger, cinnamon, cummin, mustard seed, black pepper

USAGE

Vadouvan masala is the mildest spice mix of the four. The taste is subtle but distinctive and it is a masala which gives an Indian touch to 'delicate' main ingredients, such as fine fish, early vegetables and veal or lamb.

SAMBHAR MASALA

Sambhar or Indian lentil curry is every-day food in Southern India. It is a well-spiced vegetarian stew, in which quite a lot of chilli has been added. The spice mix used – sambhar masala – is the most highly spiced of the masalas. It is advisable to use it only with moderation.

All spices are mixed in equal parts, with the exception of the Kashmir chilli, of which a double quantity is added for extra pep.

INGREDIENTS

cummin seed, coriander seed, fenugreek, asafoetida (a typically Indian spice with an onion and garlic taste), turmeric, mustard seed, 2 × Kashmir chilli, black pepper

USAGE

Sambhar masala is actually a refined variant of chilli or cayenne pepper. This masala is used in highly spiced dishes and authentic Indian preparations, often combined with one of the other three masalas. Spices such as cinnamon, cloves or nutmeg are not added to it, which is why the sambhar masala is hot without sweet touches.

A colourful preparation of greens, ready to be used in various curries.

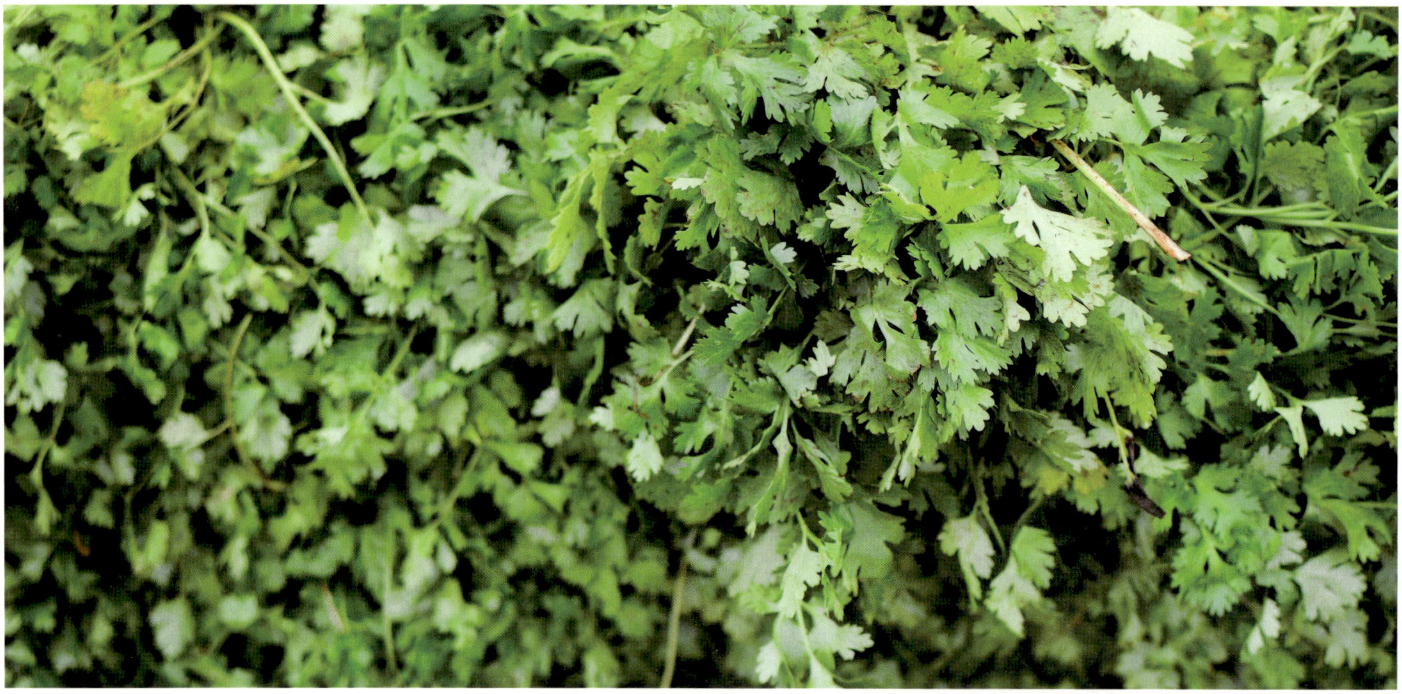

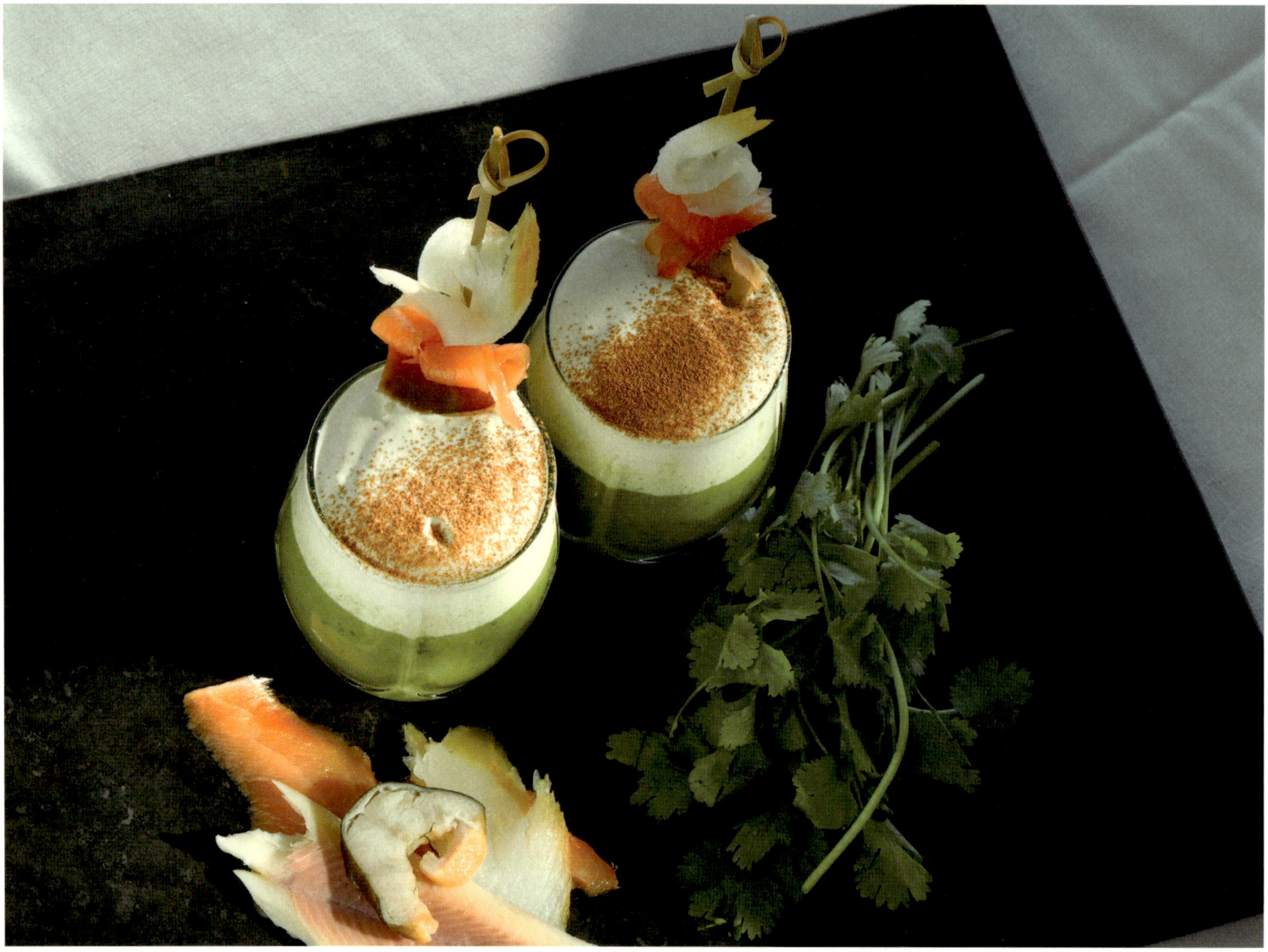

SOUP OF CORIANDER WITH SMOKED FISH AND WHIPPED CREAM WITH GARAM MASALA WESTERN

TIP

Serve the soup as soon as possible after preparing it. In this way the taste of the herbs and spices is kept at its best. Moreover, in this way the lovely green colour which makes this soup look so attractive is preserved.

Alain: 'Every time I go to India I take the opportunity to visit the Vanakam project in Tamil Nadu. The people there have become like family to me, and the reunion with the staff in charge and the children is always heart-warming. Very regularly there is a simple, but delicious coriander soup on the menu. For me one of the highlights is always when Sister Mary appears in the dining room with the steaming, fragrant soup. A feast of simplicity, quickly made but so delicious...

Without wanting to detract from the very simple recipe, I am in the habit of adding something to this simple soup when I am at home. I add a little smoked fish to it, and as a finishing touch some fragrant cream whipped with garam masala spices. An explosion of tastes, simply fantastic! Much recommended, also as a small starter soup.'

FOR 4 PERSONS

250 g red onions, 1 small green chilli, 2 cloves of garlic, 2 tablespoons olive oil, 2 tablespoons garam masala, ½ tablespoon cummin seeds, 1 litre vegetable stock, 1 bundle mint, 2 bundles coriander, ½ bundle (flat-leaved) parsley, 500 g fresh spinach, juice of 2 lemons, 250 g smoked fish (salmon, halibut, eel, herring...), 4 tablespoons cream with 1 tablespoon garam masala

PREPARATION

Peel the onion and slice it. Cut the chilli pepper open lengthways, remove the seeds and chop it finely. Peel the garlic and chop it finely. Heat the olive oil in a pan and fry the onion and the garlic. Add the garam masala, the cummin seed and the chilli pepper and leave it to simmer for a moment.

Add the hot vegetable stock to it.

Cut up the mint, coriander and parsley finely and add them to the soup. Cook for 10 minutes just below boiling point.

Wash the spinach and add it together with the lemon juice to the soup. Bring to the boil for a moment and give the soup a quick stir.

Put the fish on small sticks.

Pour the soup into bowls and put a good spoonful of cream with garam masala in each bowl. Finish off with the fish sticks.

TIP

This classic Indian dish looks even better if the chicken fillets have not been cut into pieces. Rub the marinade in this recipe into the whole fillets and bake them in the oven in the same way as the chicken pieces (but a little longer).

Mix the sauce for the cream; the shredded almonds are added as a refinement. Pour it through a sieve and then add all the other ingredients. Put the chicken fillet on the plate and add a timbale of basmati rice and quenelles of carrot puree with ginger to it.

CHICKEN TIKKA MASALA

CLASSIC & ARTISTIC

Chicken tikka masala is a rich curry with some chicken in a delicious red sauce. The dish is nicely spiced, but at the same time mild, by the addition of yoghurt and tomatoes.

This is the favourite dish of the one-time top tennis star Dominique Monami. She became familiar with it on her travels through Southern India, where she is a sponsor at Vanakam. The recipe has been specially included in this cookery book in her honour.

FOR 4 PERSONS

500 g chicken fillets, 2 tablespoons tikka masala, 3 tablespoons of peanut oil, 4 cloves of garlic, 5 cm fresh ginger, 15 g fresh coriander, 100 ml full-cream yoghurt, salt, coarsely ground, 3 large tomatoes, 1 large onion, 6 cardamom pods, 2 tablespoons tomato puree, 2 dl cream, 50 g shredded almonds, fresh coriander for a finishing touch

PREPARATION

Cut the chicken fillet into pieces of about 3 cm and put them into a large bowl. Mix the tikka masala with 1 tablespoon oil.
Peel a clove of garlic and the ginger. Chop them finely together with the coriander and mix them with the seasoned oil. Add the marinade and the yoghurt to the chicken and bring to taste with coarsely ground salt. Cover and leave overnight in the fridge.
Put the pieces of marinated chicken on a (greased) baking tray and cook them for about 15 minutes in a preheated oven at 200 °C until they are golden brown.
Remove the pips from the tomatoes and cut them into big pieces. Peel the onion and the remaining cloves of garlic, and chop them finely.
Heat 2 tablespoons of oil in a pan on a low heat and fry the onion together with the cardemom pods. Add the tomato puree and the remainder of the garlic. Finally stir the cream, the shredded almonds and the chicken fillet into the sauce and leave it to simmer for 5 minutes.
Chop some fresh coriander finely. Add the tomatoes to the dish and finish off with chopped coriander.

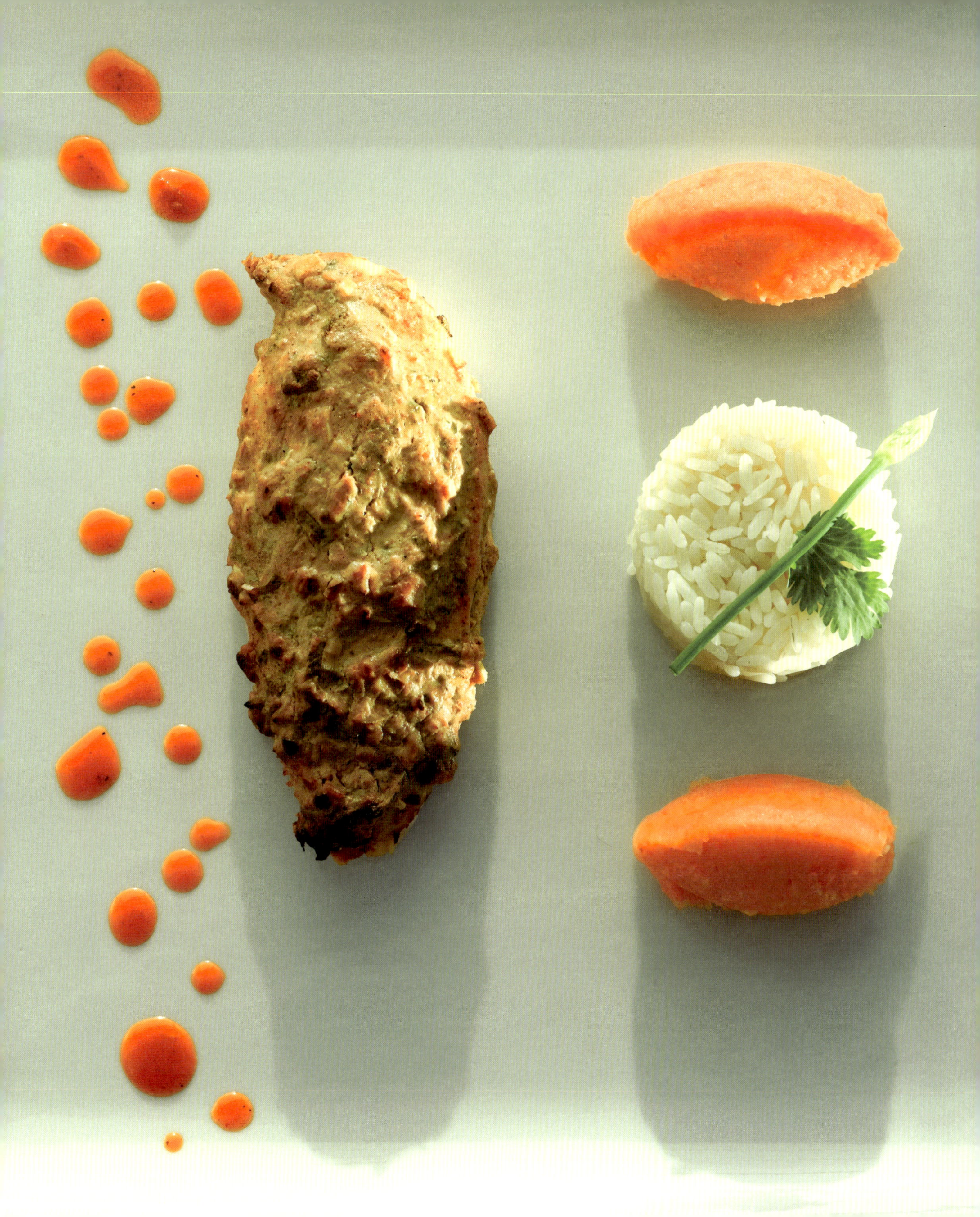

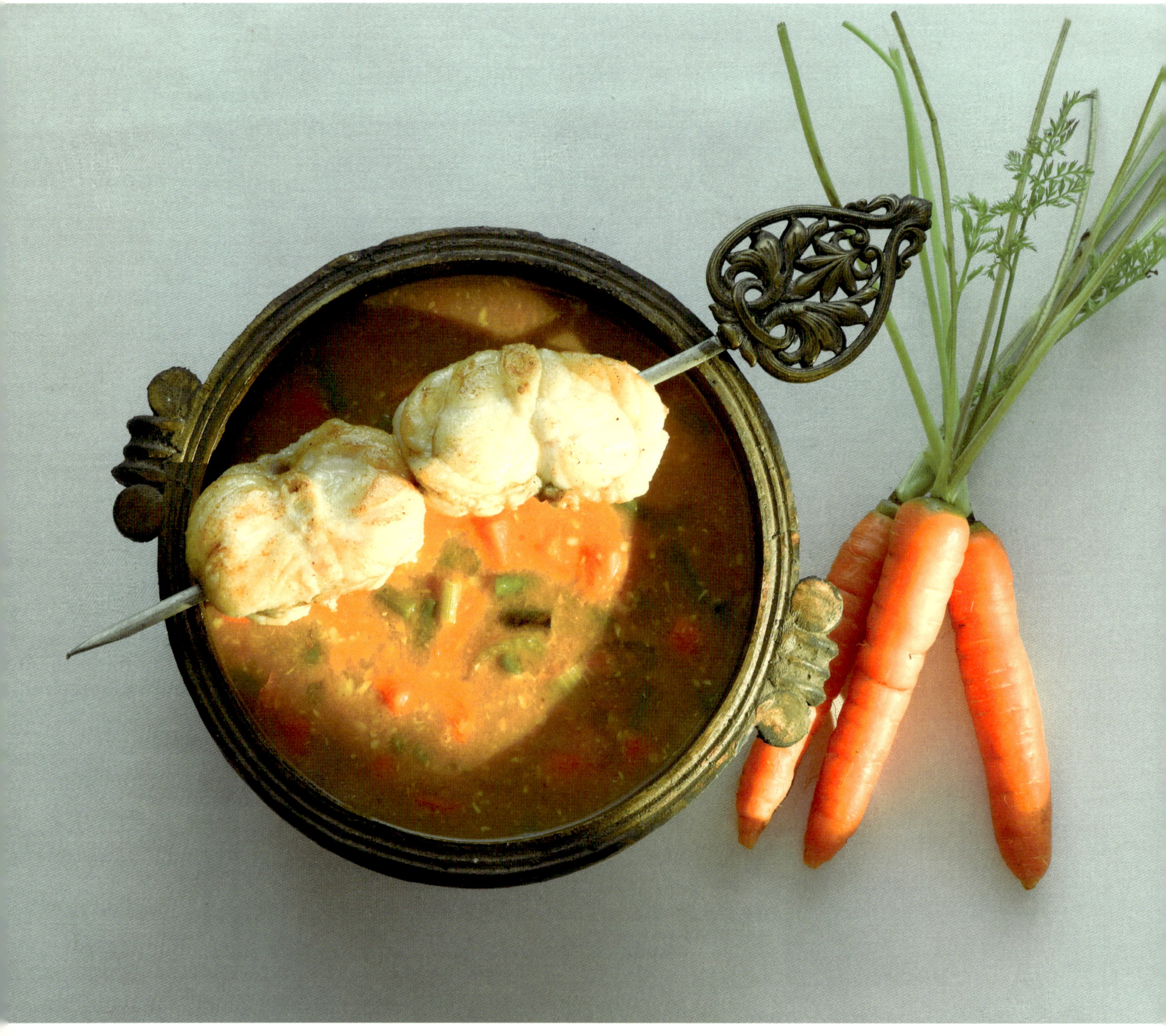

SAMBHAR OF MONKFISH   CLASSIC

In the staff kitchen of Malabar House an authentic sambhar is often prepared for the staff. This popular Indian dish is a vegetarian lentil curry. It would be difficult to give this dish of spicy lentils and vegetables a place in Flemish gastronomic culture. For that reason a slice of monkfish has been added to the original dish. A dish for those who like it spiced...

FOR 4 PERSONS

225 g yellow lentils (toor dhal in India), 200 g green beans, 2 carrots, 1 onion, ½ fennel root, 1 l concentrated fish stock, 1 tablespoon tamarind puree (or finely chopped dried prunes), 2 tablespoons vegetable oil, 1 tablespoon mustard seed, 2 tablespoons sambhar masala, 2 tablespoons turmeric, 4 monkfish steaks of 140 g each

PREPARATION

Soak the lentils for 2 hours in ½ litre water. Drain and put them in a cooking pot with 1 litre water.
Bring the water with the lentils to the boil and leave them to simmer for 15 minutes until they are soft.
Rinse the beans and carrots clean and cut them into small pieces. Boil them for 5 minutes in a large cooking pot in a litre of water.
Peel the onion and cut it roughly. Cut the fennel into pieces and add them together with the onion to the vegetables in the cooking pot. Leave it all to simmer on a low heat till done.
Add the lentils with their cooking liquid and the fish stock to the other vegetables. Add the tamarind puree to this.
Heat the oil in a pan and crisp the mustard seed in this.
Add the sambhar masala and the turmeric and stir it all well.
Rub the fish with this spiced oil and fry it briefly in the pan on both sides to a golden brown. Put the pieces of fish in the pot with vegetables and leave them to simmer on a low heat for 30 minutes, until everything is cooked. Serve this dish very hot.

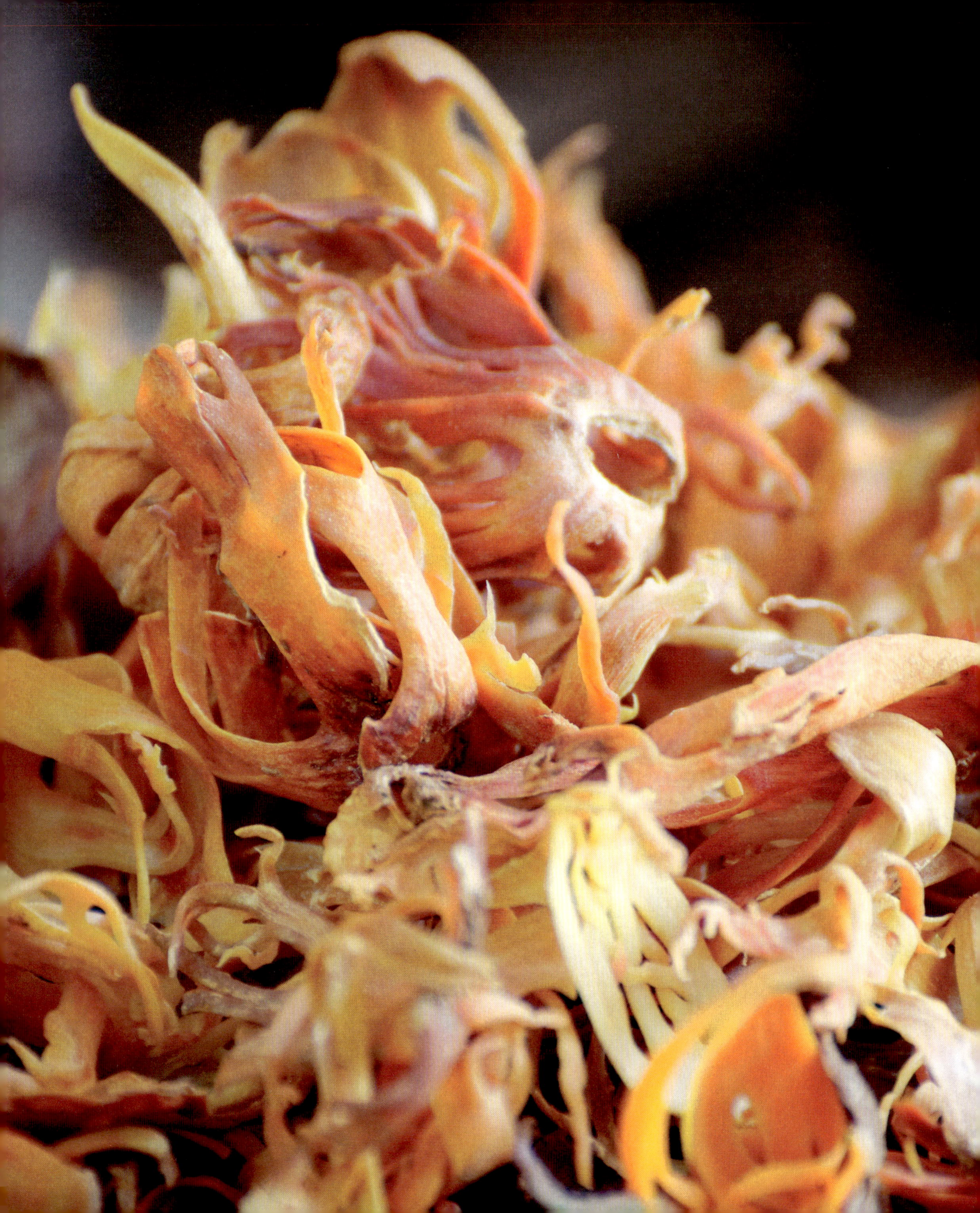

SPICES AND HERBS

AT HOME WITH GOD

'God's own Country', that is how the people of Kerala like to introduce their habitat to tourists. When I see the natural resources such as tea and spices, mostly in breathtaking settings, displayed around me, then I can quite believe that God would indeed have felt at home here…

Dr Simon John, eye surgeon and owner of the charming country estate and hotel Windermere Estate in Munnar, specialized in cardamom, the green pearl among herbs and spices. This self-made man bought this plantation of around 60 hectares around 23 years ago. He transformed the farm that was part of it into an amazing oasis of peace and comfort.

Dr. Simon John: 'You could say that Kerala was a born grocer. It has everything to make herbs and spices extremely happy here. An extensive and fruitful kitchen garden, an ideal situation and a highly suitable climate. This makes sure that from the foot of the hill to the top, specific herbs and spices grow profusely.

Here in Munnar we are at an altitude which varies between 1500 to 2100 metres above sea level. If you look around you it is reasonably clear that a carpet of green tea adorns the top. This is not at all exceptional, because tea shrubs need a great deal of sunlight to grow. They have no use for the shadow of trees, unlike cardamom which prefers to be under the tree tops; shadow is its oxygen. It makes no difference to the coffee trees; they like a bit of both. So just below the tea you will find the cardamom and coffee plantations.

Cardamom, like ginger, belongs to the family of root plants. The roots feed from the fertile soil and this results in a plant with small flowers which are fertilized by insects. Eventually the flowers produce seeds and give the spice its green colour. You see them always low down on the plant, close to the root. They are picked by hand, usually five times a year. Afterwards cardamom goes through almost the same process as tea, in the sense that we first take the moisture away and then dry them. After this we have about one-fifth left of the original quantity. To give you some idea of this: we process about 500 kilo of cardamom in 20 hours. Although we have an enormous number of trees in our plantation, we are not allowed simply to go and chop them down. They are protected by the Forestry Commission, which is not a bad thing, since most of the trees have been here for longer than there have been people. Some are even as much as 1500 years old. So with God's blessing the wood here can maintain itself and we may enjoy all its beauty.

When we leave Munnar and descend in the direction of Cochin, we have a quick view of coconut trees and we see how pepper finds its way up around the tree trunks. We also drive between many rubber plantations. Like cinnamon and cloves, all these crops grow easily in an area up to a height of 1000 metres.

Vanilla is a special case. Insects can't fertilize the flowers without getting caught, so in the early hours people move about to do this by hand. A labour-intensive activity which once was worth the effort, because of the high sales prices. But since these have come down considerably, there are increasingly fewer landowners interested in growing vanilla.

Undoubtedly the easiest spice to grow is pepper. It grows fast and needs little attention. You can find pepper growing along the whole of the Malabar coast. Malabar is the original name of the coast which embraces nearly all of Kerala. It is praised as the best pepper because black pepper had its origin here. It has, after all, been growing here for more than 2000 years. At the time of the Romans it was worth gold to the local population as a means of exchange with traders from all parts of the world, who frequented the South-Indian ports. At the time people referred to it literally as the "black gold".

Moreover, it also has a medicinal function. If you suffer from a cough or a fever, I recommend that you distill a kind of tea from it and drink that. Now we are on the subject, I will be happy to pass on some of granny's tips. If you have a toothache you hold a clove under the offending tooth and you will notice that it works like an anaesthetic and the pain goes after a little while. You may also have noticed that in the preparation of many dishes mustard seeds are crushed in the hot oil. For many this does not add anything to the taste, but it makes sure that our bodies produce Omega 3. Here in Kerala we make grateful use of everything nature has to offer us.

You know that 23 years ago, when I lost my heart to this place, I knew nothing about cardamom. Apart from some general knowledge, of course, but not how to manage a plantation. I assure you that this is unnecessary as long as you take the trouble to learn from old plantation workers. Because I was very eager to learn, I got the hang of most of it after two years.

Perhaps I am telling you something surprising for someone in my position, but cardamom is actually a luxury spice. It is relatively expensive and in fact it is only an asset in the kitchen in combination with other spices. In many poor homes you will notice that cardamom does not find the way to their spice rack. But owing to its components terpene and phenol it is thought to be useful in the fight against cancer. And chewing the seeds certainly will give you a fresh breath. Here in Windermere Estate we like our green pearls!'

Sam

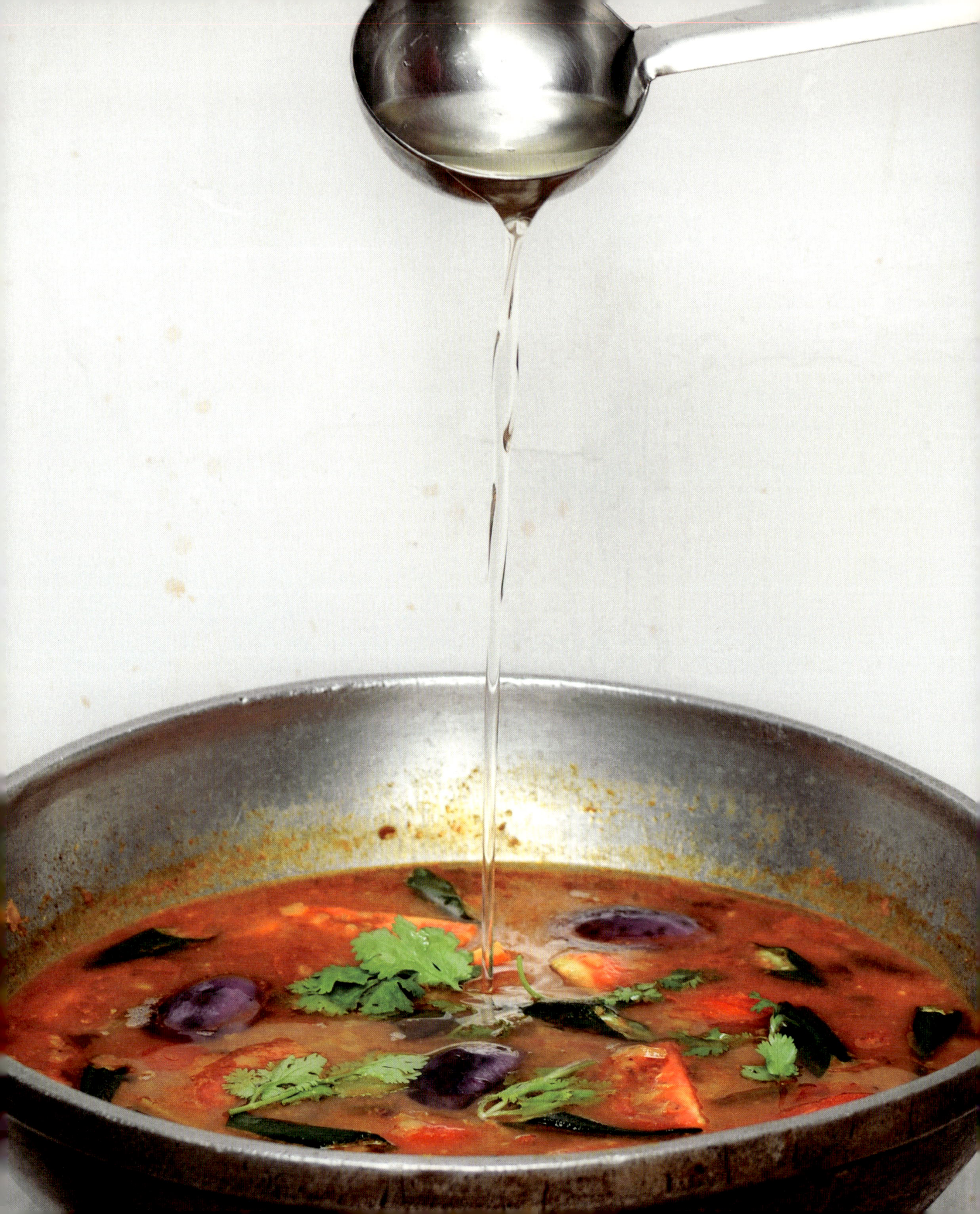

RASAM

CLASSIC

The name of this traditional soup from Southern India literally means 'juice'. It is a broth of lentils with tomatoes and tamarind.

Tamarind is a pod in which there is a sticky pulp with a sour taste, rather like sour plums, which gives the soup its characteristic taste. After harvesting, the tamarind pulp is pressed into a block and sold in pieces.

FOR 4 PERSONS

3 large ripe tomatoes, 2 red onions, 2 cloves of garlic, a pinch of cummin seeds, Kashmir chilli, Malabar pepper freshly ground, salt, 5 tablespoons olive oil, 200 g yellow lentils, ⅛ bundle of coriander, 50 g tamarind pulp, 4 tablespoons clarified butter (or ghee), 1 tablespoon vadouvan masala, 10 curry leaves

PREPARATION

Cut the tomatoes into thick slices. Peel the onion and cut it in rings. Peel the garlic and chop it roughly.
Cover the bottom of an oven dish with the tomatoes. Put the onions and garlic on this and season with cummin seed, Kashmir chilli, a generous helping of Malabar pepper, and salt. Sprinkle oil over it and allow it to cook for 30 minutes in an oven at 200 °C until done. Puree it with a hand blender and set aside.
Cook the lentils for 45 minutes in 2 litres of salted water.
Puree them and leave them to stand, so that they sink to the bottom. Remove 1 litre water.
Leave the tamarind pulp to soak in 2 dl water. Strain and keep the water separate.
Heat the butter in a pan and fry the vadouvan masala. Then add first the tomato puree, followed by the lentil stock and finally the tamarind juice. Heat it through well.

TIP

In India rasam is a vegetarian soup which is very good for the digestion. For those who wish to, pieces of chicken fillet or cooked ham can be added.

ROGAN JOSH CLASSIC

Alain: 'Riyaz and Ayaz are the managers of a small Kashmiri shop in the main street of Mahabalipuram. I have known them for many years, and the brothers have meanwhile become my friends. Ayaz is an excellent chef who can prepare delicious, typically Kashmiri, specialities. Often he uses the mild Kashmir Mirch chilli. He regularly prepares his favourite dish for us, the most popular dish of Kashmir: rogan josh, or "warm glow of the mild chilli". An ode to the culinary art of Ayaz...'

FOR 4 PERSONS

8 cloves of garlic, 6 cm ginger root, 1 teaspoon Kashmir chilli, 1 teaspoon coriander powder, 1 kg leg of lamb, boned, 1 onion, 5 tablespoons clarified butter (or ghee), 1 cinnamon stick, 6 cardamom pods, 6 cloves, 2 dl full-cream (Greek) yoghurt, saffron strands, 0.5 dl milk, salt, 1 teaspoon garam masala, 4 cups of boiled Basmati rice, 2 sprigs of flat-leaved parsley, chilli powder

PREPARATION

Peel the garlic and crush it. Peel the ginger root and grate it. Mix garlic and ginger with the Kashmir chilli and coriander powder. Cut the lamb into 3 cm pieces and put these in the bowl with the spices. Leave to stand for 3 hours.

Peel and chop the onion. Fry it in the butter and add the cinnamon, cardamom and the clove. Braise them for a moment.

Put the meat in the pan and seal it first. Leave it to simmer on low heat for 15 minutes. Add 2.5 dl water and let it stew for 30 minutes till done.

Stir the yoghurt through the cooked meat. Dissolve the saffron strands in the milk and add this to the meat. Season to taste with salt and and scatter a little garam masala over it just before serving.

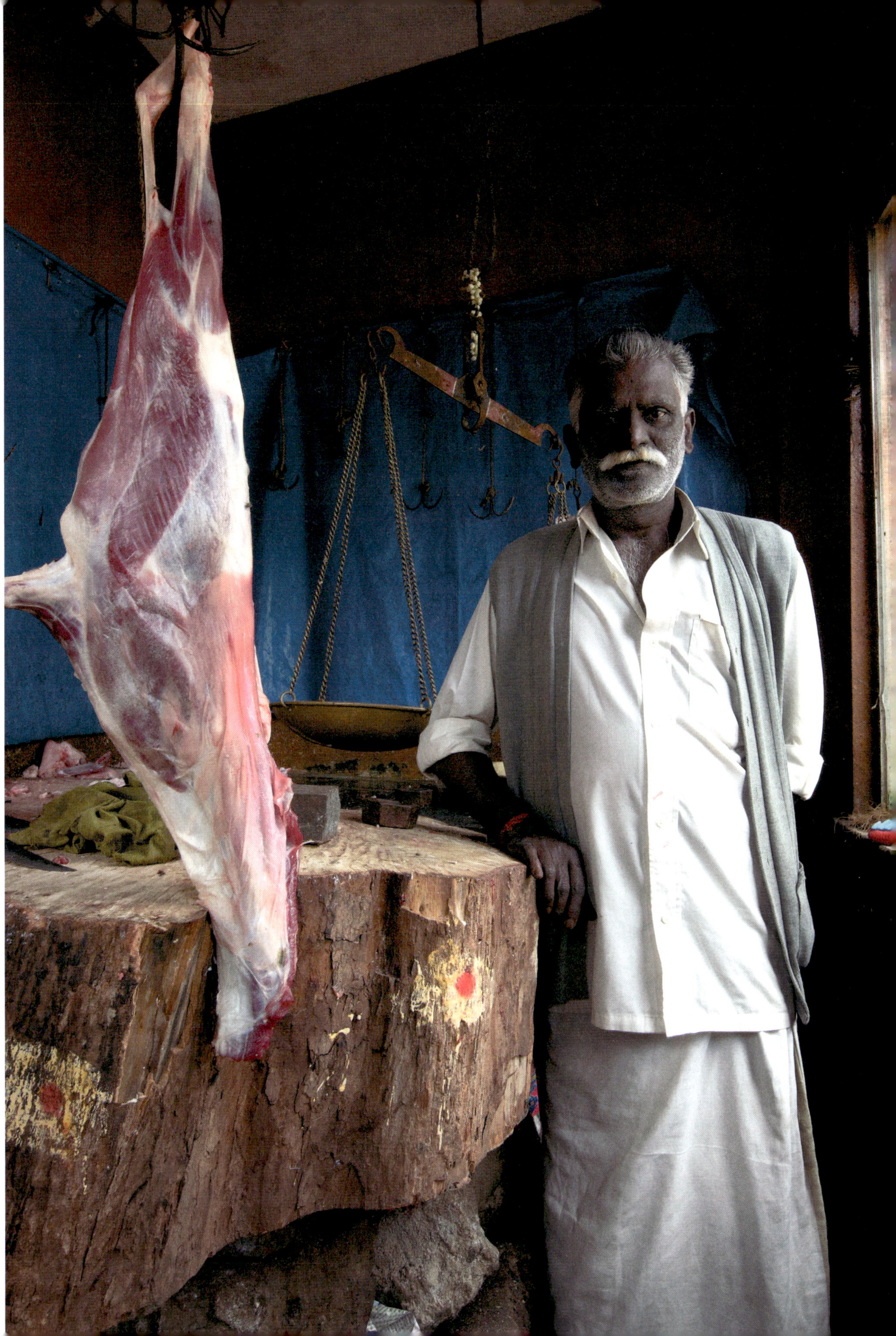

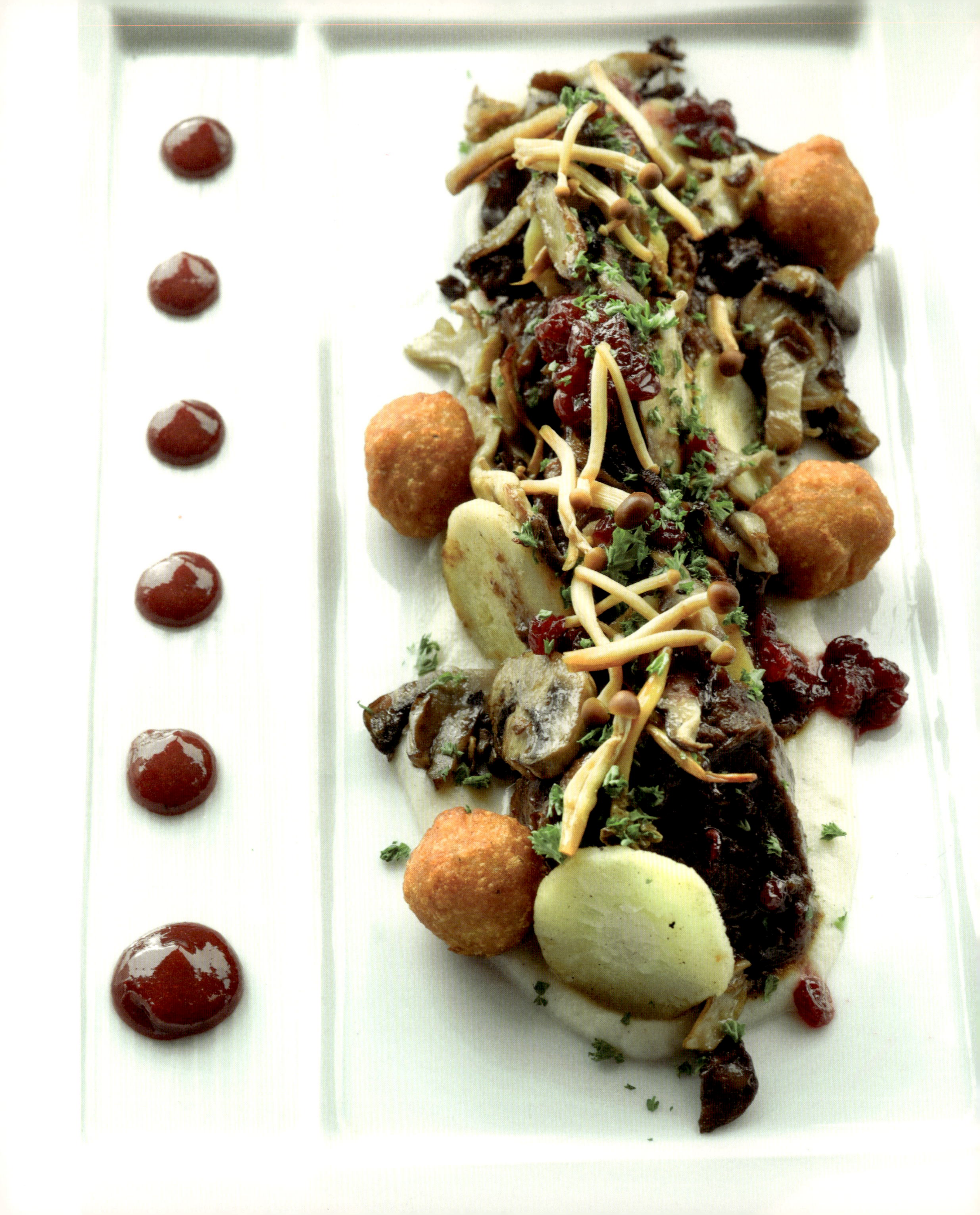

RAGOUT OF VENISON ROGAN JOSH WITH RICE CROQUETTES AND RED BEETROOT PACHADI   ARTISTIC

To dress up this classic dish in an entirely new guise a recipe has been designed in which lamb has been replaced by game.

VENISON RAGOUT 8 cloves of garlic, 6 cm ginger root, 1 teaspoon Kashmir chilli, 1 teaspoon coriander powder, 1 kg venison ragout, 1 onion, 5 tablespoons clarified butter (of ghee), 1 cinnamon stick, 6 juniper berries, 6 cloves, 2.5 dl red wine, 1 dl full-cream (Greek) yoghurt, 2 tablespoons cranberry preserve, saffron strands, 0.5 dl milk, salt, 1 teaspoon garam masala – **RICE CROQUETTES** 150 g glutinous rice, salt, 1 egg, 50 g Parmesan cheese, grated, 3 tablespoons flour, 1 tablespoon coriander, chopped, breadcrumbs, 1 tablespoon garam masala, oil for deep-frying – **RED BEETROOT PACHADI** see Roast spring chicken with pachadi of red beetroot on page 159

PREPARATION

Peel the cloves of garlic and crush them. Peel the ginger root and grate it. Mic cloves and ginger with the Kashmir chilli and the coriander powder.

Cut the venison ragout into 3 cm cubes and mix them with the spices. Leave to stand for 3 hours.

Cut the onion finely and braise it the butter. Add the cinnamon, the juniper berries and the clove to it.

Put the meat in the pan to seal it. Simmer gently on low heat for 15 minutes. Pour in the red wine and leave to simmer for 40 minutes till done.

Stir the yoghurt and the cranberry preserve into the meat. Dissolve the saffron in the milk and add this to the meat. Season to taste with salt and just before serving scatter a little garam masala over it.

Cook the rice for the croquettes in salted water till done. Pour off and allow to cool.

Separate the egg. Mix the egg yolk with the cheese and the flour through the rice and season to taste with salt. Add the chopped coriander and roll the mixture into small croquettes or little balls.

Beat the egg white loose. Mix the breadcrumbs with the garam masala. Pull the croquettes first through the egg white and then through the breadcrumbs.

Deep-fry them in oil to a golden brown.

Serve with red beetroot pachadi and winter vegetables such as wild mushrooms, chicory or slices of celeriac.

TIP

When the salmon has been marinated for the second time, it can be divided into steaks. If you wrap these steaks individually and freeze them, there will always be an appetizing dish ready in the freezer.

MARINATED SALMON WITH SAVOURY SPICES AND CHILLI OF PEAS

ARTISTIC

FOR 4 PERSONS

1 kg salmon fillet, 1 tablespoon coriander seeds, 1 tablespoon cummin seeds, 1 tablespoon fennel seeds, 2 cloves, 1 tablespoon Malabar pepper, oil, 3 tablespoons dried dill tops, 1.5 tablespoon Kashmir chilli, 5 tablespoons sugar, 10 tablespoons coarse sea salt, 1 lime **CHILLI** *250 g frozen peas, 2 dl chicken broth, 1 small green chilli pepper, cloves of garlic, 5 tablespoons olive oil, 1 tablespoon coriander powder, 2 tablespoons mustard seed, a pinch of Kashmir chilli, coarse sea salt –* **PICKLES** *4 red onions, 3 dl water, 2 dl red wine vinegar, a pinch of Kashmir chilli, 10 cloves, 100 g sugar – fresh coriander, 1 slice of lemon, mustard seeds, roasted*

PREPARATION

Cut a slice that is as long as it is broad from the best part of the salmon fillet. Heat the coriander seeds, the cummin seeds, the fennel seeds, the cloves and the Malabar pepper in a little oil. Crush them all fine in a mortar and mix them with the dried dill tops and the Kashmir chilli.
Rub the salmon slice generously with half of the spice mixture.
Mix the sugar with the coarse salt and grated lime peel. Cover the fish with this mixture and let it rest in the refrigerator for 36 hours.
Rinse the marinated salmon well under cold running water. Rub it with the other half of the spice mixture, wrap it in foil, and leave it to rest in the refrigerator for another 12 hours.
For the chilli blanch the peas in chicken broth. Plunge them into ice-cold water to preserve their colour.
Cut the chilli pepper open lengthwise, remove the seeds and chop them finely. Peel the garlic and shred them finely. Heat the oil and fry the pepper and garlic with the coriander power, mustard seed and Kashmir chilli.
Mix the mixture of herbs and spices with the peas in the blender to a smooth, thick puree.
For the pickles peel the red onions and cut them into small strips. Bring 3 dl water to the boil with wine vinegar, the Kashmir chilli, the cloves and the sugar.
Reduce to one half and finally add the onion to cook for 3 minutes. Allow to cool in the refrigerator.
Cut the salmon into slices and finish off with quenelles of green pea chilli, onion pickles, a few coriander leaves and a few roasted mustard seeds.

TURBAN SHAPES OF VANILLA AND GARAM MASALA

ARTISTIC

INGREDIENTS

850 g milk, 60 g salted butter, 500 g muscovado sugar (dark brown sugar with a taste of molasses), 1 teaspoon ground cinnamon, 1 pinch of garam masala, 40 g sugar, 3 eggs, 2 egg yolks, 2 g instant coffee, 75 g brown rum, 240 g flour

PREPARATION

Bring 600 g milk to the boil with 60 g butter.
Mix the remainder of the milk with the muscovado sugar, the cinnamon, the garam masala, sugar, eggs, egg yolks, instant coffee, rum and the flour. Pour the boiling milk with the butter over it and stir well. Leave the mixture to cool and mix it with an electric hand blender.
Fill 'cannelé de bordeaux' moulds (mini turban shapes) one quarter full with the batter.
Bake for 45 minutes in a preheated oven at 170 °C.
Allow them to cool and remove them from the moulds.

THE COFFEE RITE

Nowhere in India is coffee considered more sacred than in the two southern states,
Tamil Nadu and Kerala. It is particularly in Tamil Nadu that drinking coffee is a true ritual.

The cool of the early morning
The aftermath of a hot day
Twice time stands still for a moment
That's when the coffee booth opens

A moment of joy and release
Of equality and social fraternity
Of enjoyment and briefly dreaming away
The opening of the coffee booth

In a large copper kettle hot water is waiting
On a poor little fire the milk foams
A pot is opened of sweet-smelling coffee
Sugar is within reach

Quickly the glasses are rinsed and put ready in rows
Lastly sleeves are rolled up
With a brisk tap against the first glass
The show can now begin

Everybody looks on with approval
The coffee booth is open
Rich aromas welcome the guests
The atmosphere is cordial, everyone is ready for it

A sniff of coffee
A great assumption of sugar
And a rich and damp cloud of milk
Fill the glass with colours

Then all happens fast
A hand goes up
The coffee takes on a different guise
Snakes go from glass to glass

They squirt white foam in the hot glasses
And come sliding in from higher every time
Till, with a little nod, the glass is put in front of you
And with burning fingers you can enjoy it all

Christophe

KERALA MASALA COFFEE

WESTERN

INGREDIENTS

½ litre full-cream milk, 2 tablespoons sugar, 2 cm ginger root, 5 cardamom pods, 2 tablespoons instant coffee, 1 cinnamon stick, ground cinnamon

PREPARATION

Bring the milk to the boil with the sugar.

Peel and grate the ginger root. Crush the cardamom pods. Add the ginger with the cardamom, the instant coffee and the cinnamon stick to the milk. Allow everything to infuse for 5 minutes just below boiling point. Pour it through a sieve.

Pour the coffee into a beaker. From a great height pour the coffee from one beaker into another, until it foams properly. Serve hot and scatter a little cinnamon powder on it.

UPAMA WITH CINNAMON AND VANILLA WITH A STRAWBERRY SALAD

WESTERN

Upama is traditionally a breakfast dish made of rava or sooji (a kind of semolina), onion and spices. Because in Western households people are not used to such a well-seasoned dish, there is this sweet variant.

FOR 4 PERSONS

1 dl clarified butter (or ghee), 140 g semolina, 1 teaspoon mustard seeds, 1 teaspoon cinnamon powder, 75 g cashew nuts, 20 g raisins, 2.5 dl water, 75 g sugar, juice of 1 lime, 250 g small strawberries, 1 vanilla pod, 2 dl cream, 2 tablespoons honey, 2 cinnamon sticks, 2 ginger biscuits

PREPARATION

Heat half of the butter and while stirring continually fry the semolina light brown. Remove from the heat.

Heat the remainder of the butter and crisp the mustard seeds in it. Add the cinnamon powder, chopped cashew nuts and raisins, and wet this with 2.5 dl water. Mix in the sugar, let it come to the boil, and little by little stir in the semolina.

Remove from the heat and add the lime juice. Distribute this over some small bowls.

Remove the stalks from the strawberries.

Cut the vanilla pod open lengthways and scrape out the seeds. Add the honey and the vanilla seeds to the cream and let it slowly thicken on the heat. Allow to cool.

Turn out a small bowl of tepid upama onto the middle of a plate. Arrange the strawberries around it. Put a cinnamon stick on the opama and spoon a little of the honey cream over it. Crunch the ginger biscuits and finish the dish off with the crumbs.

An authentic upama

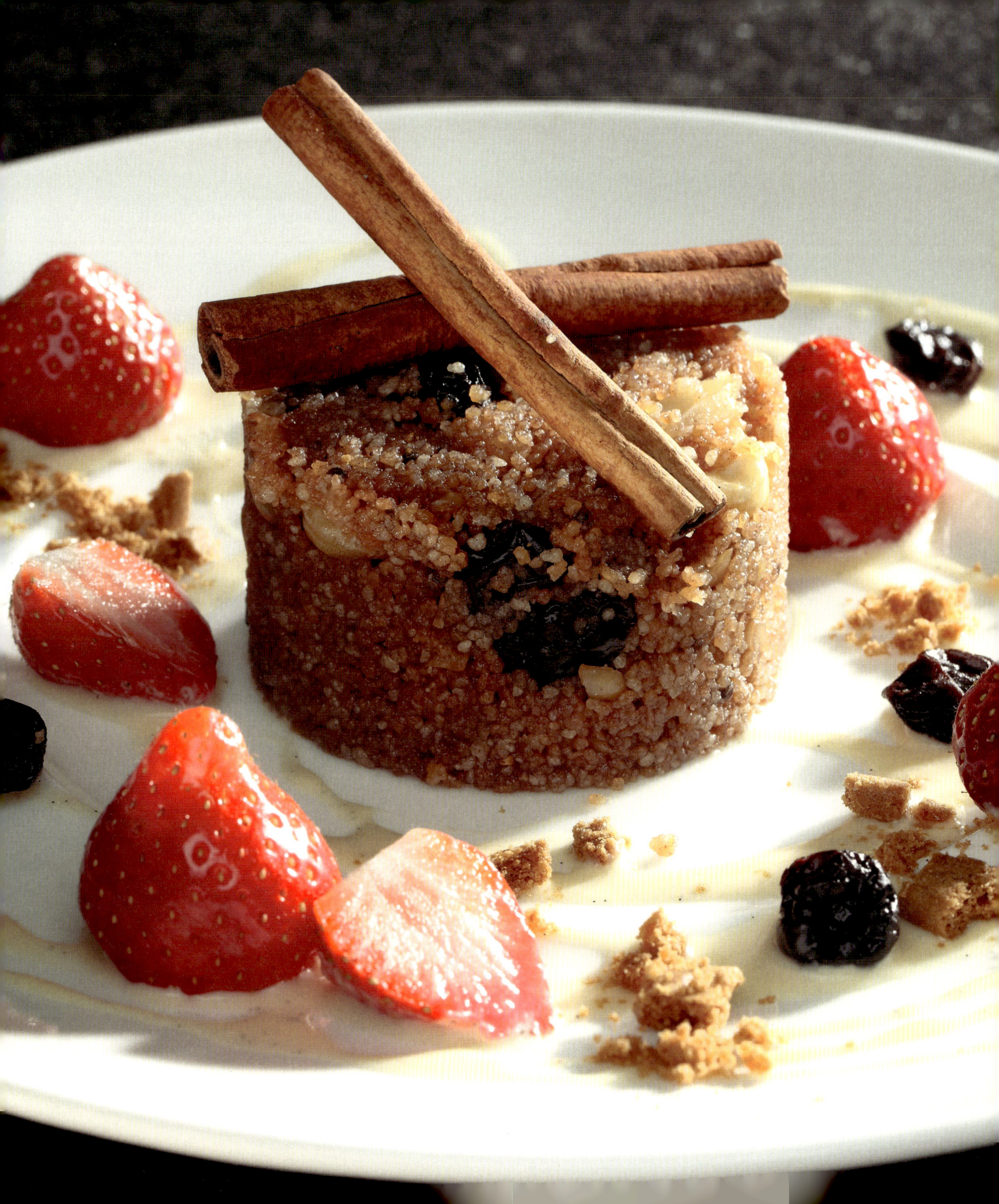

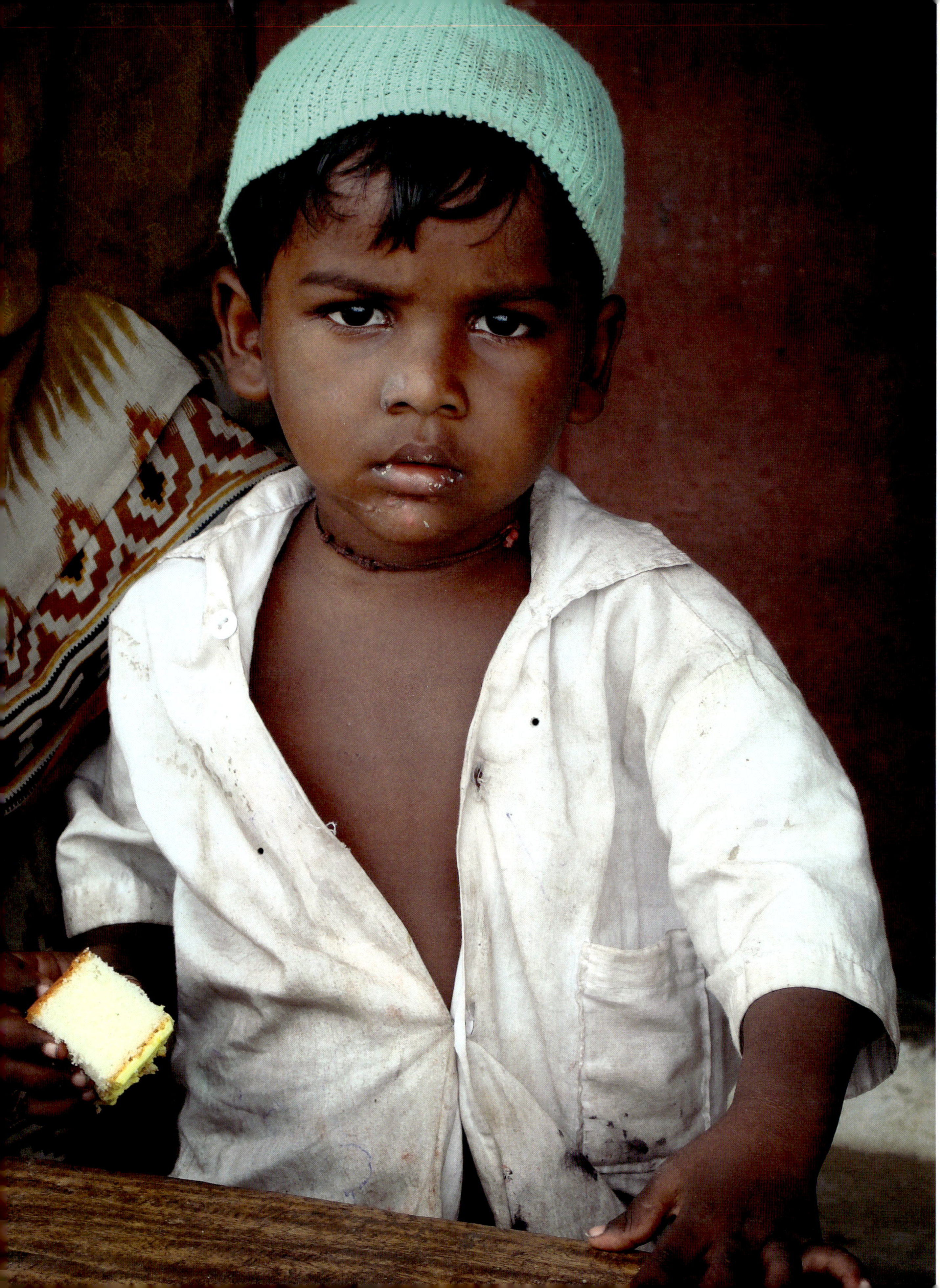

KULFI OF CARDAMOM AND NUTS

CLASSIC

FOR 4 PERSONS

20 green cardamom pods, 2 litres milk, 120 g sugar, 3 tablespoons pistachio nuts, peeled, 3 tablespoons almonds, roasted, 50 g butter, 75 g sugar

PREPARATION

Peel the cardamom pods and grind the seeds to a powder in a mortar.
Bring tne milk to the boil and add the cardamom powder to it. Boil to reduce the quantity to a third of the original quantity (7.5 dl).
Add the sugar to the milk and continue cooking until it has dissolved completely.
Pour the mixture through a sieve.
Chop the pistachio nuts and the almonds finely. Heat a little butter in a pan, add the nuts and the sugar and let it caramelize lightly.
Empty the nuts onto a baking tray covered with baking paper or onto a marble working surface and chop them roughly. Add the nuts to the sugared milk and place this in the freezer. Every 20 minutes stir the kulfi with a fork until all of it has frozen.
Fill (preferably conical) moulds with the mixture and return it to the freezer to freeze solidly again.
Remove the kulfi from the moulds by dipping the mould in hot water for a moment.

POACHED SAFFRON PEARS
WITH A RAISIN-AND-YOGHURT FILLING CLASSIC

FOR 4 PERSONS

1 litre water, 175 g sugar, 1 vanilla pod, 1 tablespoon turmeric, saffron strands, 4 pears, type Williams or Durandeau, ½ tablespoon raisins, 1 tablespoon sugar, 100 g full-cream (Greek) yoghurt

PREPARATION

Put the water with the sugar in a pan which will just hold the pears. Cut the vanilla pod open lengthways and put it in the sugar water together with the turmeric and the saffron. Peel the pears with a parer but leave the stalks in place. Cut off a little slice at the bottom so that the pears will stand upright.

Put the pears in the water, bring the water to the boil and remove the cooking pot from the fire. Leave the pears to cook till done for about 12 minutes, but be careful they don't become too soft. Check this with a skewer.

Remove the pears from the liquid with a skimmer and put them upright on a plate.

Boil the leftover liquid to a syrup.

Soak the raisins in warm water, drain them well and mix them with the sugar through the yoghurt.

Use an apple corer to remove the core from the pears and fill the hole with the yoghurt mixture. Spoon a little sugar syrup over it.

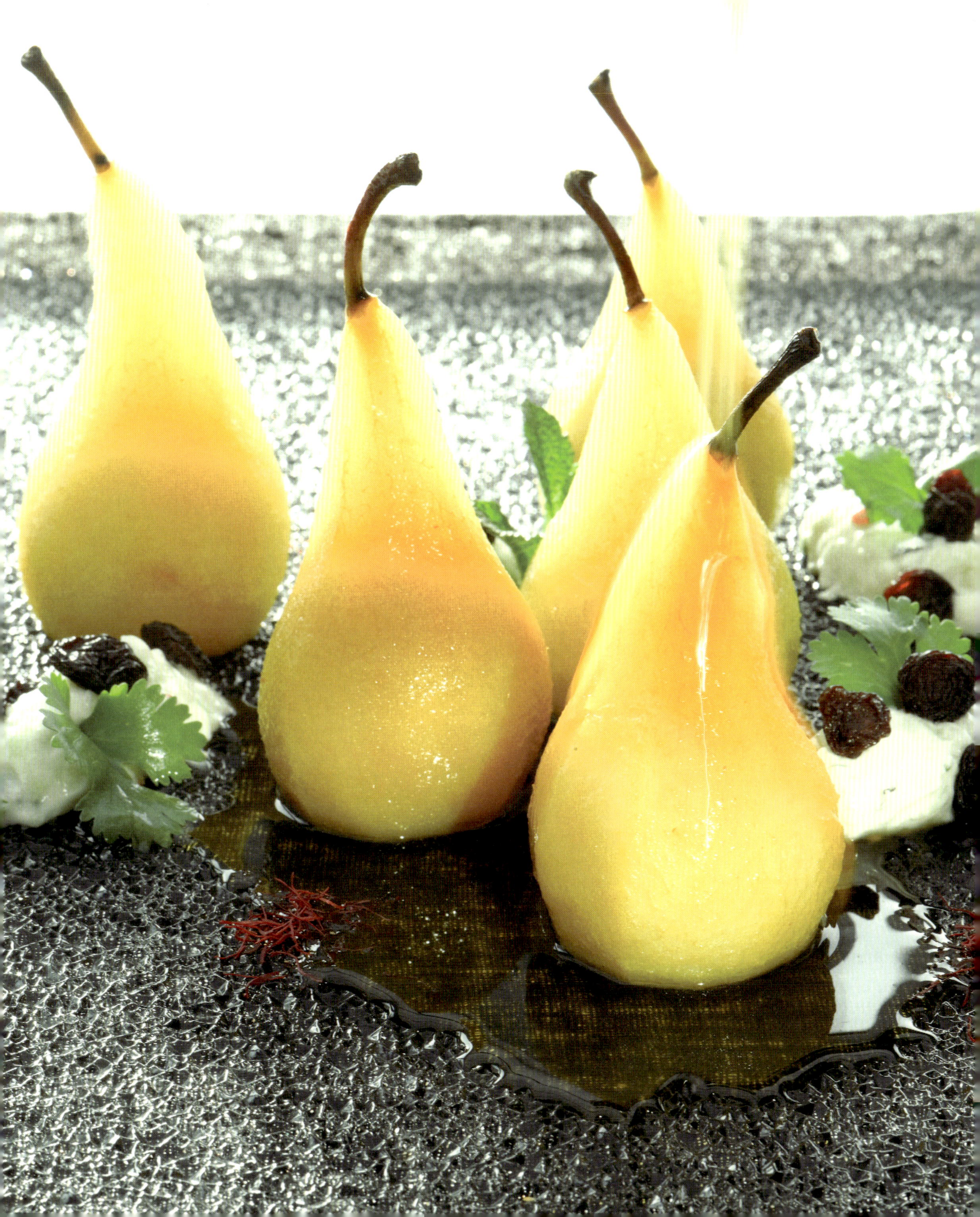

GAZPACHO OF CARROT AND PUMPKIN
WITH TURMERIC AND POMEGRANATE   WESTERN

TIP

Serve the soup in small glasses as an appetizer. This soup can also be eaten hot as a special variant of ordinary pumpkin soup.

FOR 4 PERSONS

120 g pumpkin, 120 g carrots, ½ litre chicken stock, 6 shallots, 1 clove of garlic, 2 tablespoon peanut oil, 2 tablespoon turmeric, 1 tablespoon vadouvan masala, 1 dl cream, 2 dl coconut cream, pepper, salt, fresh coriander, ½ pomegranate

PREPARATION

Peel the pumpkin and the carrots and cut them into large pieces. Cook them in chicken stock till done.

Peel the shallots and the garlic and chop them finely. Fry them in the oil and add the turmeric and the vadouvan masala.

Pour the stock with the vegetables onto the onion and garlic. Return it to the boil and mix it with a hand blender.

Add the cream and the coconut cream and leave the soup to thicken. Season with pepper and salt.

Allow the soup to cool down, distribute it over some glasses and finish off with coriander leaf and pomegranate pips.

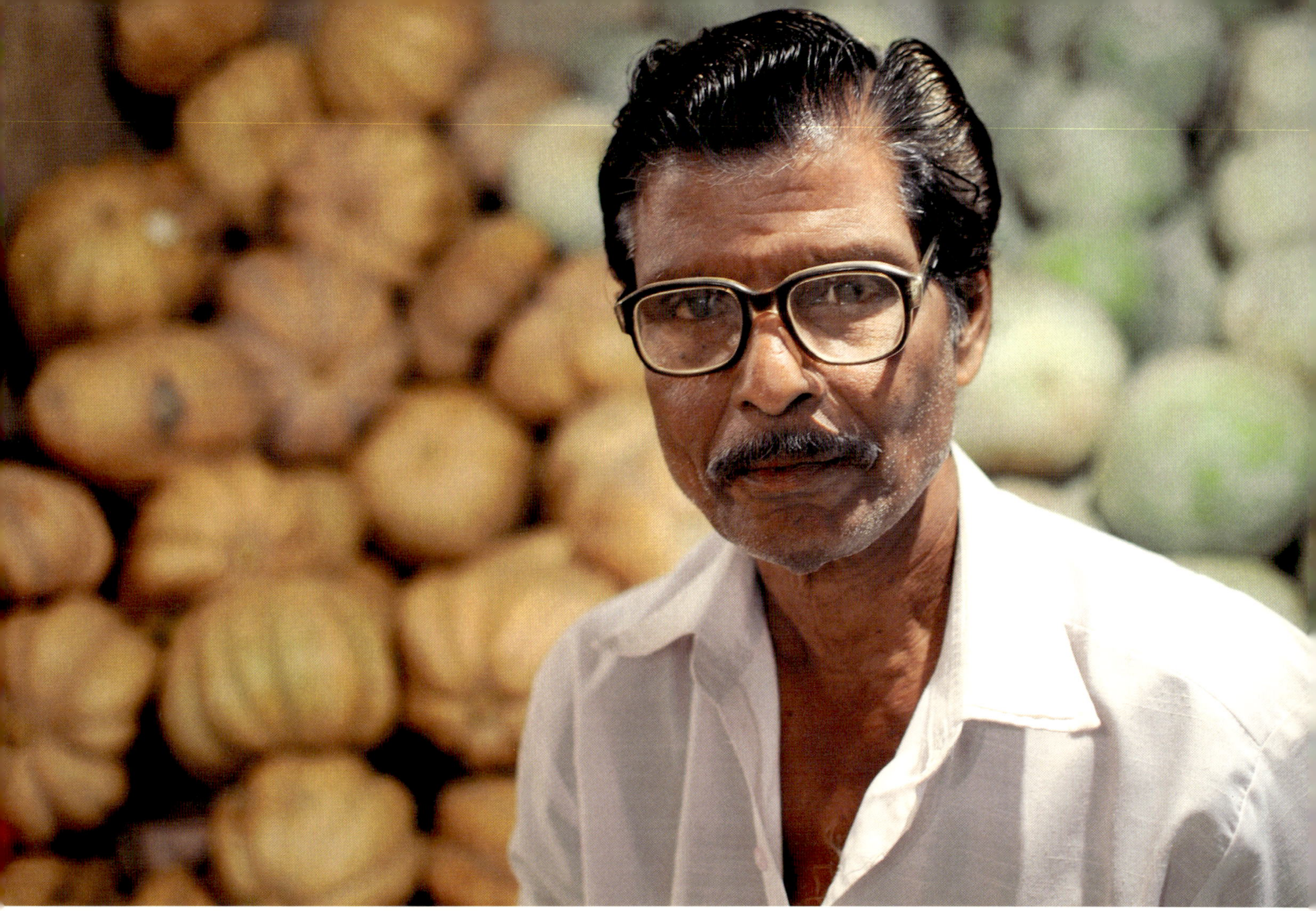
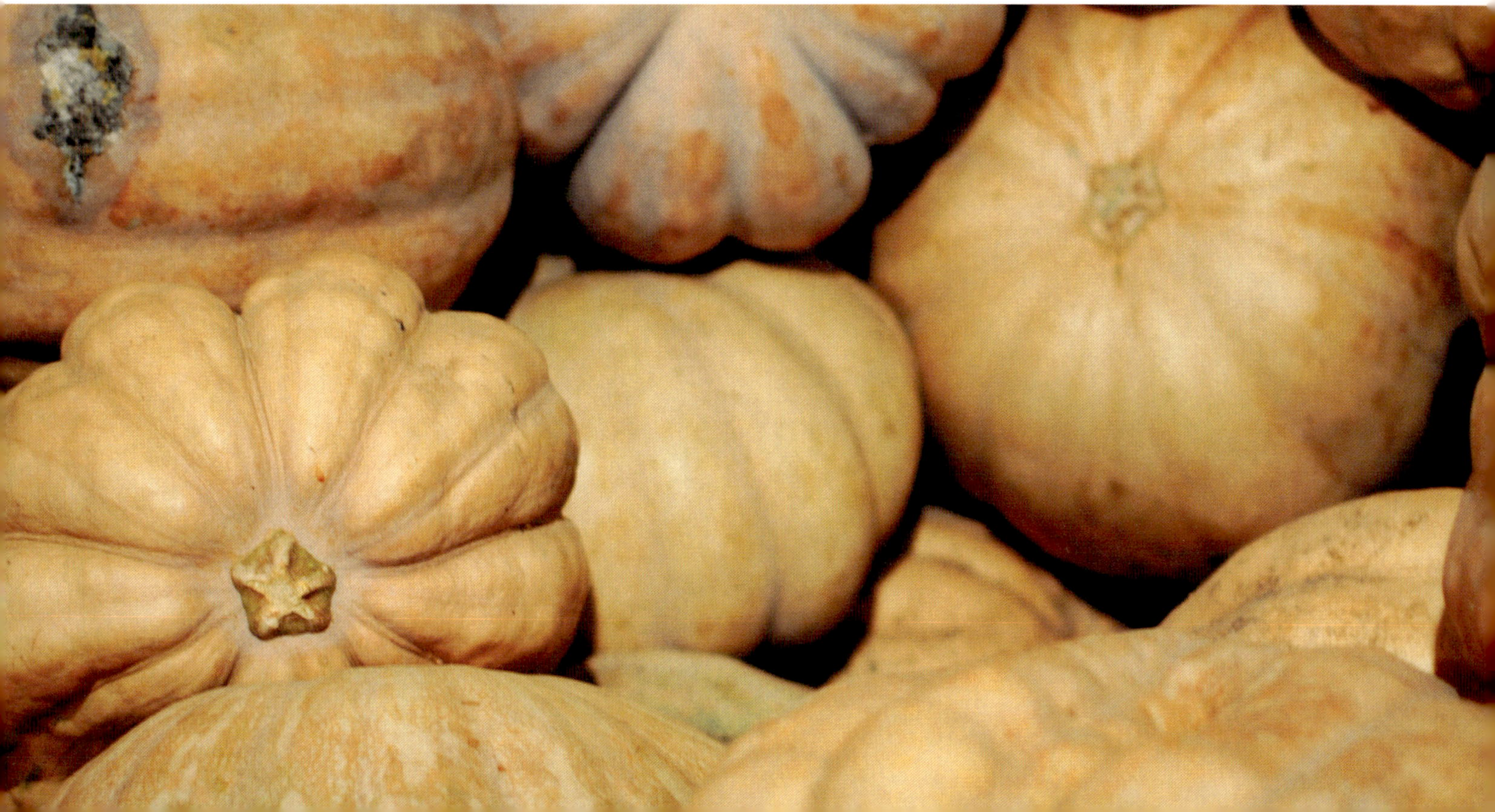

ANJOU PIGEON WITH THREE CARROT PREPARATIONS WITH AROMATIC SPICES

> ARTISTIC

FOR 4 PERSONS

PIGEONS 4 shallots, 1 clove garlic, 2 cm ginger root, oil, 1 teaspoon saffron, 1 teaspoon turmeric, 10 cardamom pods, juice of ½ lime, 100 g full-cream (Greek) yoghurt, 2 Anjou pigeons, pepper, salt

CARROT PUREE 5 large carrots, 4 dl water, 1 dl vinegar, juice of 1 orange, 50 g sugar, 1 teaspoon turmeric, salt

CARROT STRINGS 3 large carrots, juice of 2 oranges, juice of ½ lime, 2 tablespoons olive oil, 2 tablespoons sushi vinegar

CARROT VELOUTÉ 2 large carrots, 3 dl chicken stock, 1 teaspoon turmeric, 1 teaspoon saffron, 10 cardamom pods, ½ dl coconut cream, 80 g salted butter, ½ small red chilli pepper, 12 leaves young blood sorrel

PREPARATION

Peel the shallots and the garlic and cut them finely. Peel the ginger root and chop it fine.

Braise the shallots with the garlic and ginger root in oil. Add the saffron, the turmeric and the cardamom seeds. Dowse with lime juice and stir through the yoghurt.

Fillet the pigeons and season them with pepper and salt. Fry them briefly on all sides. They should not be cooked till done.

Put a fillet and a thigh onto a skewer and generously rub in the yoghurt marinade. Roast them in a pre-heated over at 200 °C until the yoghurt is a golden brown.

For the puree clean the carrots and cut them into pieces. Boil them till done in water with vinegar, sugar, orange juice and turmeric. Drain the carrots and mash them with part of the cooking water to a smooth puree. Season to taste with salt.

Clean the carrots for the second preparation and cut them with a mandolin (or a fine peeler) into fine, long strings.

Bring the juice of the oranges and the lime to the boil and allow it to thicken to a light caramel. Mix 2 tablespoons of this with the olive oil and vinegar. Put the carrot strings in this marinade and leave it to rest for some time.

For the carrot velouté clean the carrots and cut them into pieces. Cook them until done in the chicken stock and mix it with a hand blender. Season with turmeric, saffron and cardamom and bring back to the boil for a moment. Add the coconut cream to it and allow it to thicken.

Take the cardamon pods out of the pan and finish off the velouté with the ice-cold butter. Cut the chilli pepper into very fine strips and then add it to the dish.

Serve the pigeon with quenelles of carrot puree and carrot strings. Spread the velouté round it and finish off with the blood sorrel.

Turmeric

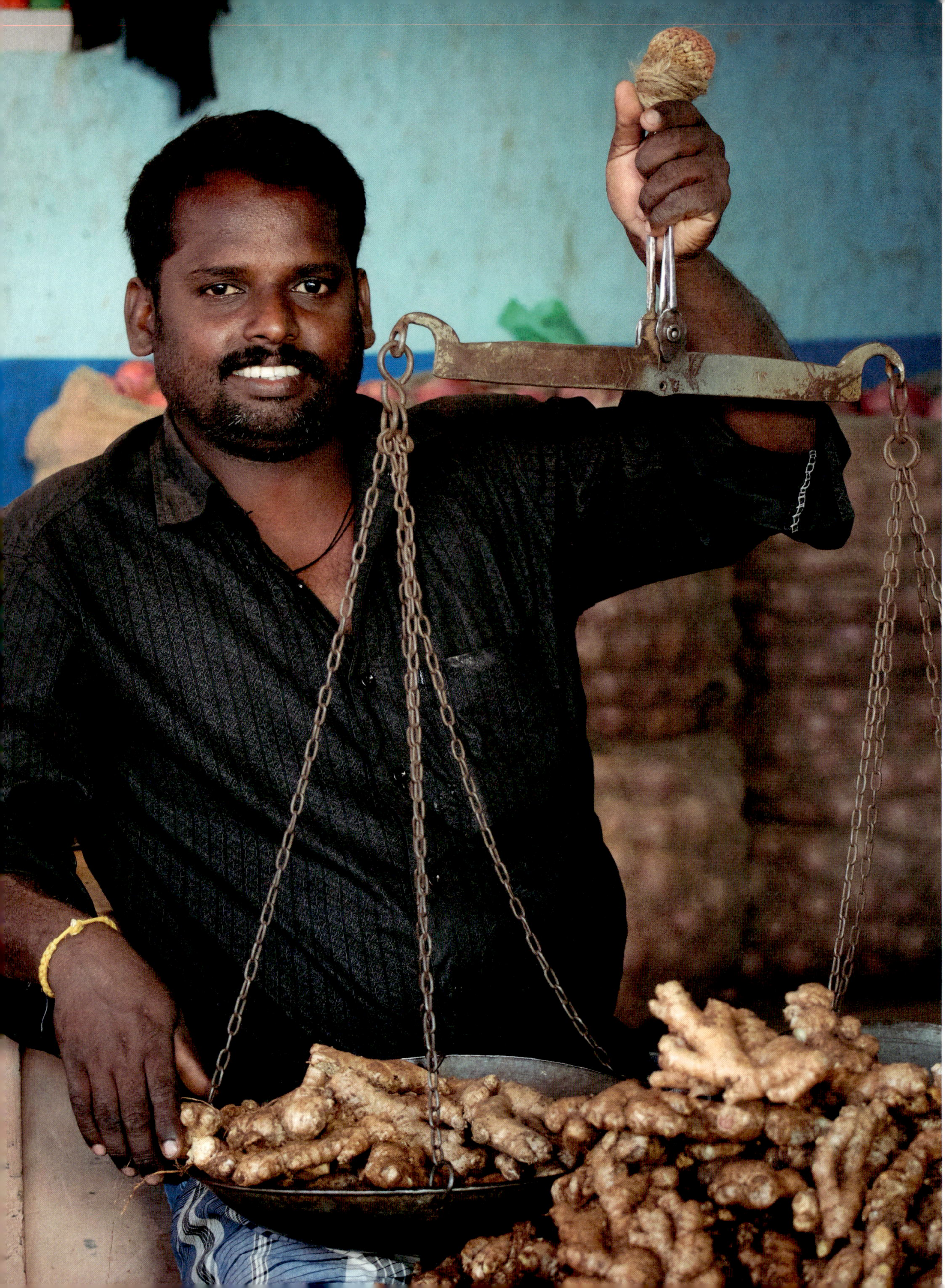

GINGER

A VISIT TO THE GINGER FACTORY

It is still the depth of night. At this virginal hour the playground in front of the Malabar House is still an oasis of peace and quiet. Even the irritating crows don't make themselves heard yet in this early break of day. The only sound that fills the dusky sky is the rhythmic, dominant clatter of large raindrops that in no time at all flood the road. Because of the intensity of the curtain of rain, we can hardly distinguish St Francis's Church, where Vasco Da Gama lay buried before he was returned to Portugal, the land of his birth. I love these intense downpours of July rain in Kerala. They never last very long, they give you some oxygen for the day and above all, feel pleasantly refreshing.

Even before we reach the little shopping streets, the water gods decide it's been enough. The rain stops as suddenly as it started. The air immediately begins to feel sultry and everywhere plumes of moisture rise dancing to the skies. Until the next shower. This is the monsoon…

We pass the fish market. Always pleasantly busy. The day's catch is being sold with loud shouts and handclapping. It is certainly a sight worth seeing. Today, however, we ignore the fishermen. We go parallel with the inlet of the sea beside us towards the bus station and beyond.

The stretch which we now continue on foot is usually undeservedly missed out by visitors. For them Fort Cochin consists of two areas. One side of the island with the Dutch Cemetery, St Francis's Church, the basilica, the little shopping streets and the Chinese fishing nets; the other side with the Jewish Synagogue, the Dutch Palace, the many antique shops, the shops selling spices, and the obligatory souvenir shops which serve to provide a permanent reminder of the visit.

For those who want to discover everyday life in its purest form, the midpoint between these two poles is far more interesting. It is the authentic socio-cultural centre of the town, far away from the continual stream of tourists. It is a chain of little living areas, markets, minuscule inner courts

---

Your green stalk
looks delicate and frail
and one would never suspect
the powers
you keep hidden underground

An Indian truffle you might be
a pregnant cluster of roots
hidden deep under the dark earth

Your antlers look elegant
your shapes freakish and mysterious
who are you?

I am the spice that gives body
to all your fish and chicken dishes
that makes lemonade refresh
and tea revive you
I'm also the one who can revitalize
that pudding and cake
and make biscuits
squeal with pleasure

I have the gift to heal you
to wrap you in warmth
when you are cold
I am
Ginger

where the local population lives and works. Here Indian society still brims over in all its facets. From the houses comes the sound of singing at pujas, in the morning women wash their laundry in the swollen stream round the corner, and then, between showers, quickly spread them out to dry. Still in the last quarter of an hour of the night, just before the sun shows itself, the first children leave their living quarters, neatly dressed in uniforms, on their way to school in crammed rickshaws, overcrowded buses, by bicycle or in colourful rows on foot. In the Muslim quarter, the butcher sharpens his knives and the shoemaker starts on his first repairs. In the markets flowers and fruit are being sold. You can spend hours here.

However, we don't turn away from the main road. What interests us today is just a little further away in this area. Adjoining the water we discover majestic spice warehouses. Pearls of Dutch and Portuguese architectural heritage. Often neglected until recently, but gradually rediscovered and upgraded as a cultural patrimony, they are sparsely restored. They are truly splendid buildings that take us back immediately to the heyday of the mercantilism of the fifteenth and sixteenth century. When countless trading companies stopped in Kochin and had the holds of their merchant ships filled with the aromatic spices which were brought here every day.

The buildings are fortunately more than silent witnesses of this illustrious past. When we get closer to the warehouses, we see more and more activity. Carts drawn by oxen and other animals have now mainly been replaced by creaking lorries, laden to the limit of their capacity. Yet the sight of men carrying sacks in and out of the sheds remains impressive. We navigate our way through this chaotic tangle and continually come up against the aromas of pepper, nutmeg, chilli, ginger and cardamom hanging in the air. We enter one of the big sheds and arrive in an impressive and completely walled-in inner yard where people are pickling ginger. To our left is a shed filled to the rafters with the ever so popular brownish-yellow root. We pull ourselves up the narrow stairs along the front. In a space that easily takes us back centuries, women are assembling all kinds of derivatives of ginger. Ginger tea, ginger soap, chutney, biscuits, oil... The charming little sales girls fetch the whole collection of ginger products upstairs. The noble aroma of ginger is present everywhere. About an hour later we leave the old building and go back to the Malabar House. Chef Biju has no trouble guessing where we have been this morning. Our clothes, our pores, everything appears to breathe ginger. He takes us along to his kitchen.

Christophe

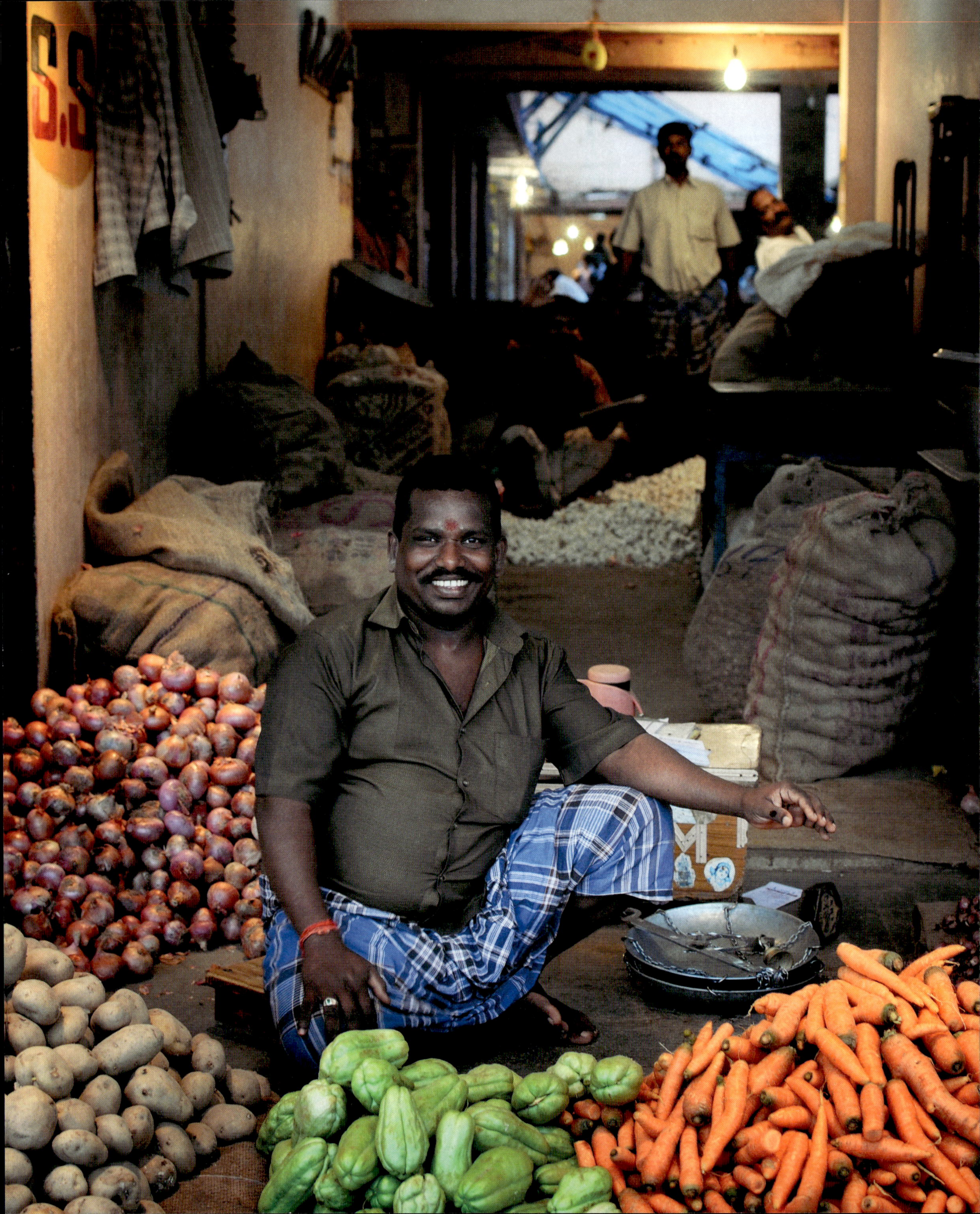

GINGER ORANGEADE CLASSIC

This appetizing, non-alcoholic orangeade of oranges and ginger is very refreshing on a warm day.

FOR 2 LARGE GLASSES

    4 oranges, 1 lemon, 2 cm ginger root, a pinch of ginger powder (djahé), 2 tablespoons ginger syrup

PREPARATION

    Press the oranges and the lemon.
    Peel the ginger root and grate it finely. Mix 1 tablespoonful of the grated ginger into the juice. Add the ginger powder and the ginger syrup.
    Leave to infuse for two hours in a cool place (but not in the refrigerator). Strain the drink through a coffee filter and put it in the refrigerator.

TIP

On a hot summer's day add some ice cubes to the glass and finish off with a slice of orange.

GINGER LEMONADE CLASSIC

Ginger lemonade is not only delicious; it also has wonderful properties. It refreshes the breath, helps to combat nausea and has a relaxing influence.

INGREDIENTS

    5 cm ginger root, juice of 3 lemons, 50 g sugar, 1 vanilla pod, 4 cinnamon sticks, 1 litre boiling water, 4 twigs of mint, lemon for a finish

PREPARATION

    The ginger gives the traditional lime juice a real upgrade.
    Peel the ginger root and cut it fine. Mix 4 tablespoons of ginger with the lemon juice and the sugar. Put the vanilla pod and the cinnamon stick in the juice and pour 1 litre boiling water over it. Leave to infuse for 2 hours.
    Serve the lemonade with a lot of ice cubes. If necessary sweeten it with sugar syrup and finish off with mint leaves and a small slice of lemon.

TIP

Use cinnamon sticks for stirring.

TIP

Serve the punch in attractive cups and add a cinnamon stick to stir with. A few bits of preserved ginger are a delicious addition...

GINGER PUNCH

CLASSIC

Punch is thought to date from the eighteenth century in India and to have come to Europe via the British East-Indian Company. The name is derived from the Hindi word "panch", five, in reference to the five ingredients of the original mixture: water, tea, arak (an alcoholic drink), lemon and sugar.

The most famous punch is ginger punch, undoubtedly because of its healing qualities. It is indeed still a warm pick-me-up in the cold months.

INGREDIENTS

1 litre water, 3 tea bags of black tea, 100 g light brown soft sugar, ½ litre fresh apple juice (from the liquidizer), 3.5 dl white rum, 4 tablespoon ginger powder (djahé)

PREPARATION

Bring 1 litre water to the boil in a saucepan. Take it off the heat, put in the black tea and leave to draw for 5 minutes. Take the teabags out of the water and put the soft sugar, the apple juice, the rum and the ginger powder in it. Heat the punch until it begins to steam but not boil. Serve at once.

GINGER TEA

CLASSIC

The aroma of a ginger root is warm and spicy. Its taste is delicate and piquant. Ginger tea smells of pepper, lemon and a touch of camphor. Hot drinks such as punch and tea are combined with sweet treats such as ginger cake, ginger biscuits, ginger pudding, etc...

FOR 2 CUPS

4 cm ginger root, 1 cinnamon stick, black pepper, 2 oranges, honey (to taste)

PREPARATION

Put 3 cups of water in a saucepan.

Peel the ginger root and grate it finely. Put the ginger pulp in the saucepan and put it on a low heat, with the lid half open. Add a small piece of the cinnamon stick.

Leave the ginger tea to boil gently until part of the water has evaporated and the tea is light brown in colour. Stir occasionally to stop the pulp from sticking to the bottom.

Add a good touch of black pepper to it.

Press the oranges and pour the hot tea onto the juice. Mix well.

Drink the tea hot and sweeten it with a little honey if desired.

The ginger pulp is very healthy and can be drunk with it.

TIP

You may have to get used to the taste, but after a few times you will certainly enjoy this tea. The tea gives an enormous boost in the afternoon, and in the evening it is heart-warming.

CRÉCY SOUP WITH GINGER POWDER

WESTERN

TIP

Put a spoonful of whipped cream with lemon and fine strips of ginger in the middle of the plate.

By adding a little ginger powder to grandmother's stewed carrots, the dish acquires a completely new touch.

FOR 4 PERSONS

500 g carrots, 2 cm ginger root, 1 large sweet onion, 50 g butter, 1 red chilli pepper, 1.5 litre vegetable stock, 1 dl ginger syrup, 1 tablespoon ginger powder, 2.5 dl cream (40% fat content), juice of ½ lemon, coarse salt, Malabar pepper

PREPARATION

Peel the carrots and cut them into thick slices.

Peel the ginger root and grate it finely. Save the sap and the pulp.

Peel the onion and cut it into coarse pieces. Cut the chilli pepper lengthways, remove the seeds, and chop it finely.

Melt the butter in a saucepan. Braise the onion with the carrot, the ginger and the chilli. Pour in the stock and leave it to simmer for half an hour.

Mix the soup with a hand blender and add the ginger syrup and the ginger powder.

Just before serving add the cream and the lemon juice.

Season to taste with coarse salt and freshly ground pepper.

SCOUBIDOU OF SOLE FILLED WITH TOMATO-AND-GINGER COMPOTE IN A CRÉCY SOUP

ARTISTIC

FOR 4 PERSONS

4 soles divided into 16 fillets, 2 cm ginger root, 1 tablespoon ginger powder (djahé), 4 tablespoons tomato chutney (see Pollitchatu of swordfish on page 197), ½ litre fish stock, 1 litre Crécy soup with ginger powder (see Crécy soup with ginger powder on page 90), 2 sprigs of Thai chives (or Thai soy)

PREPARATION

For each person put 2 fillets of sole next to each other. Weave a third fillet through it. This fillet lies on top of the first and underneath the second fillet. Weave the fourth fillet of sole also through the first two, but now under the first and on top of the second fillet. The centre of the fillets now forms a solid square.

Peel the ginger and grate it finely. Mix it with the ginger powder and the tomato chutney.

On each square put a generous tablespoonful of this mixture and fold the outer pieces of the fillets inwards. Turn the parcel round. It forms a firm 'scoubidou'.

Put the parcels in a shallow cooking pot or pan, pour fish stock over them and cover with a lid. Keep for 8 minutes just below boiling point. Heat the Crécy soup and divide it over four soup plates. Put the scoubidous in the middle of the plates and finish off with Thai chives.

INDIAN MEAT BALLS CLASSIC

You meet kofta almost anywhere in the Middle East and in South Asia. The minced meat is always well seasoned and often mixed with other ingredients, such as rice, eggs or vegetables. Only then are small balls formed and fried. Because of the spiciness of the minced meat the kofta is usually served without an accompanying sauce.

TIP

Serve this Indian kofta with basmati rice and a curry of green beans with ginger (see next page).

FOR 4 PERSONS

½ large onion, 1 clove of garlic, 2 cm ginger root, 15 black peppercorns, 15 coriander seeds or a pinch of coriander powder, a pinch + 1 tablespoon garam masala, juice of ½ lemon, coarsely ground salt, 650 g mixed mince, pork/veal, 1 teaspoon tikka masala, 1 teaspoon ginger powder (djahé), 2 tablespoons flour, 1.5 dl olive oil

PREPARATION

Peel the onion and the garlic. Peel the ginger. Chopped them all very fine.

Grind the peppercorns and the coriander seed finely in a mortar. Add a pinch of garam masala, the lemon juice, and a pinch of coarsely ground salt, then add the onion, garlic and ginger.

Season the minced meat with tikka masala and ginger powder.

Roll into small balls the size of a golf ball and push a hole in the middle with your thumb. Fill this with the spiced onion mixture, close it again and roll it into a smooth ball.

Mix the flour with 1 tablespoon of garam masala and a pinch of salt. Dip the meatballs in the flour and fry them in a deep pan in hot olive oil.

SPICY CURRY OF YOUNG GREEN BEANS AND GINGER

CLASSIC

TIP

Serve the curry with Indian meat balls and basmati rice (see previous page).

In India this authentic and well-spiced Indian green bean curry is prepared in a wok or karahi. The frying is done very fast so that you will have to stir continually to avoid it sticking to the pan. Even while it is simmering it has to be stirred until the water has evaporated.

FOR 4 PERSONS

500 g young green beans, ½ large onion, 5 cm ginger root, 20 g (a handful) fresh coriander, 1 dl olive oil, 2 teaspoons vadouvan masala, 3 dl poultry stock, juice of ½ lemon, coarsely ground salt, a pinch of ginger powder

PREPARATION

Cut the beans into 2 cm pieces. Peel the onion and cut it into rings. Peel the ginger root and chop it very fine. Chop the coriander coarsely.

Heat the oil in a wok and fry the finely chopped ginger in it. Add the vadouvan masala and the fresh coriander, let it stew for a minute and then add the beans and the onions.

Dowse with the stock and leave it to simmer for 10 minutes until all moisture has evaporated. Add the lemon juice, the salt and the ginger powder.

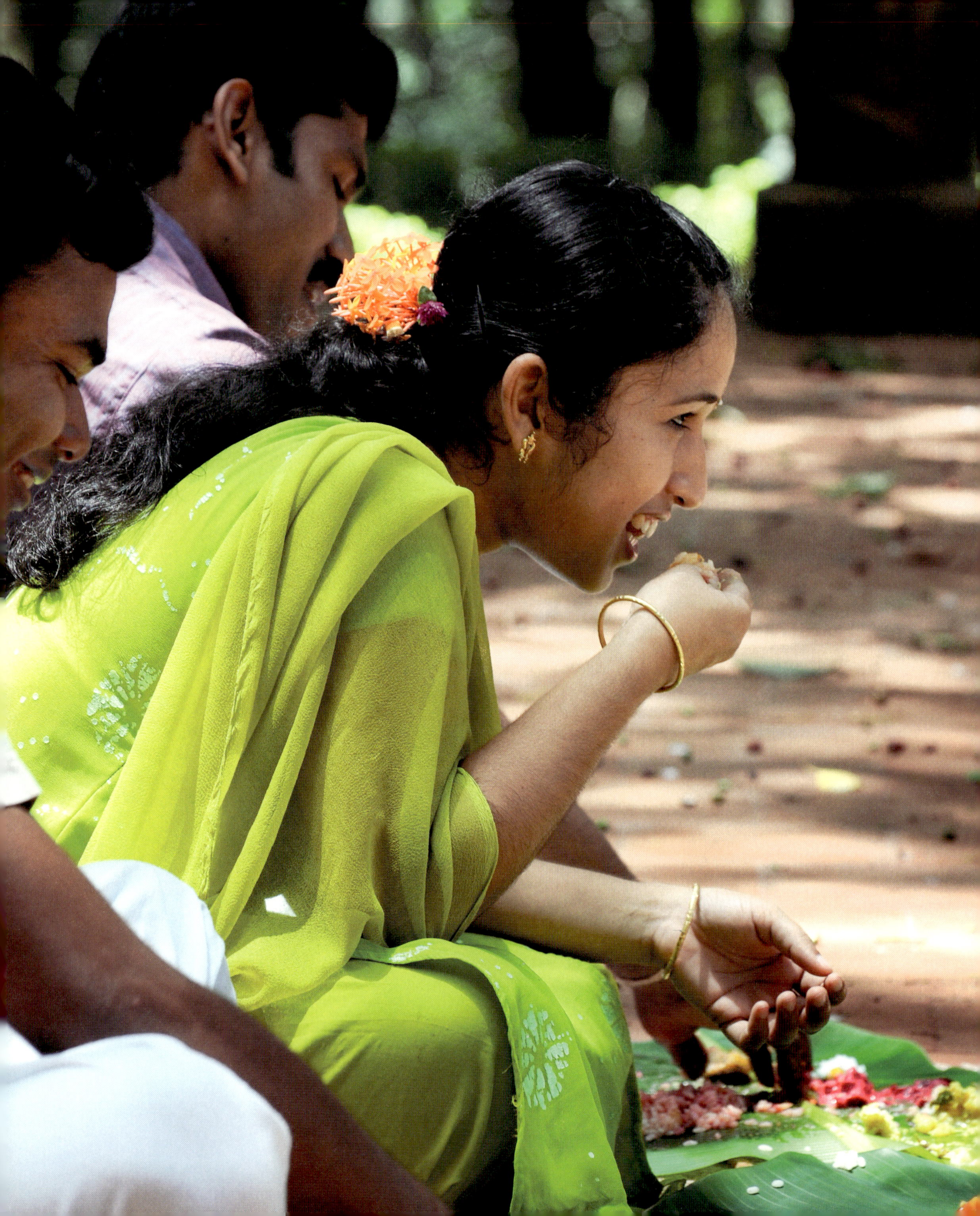

SALAD OF FRESH FRUIT WITH
WHIPPED GINGER CREAM AND CHUTNEY   WESTERN

The refreshing lemon scent of ginger combines well with sweet kinds of fruit. A dollop of ginger cream on a coupe with summer fruits tastes delicious. If desired you can add a spoonful of ginger chutney for extra taste.

FOR 4 PEOPLE

2 oranges, 2 lemons, 10 tablespoons sugar, 5 tablespoons ginger syrup, a pinch of ginger powder, ½ Cavaillon melon, ½ pineapple, 2 sweet pears, type Durondeau, 1 mango, 7 cm ginger root, 100 g strawberries, 50 g raspberries, 2.5 dl whipping cream, 2 tablespoons preserved ginger, chopped fine, 100 g raisins, salt, 4 twigs of redcurrant

PREPARATION

Press the oranges and 1 lemon. Bring to the boil with 7 tablespoons of sugar, 3 tablespoons of ginger syrup and a pinch of ginger powder. Take off the heat and let the marinade cool down.
Peel the melon, the pineapple, the pear and the mango. Remove the hard core of the pineapple and cut the pineapple into small cubes.
Cut the melon into little balls with the aid of a parisienne cutter.
Cut the pear into thin slices and make fans of the mango.
Arrange the fruit in a shallow bowl and pour the cooled-down marinade over it. Leave to stand for an hour.
Peel the ginger and cut 2 cm into very thin strips.
Divide the fruit over four plates and put the cleaned strawberries and raspberries with it. Sprinkle with ginger strips and spoon some of the marinade over it.
Whip the cream till firm and mix it with 1 tablespoon ginger syrup and 2 tablespoons of preserved ginger.
Soak the raisins in water with 2 tablespoons of heated ginger syrup. Strain and let it drain well. Chop the remaining ginger root very fine and add it with 3 tablespoons sugar, the juice of 1 lemon and a pinch of salt to the raisins. Preferably make this chutney a few days beforehand.
Put three quenelles of ginger chutney and ginger cream with the fruit. Finish off with redcurrant.

TIP

Replace a plain whipped cream by this ginger cream to go with a strawberry coupe on a summery day. It tastes heavenly!

COLONIAL GINGER CAKE

CLASSIC

This unadulterated English cake is highly recommended. It gives a warm feel in the mouth because of its rather aromatic and even slightly peppery taste. The cake is at its best after a few days, so bake it in good time and in a sufficiently large quantity.

INGREDIENTS

250 g self-raising flour, 10 g ginger powder, 160 g oat flakes, 150 g soft brown sugar, 150 g butter, 100 g acacia honey, 3 dl milk, 2 eggs, 50 g preserved ginger, butter for greasing, flour for dusting, 2 tablespoons of clarified butter (or ghee), 80 g flaked almonds

PREPARATION

Mix the flour with the ginger powder, the oat flakes and the brown sugar.

Melt the butter and stir in the honey and the milk. Put the mixtures together and stir them well.

Beat the eggs and add them to the batter. Cut the preserved ginger into pieces and stir them into the batter.

Grease a baking tin with butter and dust it with flour. Put the batter into the baking tin, coat the cake with clarified butter and finish off with flaked almonds. Bake it in a preheated oven at 150 °C for one hour and 15 minutes.

GINGER PUDDING

CLASSIC

INGREDIENTS

4 dl milk, 200 g old bread without the crust, 3 eggs, 30 g butter, 75 g sugar, 100 g raisins, 200 g preserved ginger, 3 tablespoons ginger powder, a pinch of salt, butter for greasing, flour for dusting

PREPARATION

Bring the milk to the boil. Tear the bread into small pieces and stir it till it dissolves in the milk.

Separate the eggs. Take the saucepan from the heat and stir in the egg yolks, the butter, the sugar, the soaked and well squeezed out raisins, the cut pieces of preserved ginger and the ginger powder.

Whisk the egg whites until they peak and use a spatula to work them into the mixture.

Grease a baking mould and dust it with flour. Pour the batter into the baking tin and put it in a larger basin filled with hot water. Put it in a preheated oven at 180 °C for an hour and a half.

Take the mould out of the oven, carefully loosen the pudding and turn it over onto a warm dish.

CRUNCHY GINGER BISCUITS

CLASSIC

FOR 15 BISCUITS

2 limes, 8 cm ginger root, 210 g flour, 125 g clarified butter (or ghee), 120 g sugar, 1 egg, 2 tablespoons ginger powder (djahé)

PREPARATION

Scrub the limes clean. Grate the peel and press them.

Peel the ginger root and grate it finely.

Knead the flower with the melted butter, the sugar, the egg, the ginger powder, half of the grated ginger, half of the grated lime, and half of the lime juice to a smooth dough. Shape it into a ball, wrap it in plastic foil and put it into the refrigerator for an hour.

Roll out the dough into a sausage shape of the desired diameter. Cut into 3 mm slices, put these on a baking tray covered with baking paper or greased, and push into the centre of each biscuit some of the leftover grated lemon and ginger.

Bake for 20 minutes in a preheated oven at 180 °C.

Take the biscuits out of the oven and leave them to cool on a wire tray.

TIP

Leave the biscuits to cool after baking and serve them fresh and crisp with a cup of ginger tea.

Real ginger lovers add some small pieces of preserved ginger to the dough.

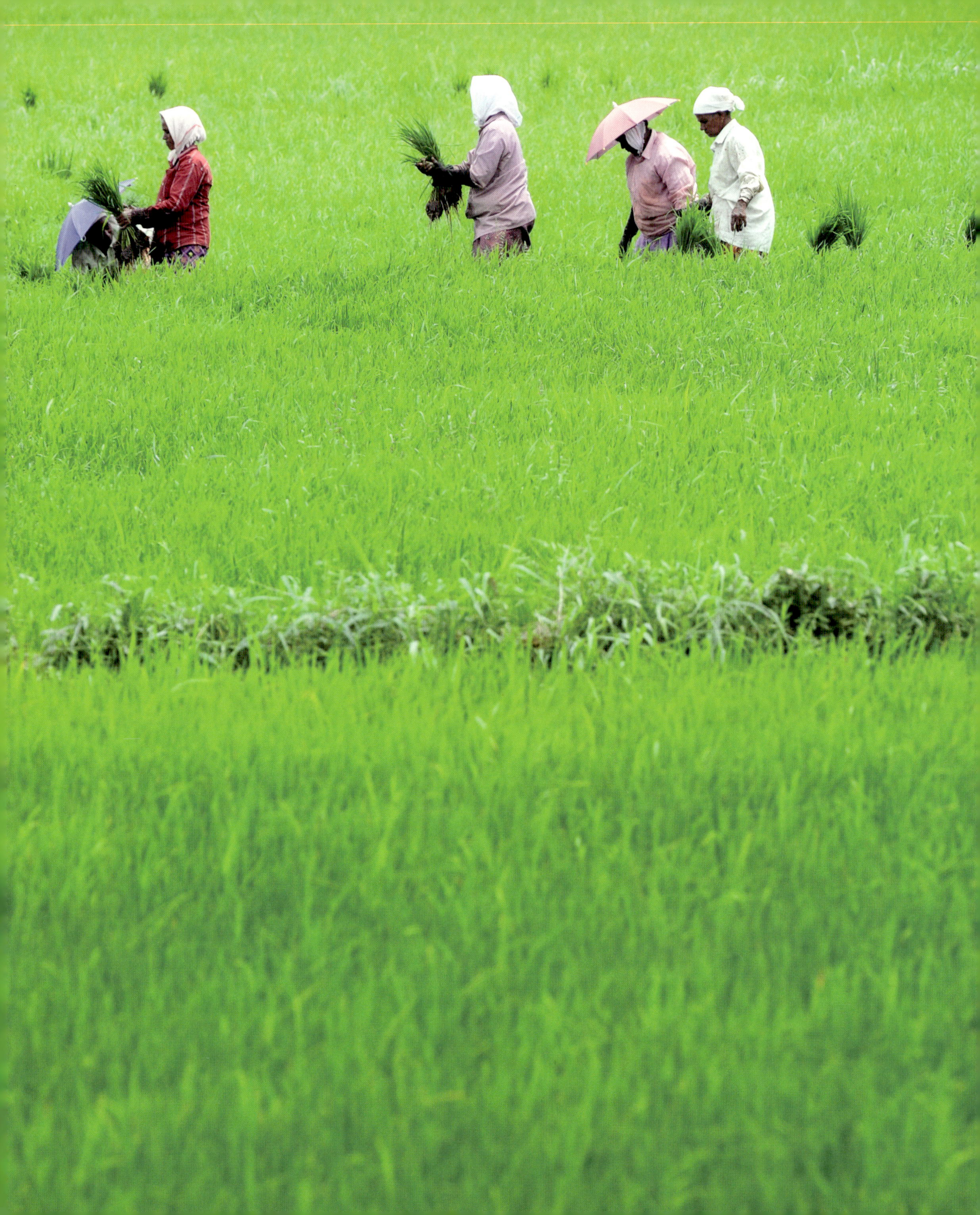

RICE, LENTILS AND BREAD

SWEET OXYGEN

Rice and India go hand in hand. When the seeds are being planted under water by bent-over little women in colourful saries, they are already destined to serve someone's stomach, from the toiling labourer nearby to the highest official far away. They accept it. More than that, they are proud when the plants grow and the barren field is transformed into a bright green plain. Three times a day they are the oxygen for every Indian…

Idly, dosa, uppuma, Biryani… familiar names on the menu card, all of which have rice as their basis. Biryani is popular everywhere in India, although its origins are in Iran. The name comes from the Persian word 'bērya(n)', meaning 'fried' or 'roasted'. It found its way to Southern Asia via Iranian travellers and traders. Traditionally it is a vegetarian dish, but in India the rice is often fried together with both fish, meat or eggs as well as vegetables. And the grain of rice also has well-defined properties, as you might expect…

Mr Shamboo: 'In Kerala you can't escape rice. It is, perhaps even more than in other areas of India, pre-eminently the staple food. For breakfast we already have six or seven different rice dishes, including the idly, the soft little cake made of rice flour well-known to you, and the dosa. Many sweet desserts such as payasam start with the rice grain, to which milk, yoghurt or curds are then added.

The rice harvest differs from region to region. Here in Kerala we have only two per year. It depends on the kind of rice you are growing. The first cultivation is between March and July, when a thicker rice is planted. This needs ninety days to reach maturity. The second is a white rice and is harvested after sixty days. If you look at our neighbouring state Tamil Nadu, you sometimes have three harvests a year, because the variety they plant is ripe after forty-five to fifty days.

Biryani belongs to the "Malabar" region, in Kerala home mainly to Muslims. In the preparation of Biryani you can actually see that it is influenced by another cuisine. In this case the Arabic cuisine. The fact that no curry leaves and chilli powder are used shows that the dish does not come from Kerala. Yet you can eat the "Malabar Biryani" anywhere here as the Kerala Biryani.

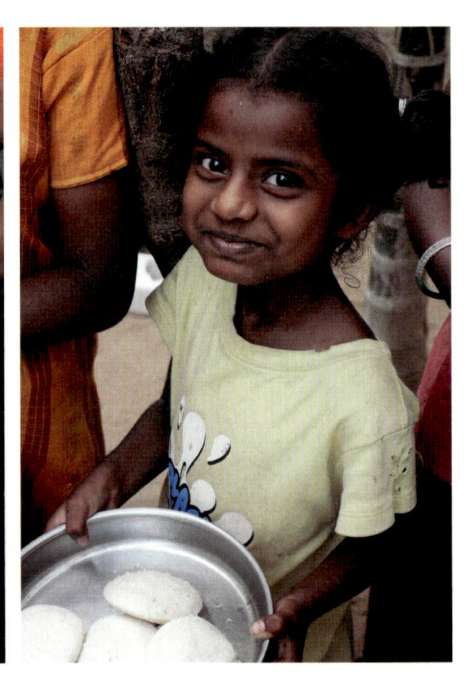

In Wayanad, a remote area in Kerala, you can even get "bamboo rice". The Adivasi take a piece of bamboo and remove everything from it, fill it up with rice and close it with banana leaves. Then they throw it into the fire and when ready they cut the bamboo in half. The taste of this rice is said to be exceptional and it is moreover also medically beneficial.

As you see, even if you have little to eat, there will always be rice. But if you look at the health situation of the Kerali, you will alas find many diabetic patients. That is the result of the high sugar content in rice. The bamboo version, however, is thought to reduce this a little. Rice contains many carbohydrates and calories. These give you energy and oxygen to keep you working. An asset to anyone, particularly to those who have to do much physical labour. They will easily work off all those calories. People with a sedentary job are saddled with it and that is why many among us put on weight rather too quickly. Indeed, I should be working in the field more or avoid rice a little more (laughs)...

Sam

For the Southern Indian *idly* is a festive breakfast, served with a spicy sambhar and a refreshing coconut chutney.

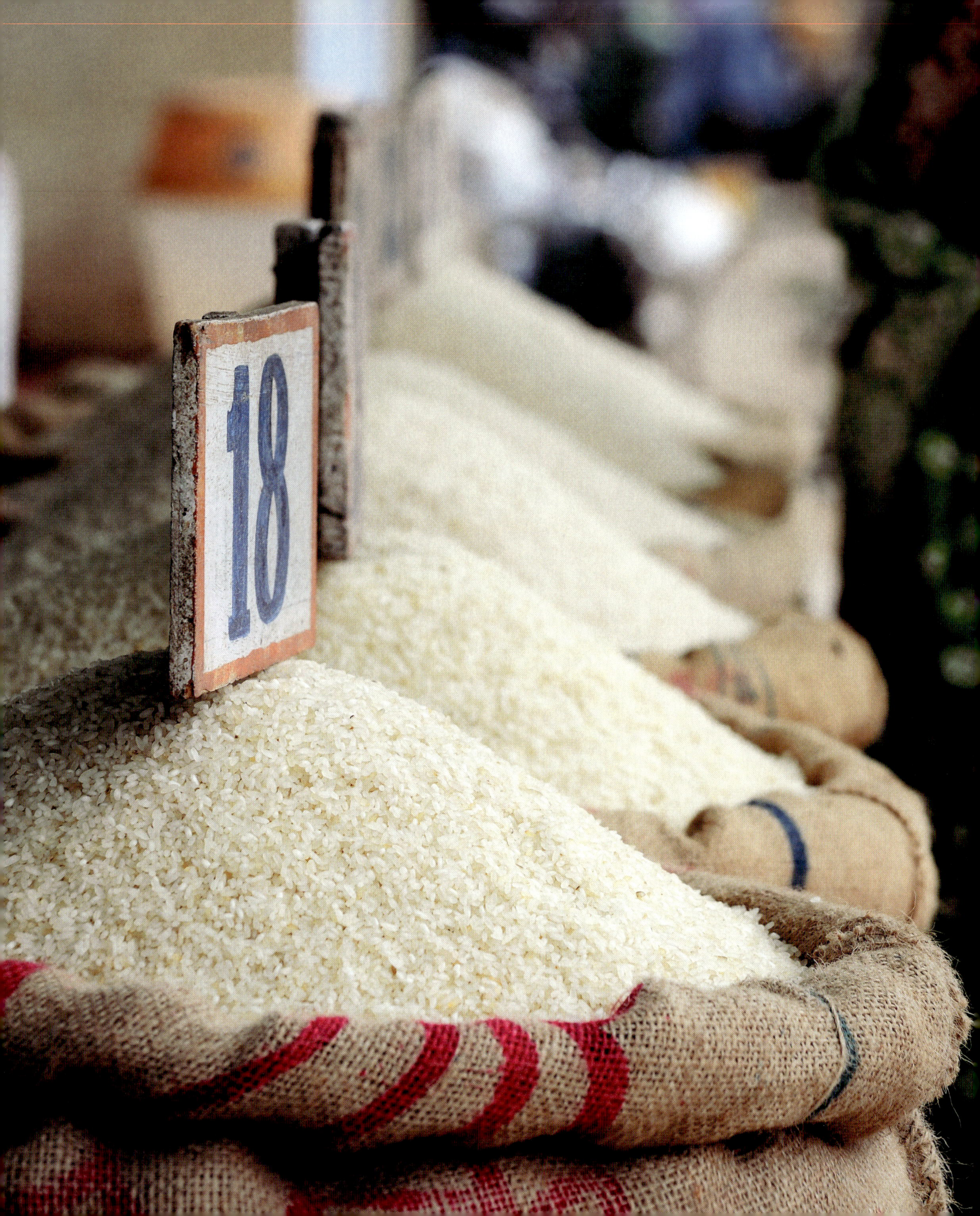
18

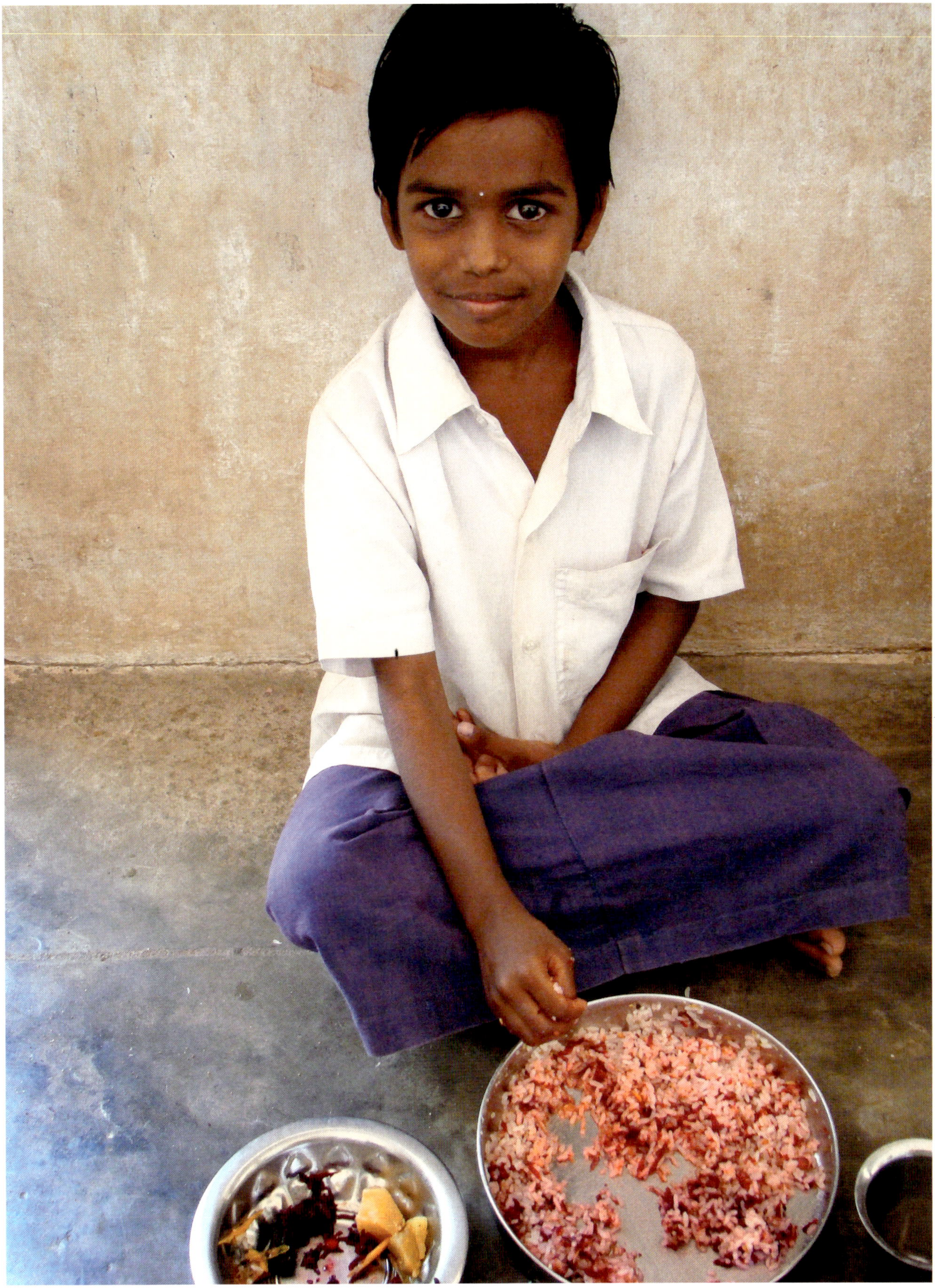

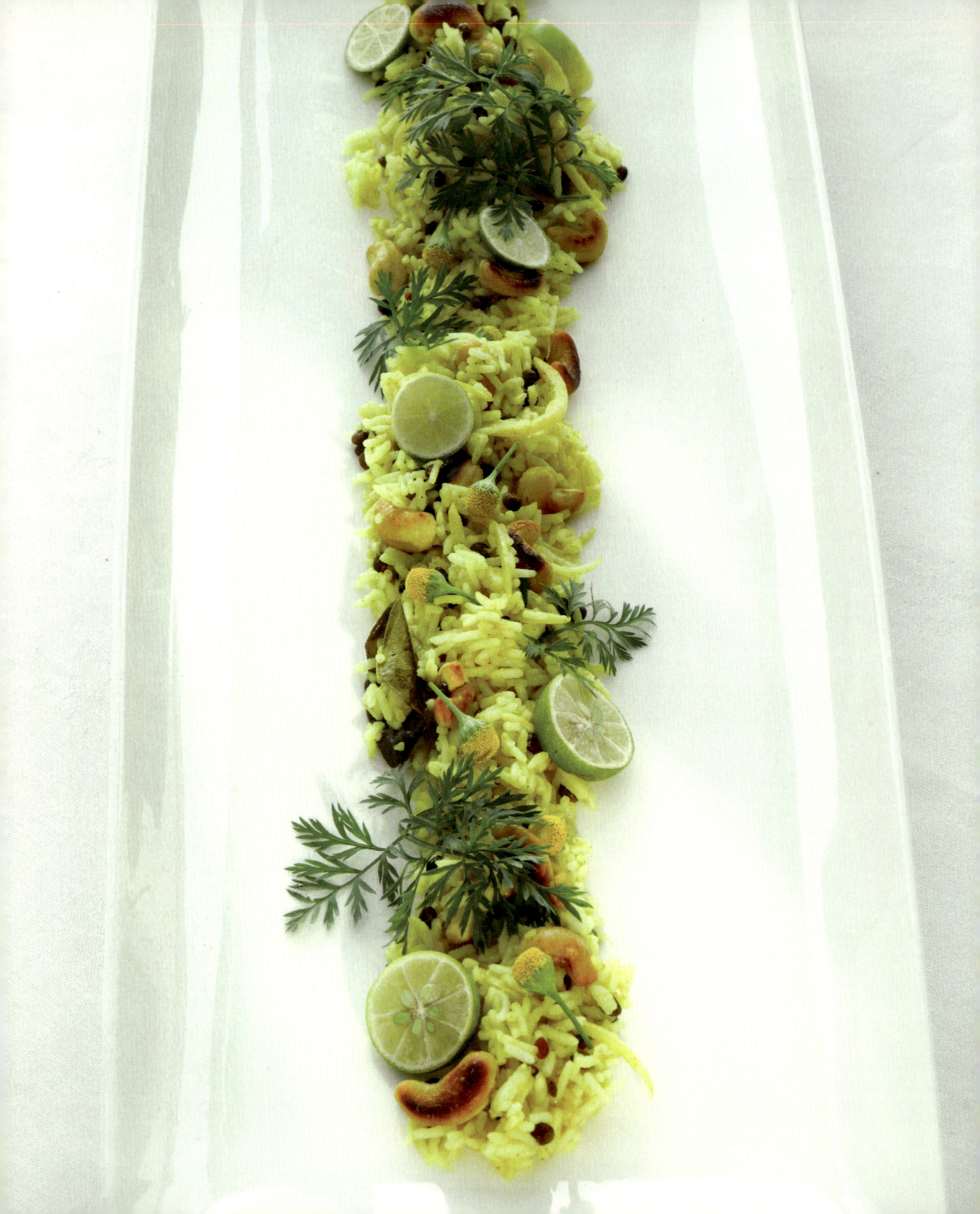

LIME RICE PULIHORA

CLASSIC

Pulihora literally means 'sour rice'. In Southern India, in Tamil Nadu and particularly in Andhra Pradesh, it is a very popular rice dish. Pulihora tastes both sour and salt. During festivals and in the temples turmeric, the symbol for prosperity, is added to it. The dish is then called 'prasadam'.

This recipe is for a slightly more elaborate rice dish, with a splendid lemon-yellow colour and a fantastic range of tastes.

FOR 4 PERSONS

400 g basmati rice, salt, 3 tablespoons peanut oil, 25 g lentils, 50 g cashew nuts, 1 tablespoon mustard seeds, 20 curry leaves, 1 tablespoon turmeric, 1 lemon, juice of 2 limes, 1 limequat, a few sprigs of dill

PREPARATION

Rinse the rice under cold running water and leave it to soak in cold water for 20 minutes.

Cook the rice *al dente* in 8 minutes in 1 litre salted water. Pour off the water and leave to drain properly.

Heat the oil in a pan and fry the lentils and cashew nuts in it.

Add the mustard seeds, the curry leaves and the turmeric, stir well and add a little water.

Peel the lemon and cut the yellow peel into thin strips. Blanch them in boiling water.

Add the rice to the lentils and season to taste with the salt, the lime juice and the lemon strips.

TIP

To give the lime rice more colour, add acid accents such as pieces of unripe mango or pomegranate seeds.

| TIP | # BIRYANI OF LAMB | CLASSIC |

Biryani can be made of several kinds of stewing meat. It is a popular dish in India, but also in a number of countries in Southern Asia and in Arabic coutries.

Alain: 'My first biryani, I remember it well, I had in Jodhpur, the blue city in the state of Rajasthan. At a rickety little table on an improvised little terrace above a row of houses, with a view of Mehrangarh Fort. It was a mutton biryani, prepared with shoulder of lamb. The pot was sealed with a beautiful pie crust, with a fantastic dish hidden under it. The secret of this dish is that the rice and the thick meat curry are made separately. The curry and the rice are then brought together in the pot in layers. This results in a rich dish with contrasting and intense tastes.'

FOR 4 PERSONS

LAMB CURRY 1 kg boned shoulder of lamb or leg of lamb, 5 cm ginger root, 2 cloves of garlic, 2 tablespoons garam masala, a pinch of turmeric, ⅛ bundle of coriander, ⅛ bundle of mint, 4 onions, 4 tablespoons of peanut oil, 125 g butter, 2.5 dl full-cream (Greek) yoghurt, water or lamb stock – **RICE** 400 g basmati rice, salt, ½ tablespoon saffron strands, 1 dl full-cream milk – **DOUGH** 100 g flour, 100 g wholemeal flour, salt, a cup of water

PREPARATION

Cut the meat into large pieces.
Peel the ginger and grate it. Peel the garlic and crush it with the ginger. Mix in the garam masala and the turmeric. Chop the coriander and the mint fine and add them to the marinade.
Mix the lamb with the marinade, cover, and put it in the refrigerator for a few hours.
Peel the onions and cut them into thin rings. Heat the oil with the butter and braise the onion rings till coloured. Pour off the fat and set it aside. Add the meat to the onion and allow it to colour. Add the marinade and yoghurt to it and leave it to simmer for 30 minutes until the meat is completely done. Every now and then add some water or lamb stock to the meat, until you have a fibrous sauce with pieces.
Rinse the rice until the water is clear. Let it drain well.
Cook the rice *al dente* in 8 minutes in salted water.
Arrange the lamb curry in a pan with a thick bottom. Divide the rice over the meat and pour the fat that was set aside over it.
Leave the saffron to soak in the warmed-up milk and pour this in a thin trickle over the rice.
Mix the flour and the wholemeal flour with a pinch of salt and water to a smooth dough. Roll it into a long sausage and put it round the edge of the pan. Push the lid into the dough so that the pan is sealed.
Put the pan for 3 minutes on a high heat and then for 30 minutes in a preheated oven at 200 °C.

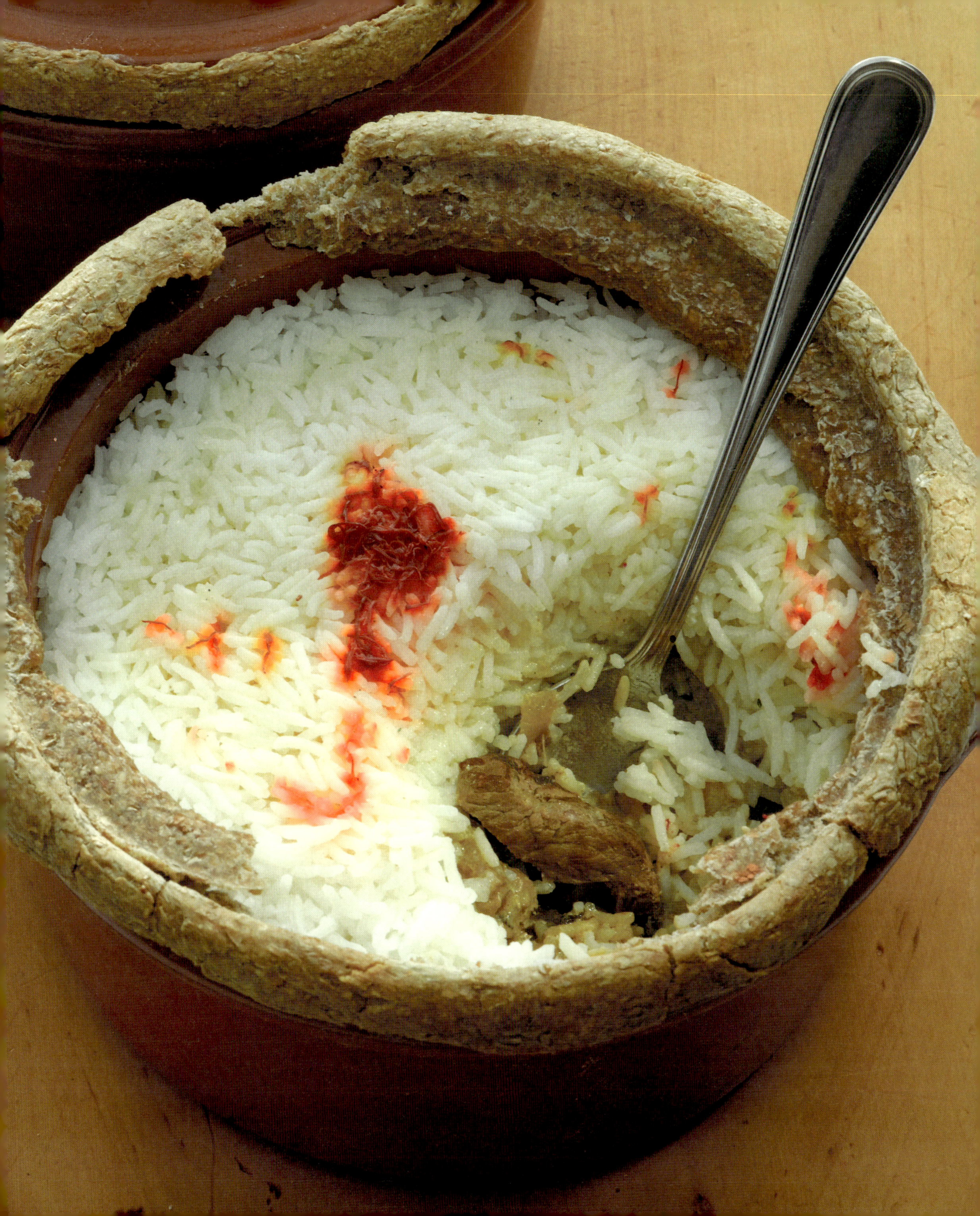

PAYASAM WITH CARAMELIZED BANANA

INDIAN

We eat our rice porridge with golden spoons in heaven; in India the payasam is prepared in the temples at Hindu festivals to please the gods. Is there some religious analogy?

FOR 4 PERSONS

RICE 100 g rice, 2 tablespoons clarified butter (or ghee), 25 g raisins, 25 g cashew nuts, ½ litre milk, 80 g cane sugar, 10 cardamom pods, 4 cloves, ½ teaspoon saffron strings

BANANAS 4 small bananas, 50 g salted butter, 100 g sugar

PREPARATION

Rinse the rice under cold running water.
Heat the butter in a pan and fry the raisins and the cashew nuts until the nuts are light brown.
Bring the milk to the boil with the sugar, the cardamom pods, the cloves and the saffron. Add the rice and let it simmer on a low heat for 30 minutes without a lid on the pan. Stir only if it is necessary.
Peel the bananas and fry them in the melted butter. Add the sugar and leave it to caramelize gently.
Serve the payasam with the caramelized bananas. Finish with the raisins and the nuts.

CHAPATI

CLASSIC

The word chapati is derived from chappa, which means 'beaten flat'. It refers to the shape of the bread which looks like a flat circle. It is a very neutral bread dough, from which you tear pieces to help yourself to curry from the many bowls set out. The neutral taste of the bread also softens the often highly spiced taste of the curries.

FOR 10 CHAPATIS

100 g white flour, 100 g wholemeal flour, 1 tablespoon salt, 1 tablespoon peanut oil, 1 dl warm water, 2 tablespoons yoghurt, 150 g clarified butter (or ghee)

PREPARATION

Knead the flour, the wholemeal flour, the salt, the oil, the water and the yoghurt to a smooth dough. Make it into a ball and leave it to rest for 10 minutes.

Roll the dough into a long sausage. Cut this into 10 equal pieces and shape them into small balls. Roll them out to circles of equal thickness.

Bake the chapatis in a hot pan and toss them continually so that they puff up. The chapatis should not be too coloured.

Rub the chapatis with clarified butter and make a pile of them.

UTTAPAM

CLASSIC

An uttapam looks a little like a dosa but it is thicker and is not folded over. It is a kind of Indian pizza, a thick pancake covered with ingredients that are baked together with it. An uttapam is served with sambhar and chutney.

FOR 4 PERSONS

BATTER *125 g rice flour, 125 g wholemeal flour, 2.25 dl water, 2 tablespoons full-cream (Greek) yoghurt, 2 eggs, salt*

GARNISHES *2 cloves of garlic, ⅛ bundle coriander, 1 green chilli pepper, 2 large onions, 3 tablespoon coconut oil, salt, 1 teaspoon tikka masala, 20 cherry tomatoes – oil for frying*

PREPARATION

Mix the rice flour with the wholemeal flour. Sieve the flour into a bowl and stir it to a thick batter with the water, the yoghurt, the eggs and a pinch of salt.

Peel the garlic and cut it into fine slices. Chop the coriander finely. Cut the chilli pepper open lenghtways, remove the seeds and chop it coarsely. Peel the onion and cut it into large pieces.

Heat the coconut oil in a pan and fry all ingredients briefly. Season with salt and tikka masala.

Cut each cherry tomato into three and fry it briefly with the rest. Heat a little oil in a pan with non-stick coating. Pour a spoonful of the batter into the pan and shape this into a pancake 1.5 cm thick and about 12 cm diameter.

Distribute the tomato and onion mixture over the pancake, turn it over and bake the other side. Turn over again and crisp the pancake underneath.

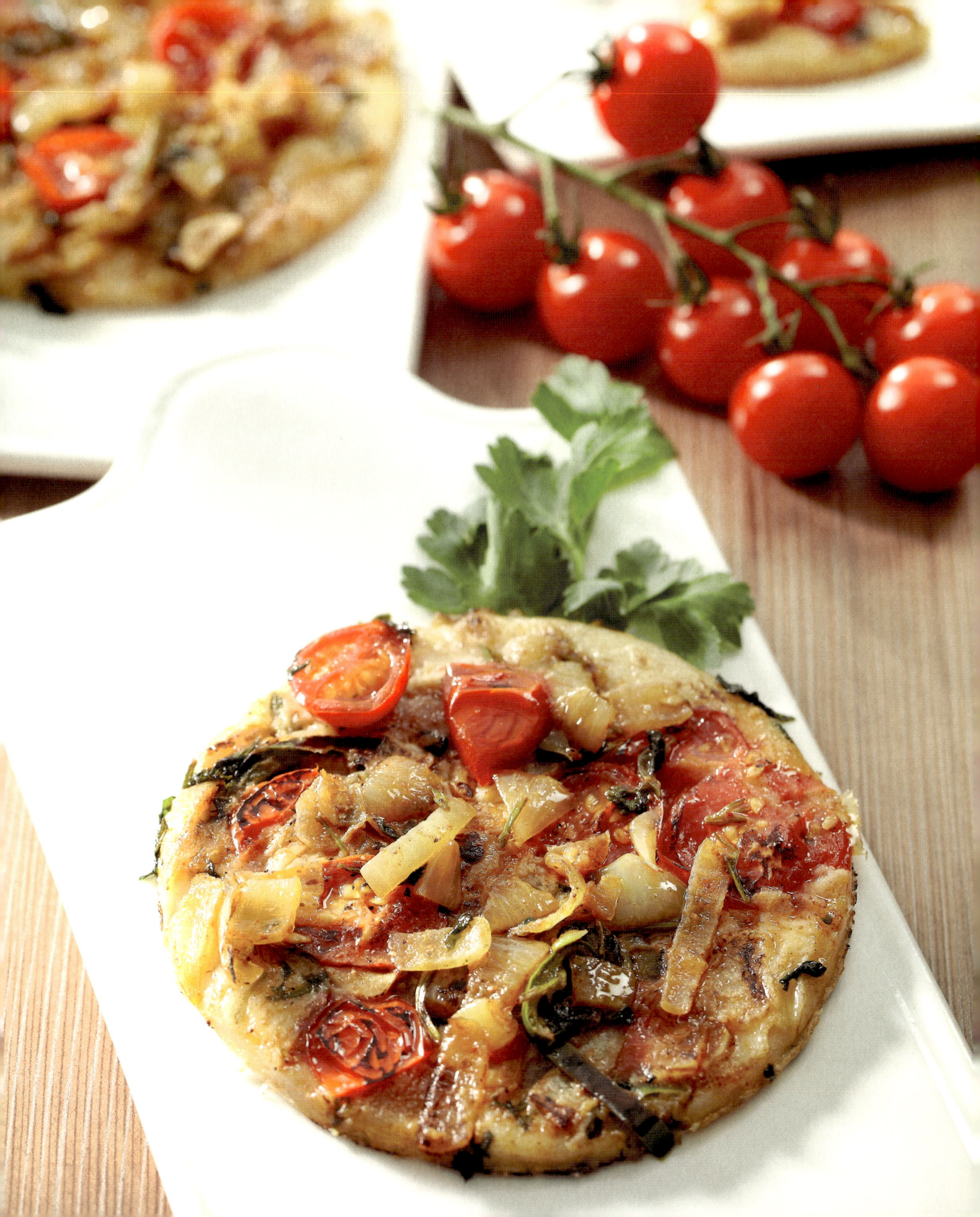

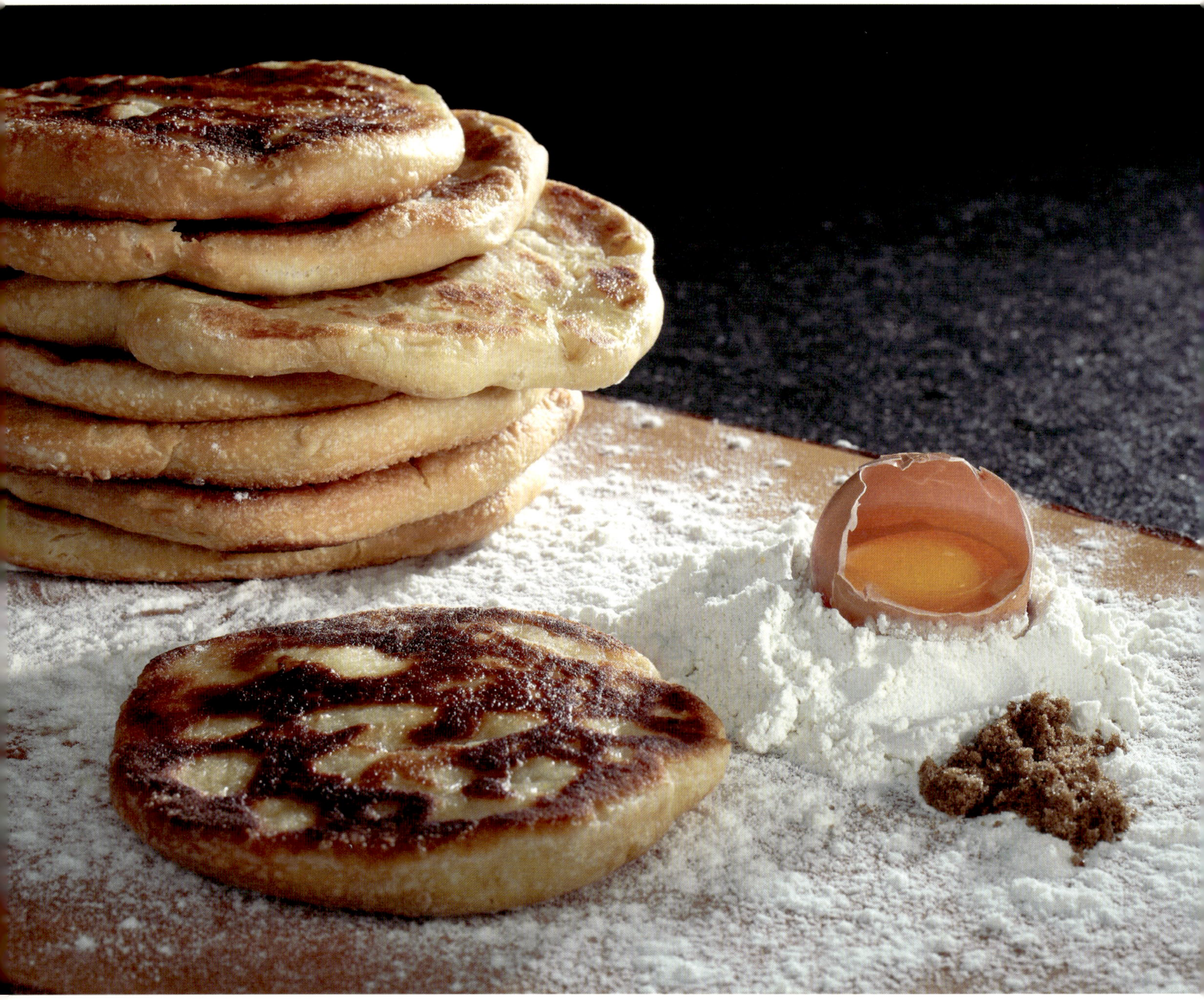

NAAN

CLASSIC

Naan is the most important side dish in almost all of Southern India and is traditionally baked in a tandoor or clay oven. This gives the naan the special taste of charcoal which you will obviously not have in this recipe. During the summer months you can bake the naan on the barbecue instead of in the oven. The naan bread will then need to be turned continually for perfect colouring.

FOR 10 NAANS

1 tablespoon caster sugar, 1 sachet of dried yeast, 1.6 dl tepid milk, 450 g flour, a pinch of salt, 1 tablespoon baking powder, 25 g clarified butter (or ghee), 3 tablespoon yoghurt, 1 egg, a pinch of turmeric

PREPARATION

Add the sugar and the yeast to the tepid milk and let it rest for 15 minutes.
Mix the flour with the salt and the baking powder. Make a little hill with a dip in the middle.
Mix the melted butter with the yoghurt and the egg. Pour this mixture together with the yeast into the dip and knead it all to a smooth dough. Leave it to rise for 1 hour, covered by a kitchen towel.
Knead the dough a little longer and form it into 10 little balls.
Roll them out, spread them with melted butter and bake them in a hot pan. Turn the naan continually during baking until they are golden brown.
Just before serving rub in a little melted butter to which a spoonful of turmeric has been added.

TIP

For garlic naan add two coarsely chopped cloves of garlic to the dough and spread the naan with some melted butter to which garlic has been added.

Experiment with naan by kneading coriander, cummin seed, turmeric, or even marinated tomatoes, olives, or grated cheese into the dough.

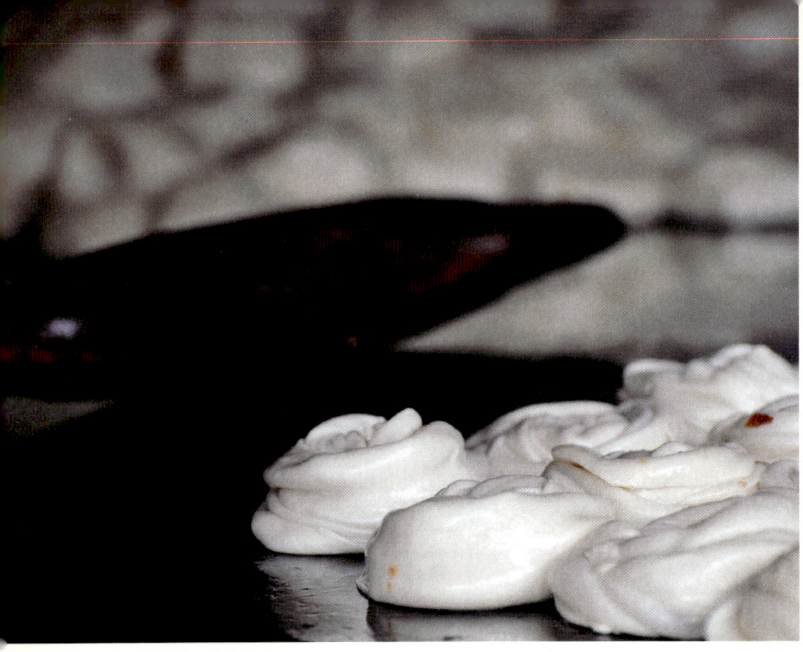
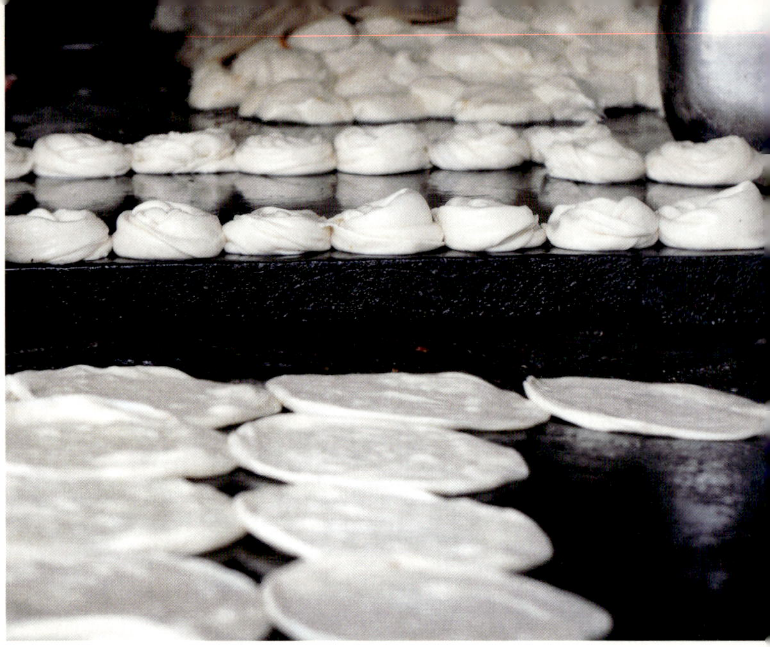
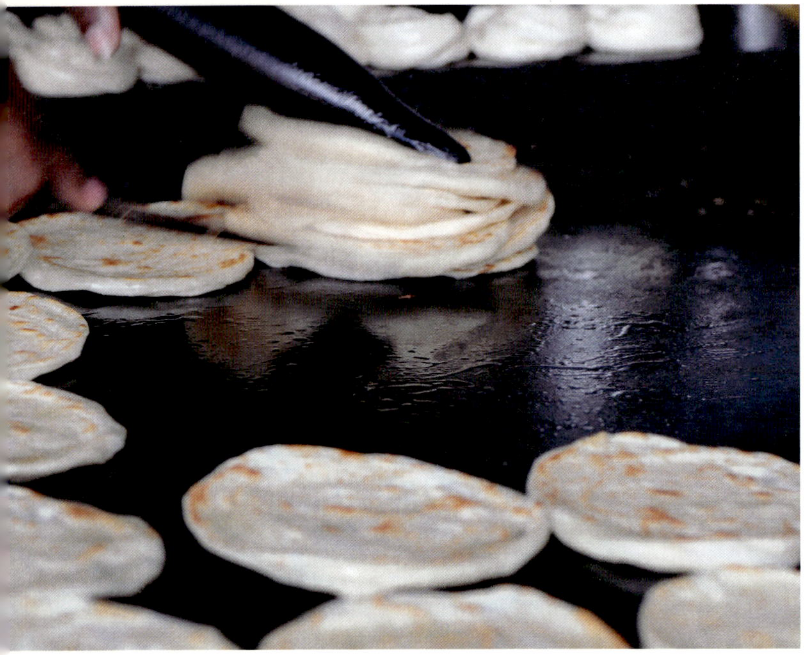
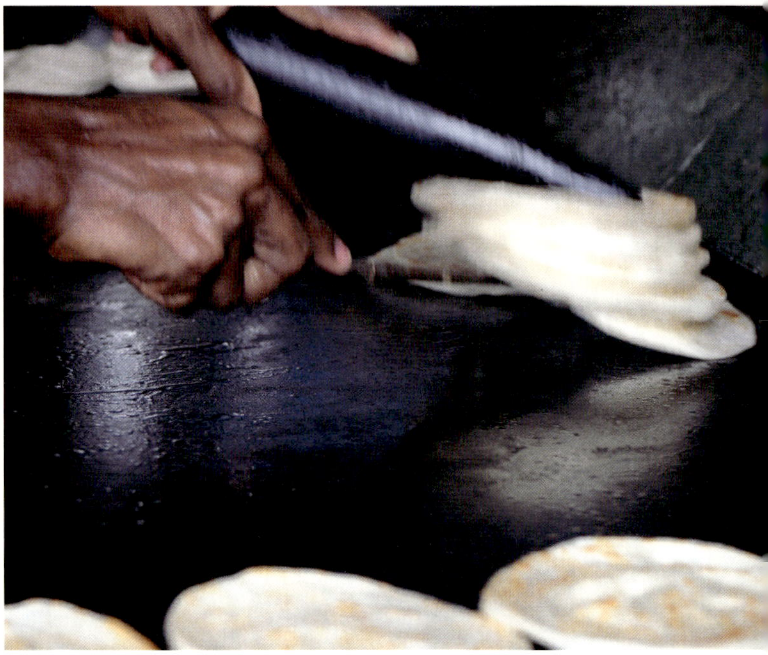
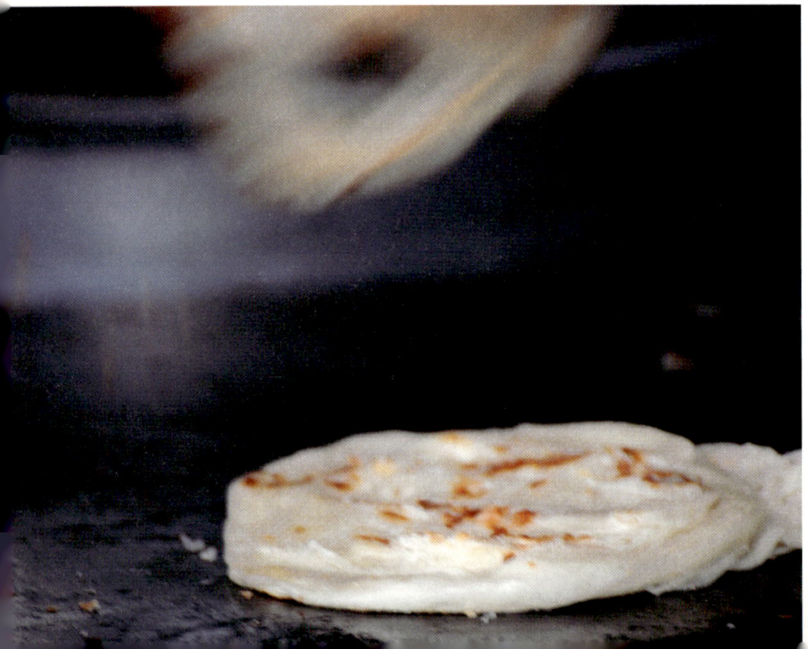
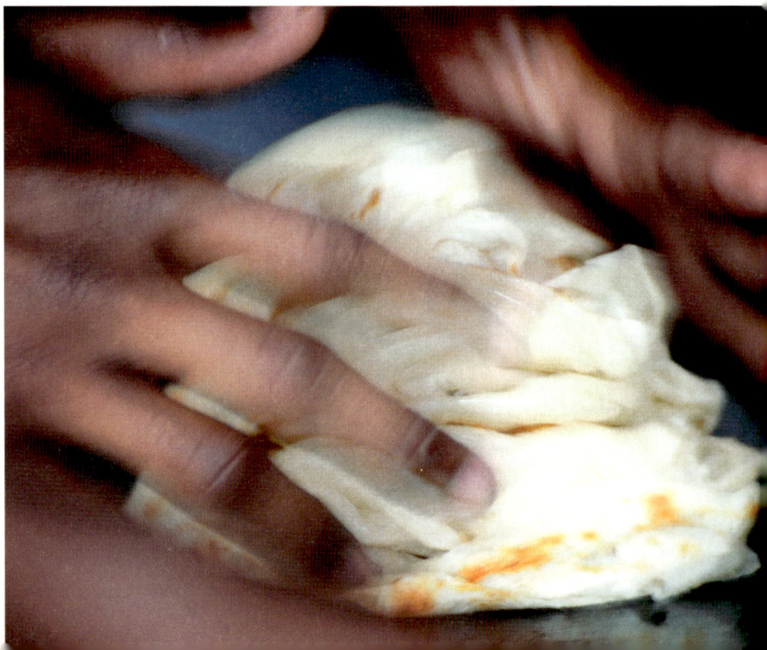

PARATHA

CLASSIC

The specific shape of the paratha comes from the special way of rolling it up to get a very light and stringy roti (bread). The process of making layers or sheets in the dough is characteristic. The taste is sublime as a result of the use of ghee or clarified butter.

FOR 10 PARATHAS

325 g wholemeal flour, a pinch of salt, 125 g clarified butter (or ghee), 1.5 dl warm water, white flour for dusting

PREPARATION

Sieve the flour and mix in the salt. Knead 50 g clarified butter at room temperature and the water through the flour. Divide it in four equal portions.

Make 4 balls and roll them out on a working surface into rounds of 20 cm diameter. Spread a spoonful of clarified butter over each circle.

Roll each circle from the bottom to the top to make a roll 2.5 cm thick and 20 cm wide. Stretch out the roll and put it on the working surface. Roll the top half to the right (clockwise) and the bottom half to the left (anti-clockwise) so that the two halves touch each other. Fold the two halves across each other and push them together firmly. Sprinkle a little flour over it and roll it out to a circle with a diameter of 20 cm.

Spread both sides with the remainder of the clarified butter and bake it golden brown in a pan. Turn over regularly and push down during baking.

ENEEN PARATHA

Pull stale parathas through a mixture of beaten egg, sugar and cinnamon powder and fry them in a hot pan. This is the Indian version of French toast and is very popular with children.

STUFFED PARATHA

Put a filling such as vegetarian curry or chutney on the paratha before you put the two halves on top of each other. Fold shut, roll it lightly and fry on both sides. A paratha with, for instance, mint chutney is refreshing.

KALI DHAL WITH PRESERVED PIG'S CHEEKS AND LOMO

CLASSIC & WESTERN

TIP

Kali dhal is also very nice with Flemish stews or baked salmon.

Alain: 'Dhal is the national dish of India. It is a lentil stew which particularly in the north is eaten almost daily. I learned that dhal is not only the name of the dish, but also of the basic ingredient. Eating lentils is not exactly part of our Flemish culture, but it really pays to try out this kali dhal.'

FOR 4 PERSONS

KALI DHAL 250 g black lentils, 1 onion, 2 cloves of garlic, 3 cm ginger root, 1 small green chilli pepper, 1.2 dl peanut oil, 2 pinches of salt, 2 tablespoons garam masala, 2 pinches of ginger powder, 50 g lomo (Spanish bacon)

PIG'S CHEEK 1 kg pig's cheeks, 1 onion, 1 dl clarified butter (or ghee), garam masala (1 pinch), ½ litre veal stock, 4 ginger biscuits, 3 star anise, 1 cinnamon stick, a few sprigs of sage, rosemary and bay leaf

PREPARATION

Put the lentils in a large saucepan with 2 litres water and bring this to the boil. Leave to simmer for one hour on a low heat until they are soft to the touch.

Drain and keep the cooking liquid.

Peel the onion, the garlic and the ginger root. Cut the chilli pepper open lengthways and remove the seed. Chop everything coarsely and mix it to a puree in the blender.

Heat the oil in a pan and braise the onion and ginger puree. Add the lentils to this and season with 2 pinches of salt, garam masala and two pinches of ginger powder.

Pour 2.5 dl of the cooking liquid onto the dahl. Add the very thinly cut slices of lomo and leave it to simmer for a moment. The fat of the lomo gives the dhal a subtle body.

By adding more or less cooking liquid, it becomes a thicker or a more liquid dhal.

Remove the membrane from the pig's cheeks.

Peel the onion and chop it coarsely. Heat the clarified butter and fry the pig's cheeks with the onion and the garam masala. Deglaze them with the veal stock and add the crumbed ginger biscuits. Put the star anise and the cinnamon into the saucepan and leave the cheeks to cook till done for about one hour.

Serve the pig's cheeks with the dhal. Finish with a slice of lomo and a few sprigs of sage, rosemary and bay leaf.

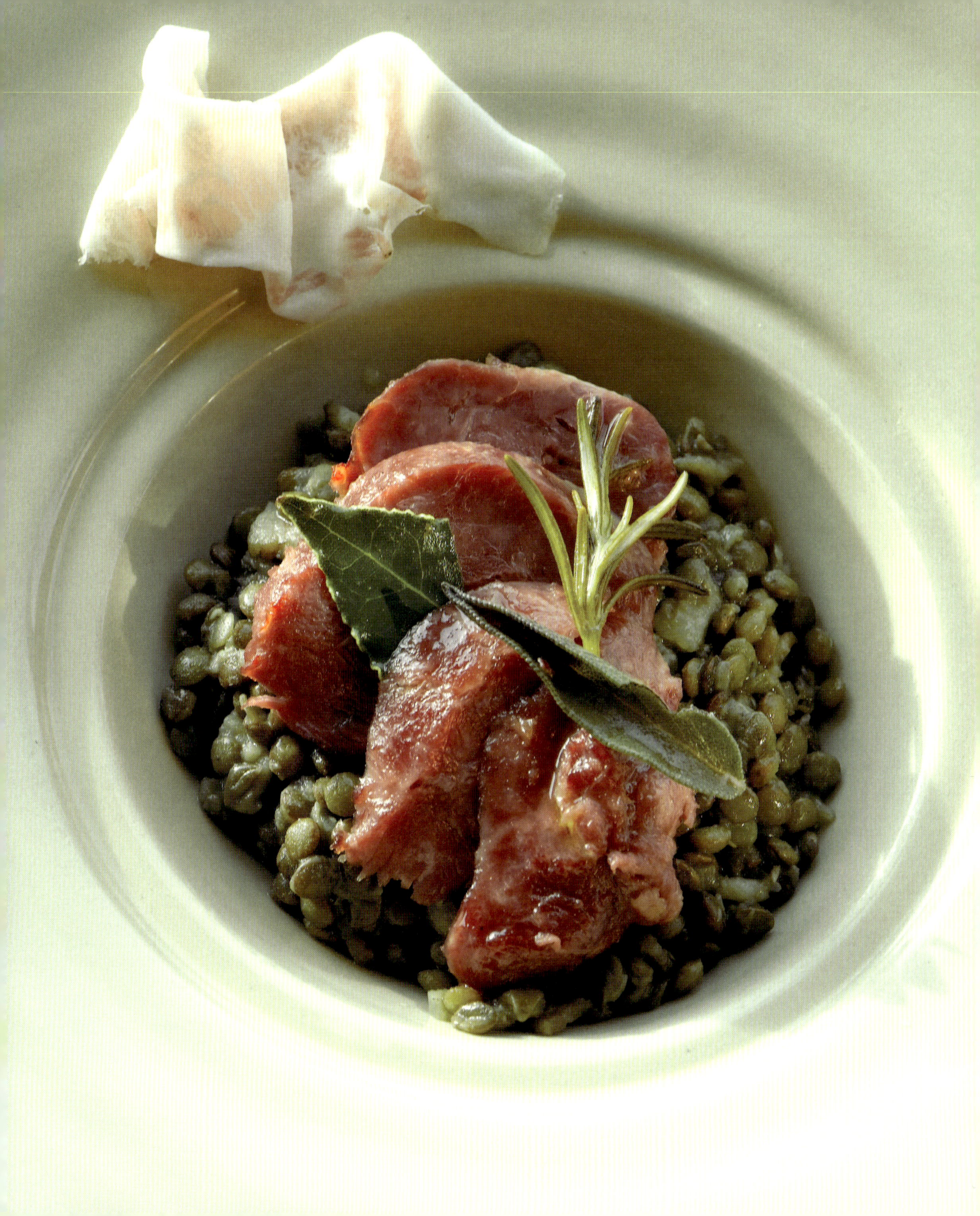

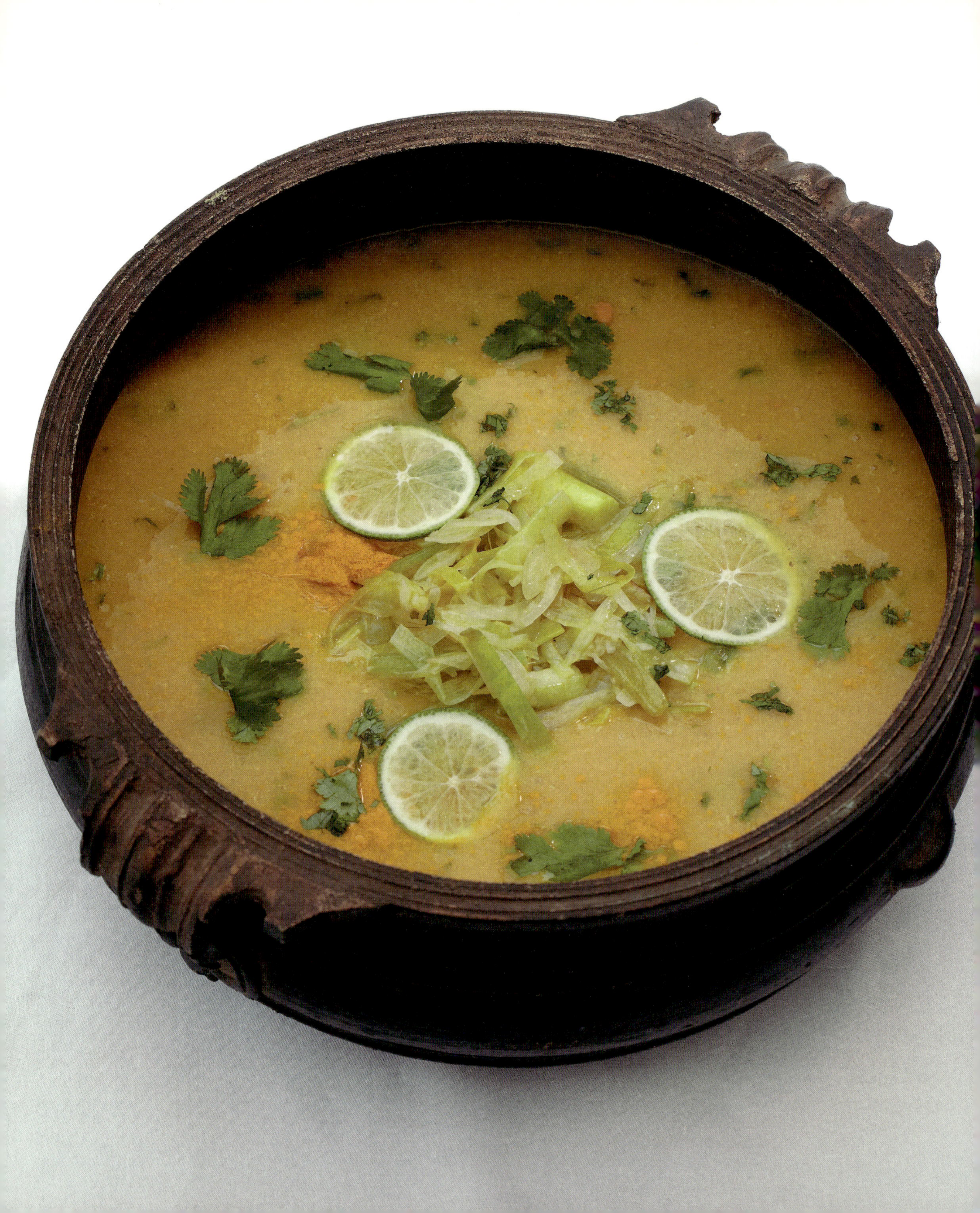

SOUP OF LENTILS, LIME AND TURMERIC **CLASSIC**

INGREDIENTS

500 g lentils, salt, 1 tablespoon turmeric, freshly grounded Malabar pepper, ½ celeriac, 2 onions, 2 stalks of leeks, 150 g butter, 5 cm ginger root, 5 cloves of garlic, ½ bundle of coriander, a few slices of lemon

PREPARATION

Cook the lentils till done in 1.5 litres of salted water. Season with turmeric and a fair amount of ground Malabar pepper. Mix the soup with an electric blender.

Clean the celeriac, the onions and the leeks and cut them into large pieces. Braise the vegetables in the butter without allowing them to colour.

Peel the ginger root and grate it. Peel the garlic and chop it fine. Add the ginger and the garlic to the vegetables. Pour in the lentil soup and continue to let it all simmer.

Pour the lime juice into the soup until it has a sufficiently sour taste. Finish of with chopped coriander.

Both in Kerala and in Tamil Nadu most of the eating booths do their cooking outside. Close to the people and the street. But with temperatures of more than 35 °C not as cool as you might like.

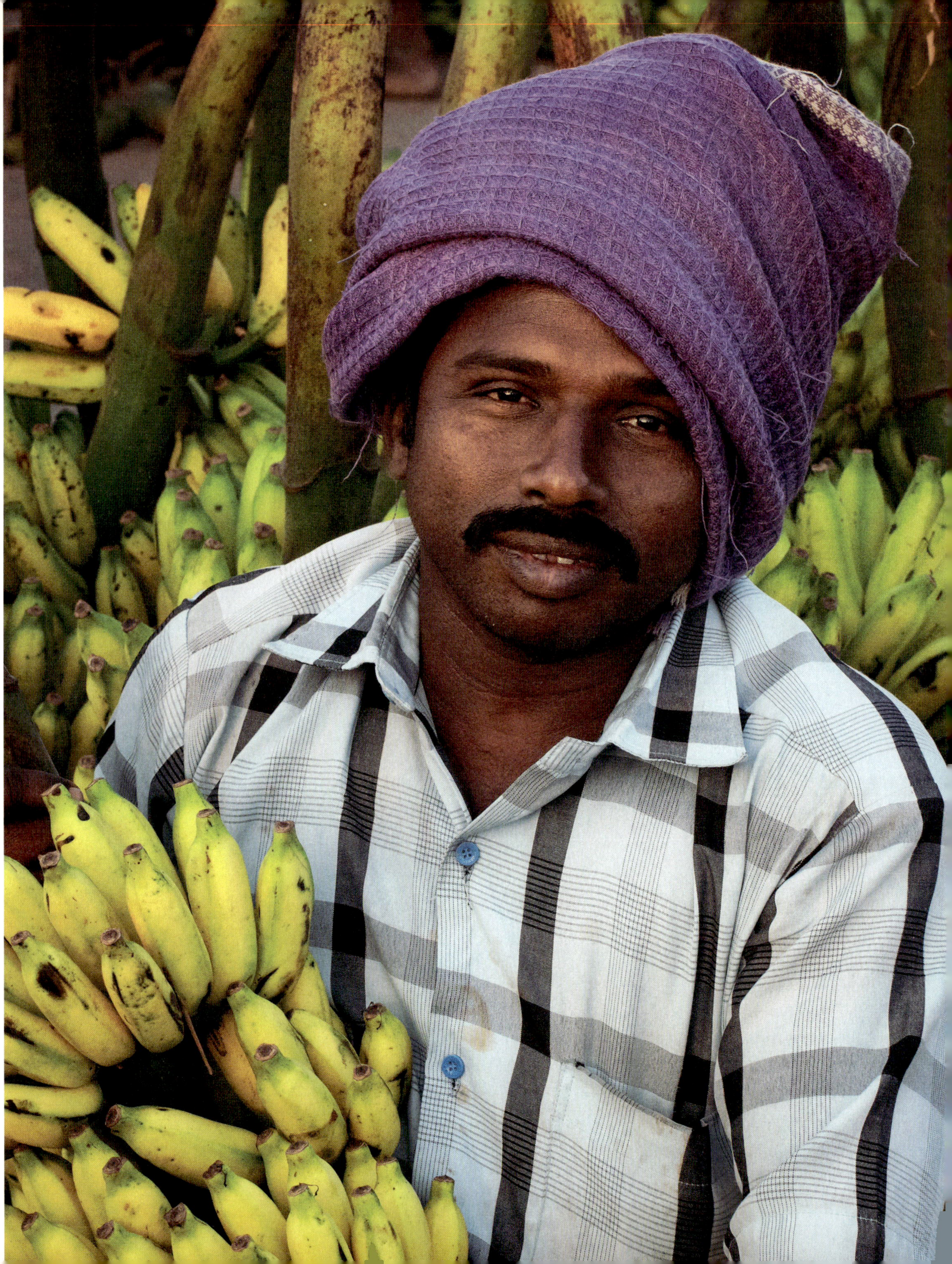

FRUIT AND NUTS

THE MORNING MARKET OF KUMBAKONAM

Today is again an early day. Around half past four our car is once more driving through the jet-black night in the direction of the temple town of Kumbakonam. We are going to visit the largest fruit and vegetable market of the entire region. The short drive of twelve kilometres reminds us that life in the countryside is already fully in motion, even before the birds have started their morning song. As if from a dark cupboard, unlit ox-carts, cyclists and pedestrians show up very briefly in our headlights, to be swallowed up promptly by the greedy darkness again. We see how, on the roadside, some locals have come out of their little houses, still drowsy with sleep. At the well a little further on, women make use of the dark curtain of the night to wash themselves discretely. A few goats, cows and dogs meanwhile risk a first dangerous crossing of the main road. The increasing traffic reveals that we are approaching the market. Here, just outside the urban belt of Kumbakonam, the buses blow their poisonous gases generously around. There is a tremendous hustle and bustle here.

The coffee booths in front of the market square are doing a roaring trade. While we too treat ourselves to this delicious brew and the obligatory shortbread biscuit, we see how a man in a spotless white dhoti and shirt confronts the buses in the middle of the crossing, like a South-Indian Don Quixote. At this early hour the show-off had clearly already helped himself to some Dutch courage. The bus drivers hoot like reckless elephants and can barely avoid the unfortunate man. It all looks very terrifying, but the onlookers are laughing at it, while they have another sip of their hot coffee. That is until a passing policeman thinks the spectacle has gone on long enough and gives the staggering Don Quixote a wallop.

We swallow the remainder of our second coffee and enter the market area via its gigantic entrance gate. As far as the eye can see, stalls are crammed full with all kinds of vegetables and fruit. It is a show of colours, with a nervous sea of people trying to battle their way through. Women heap up mountains of onions while their men loudly recommend their goods to passers-by. A stone's throw further on we go past a veritable wall of fresh coriander, green and purple spinach and fresh mint. A man with a twinkle in his eye, who is sitting on a little chair next to baskets full of bright yellow and bright green limes, gives each of us a fruit in the palm of our hands. 'In Tamil Nadu this is a token of honour. It will bring you luck,' he tells us confidently. A little further on we can taste something. A little old woman has cut up pieces of pineapple, the best of the whole of India. Her deep-red pomegranates are also not to be despised. Because of the enthusiastic crowd attaching themselves to us it is increasingly difficult to move forward. We walk past carpets of fiery red tomatoes and purple aubergines. We are beginning to feel that these farmers have brought in whole fields full of beans, peas, okras, green and red peppers, red beetroot, ginger and many more other crops.

We buy some bananas and lychees and enter the indoor part of the market. Men meander deftly with heavy jute bags on their shoulders through the market crowds. Here the voices of the sellers seem to sound even louder in our ears. An intense smell of garlic meets us. A seller of watermelons sits surrounded by his market goods and stares at us. The pumpkin seller next to

Alain in the market, talking to local farmers. The aubergine seller shows his merchandise. These bregals are used in many southern dishes.

him poses proudly for a photograph. Here we could easily have spent hours in this labyrinth of passages, with these simple, friendly people. Here the Indian countryside brims over, here the visitor can find the true identity of the average Indian again. And so the visit to this market has been a feast for the eye and has done us a power of good.

On the way back, leaving the market, we hear again the turbulent hooting of the buses. Don Quixote has come back...

Christophe

The morning market of Kumbakonam is one of the largest fruit and vegetable markets in the region.

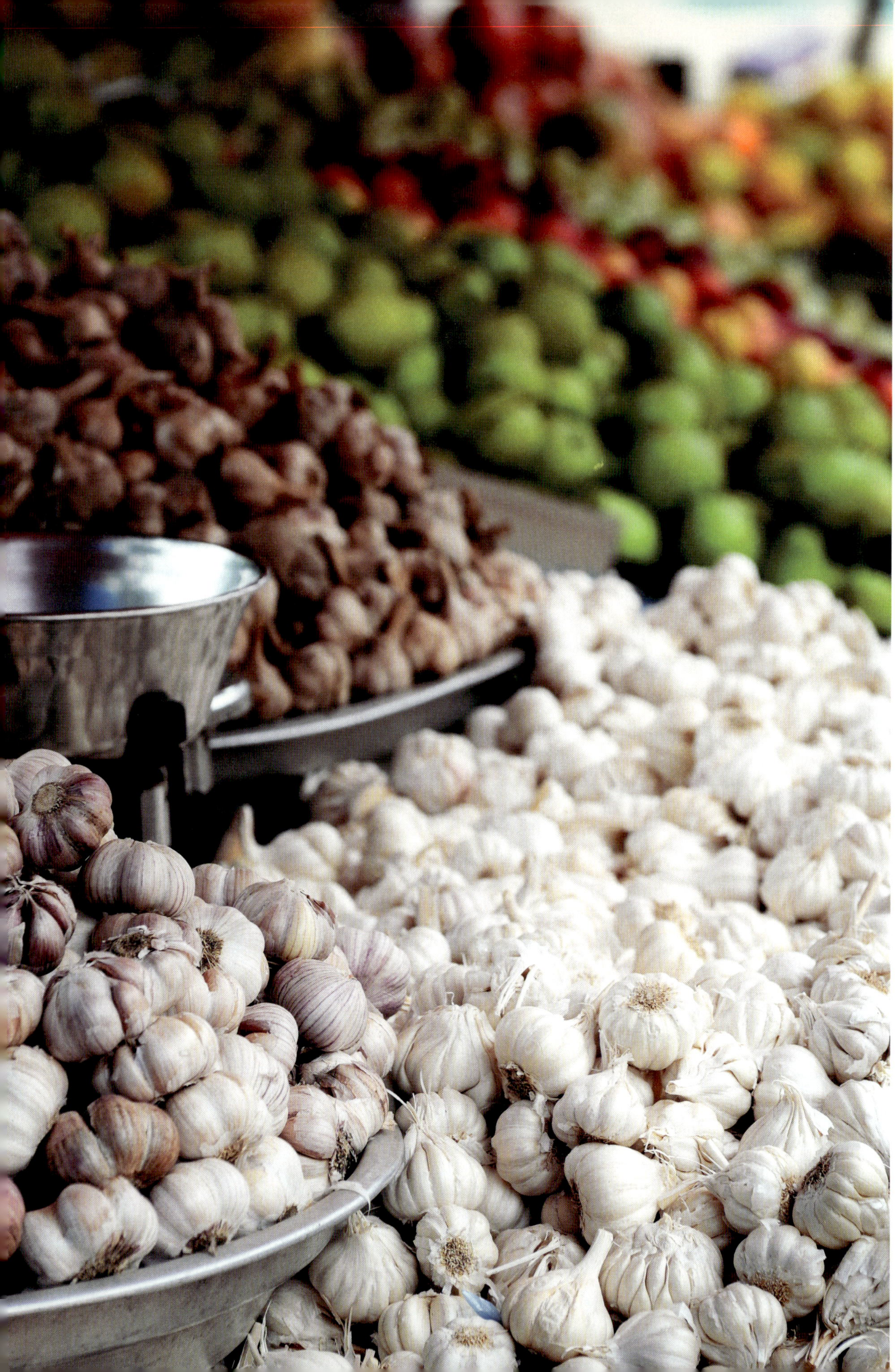

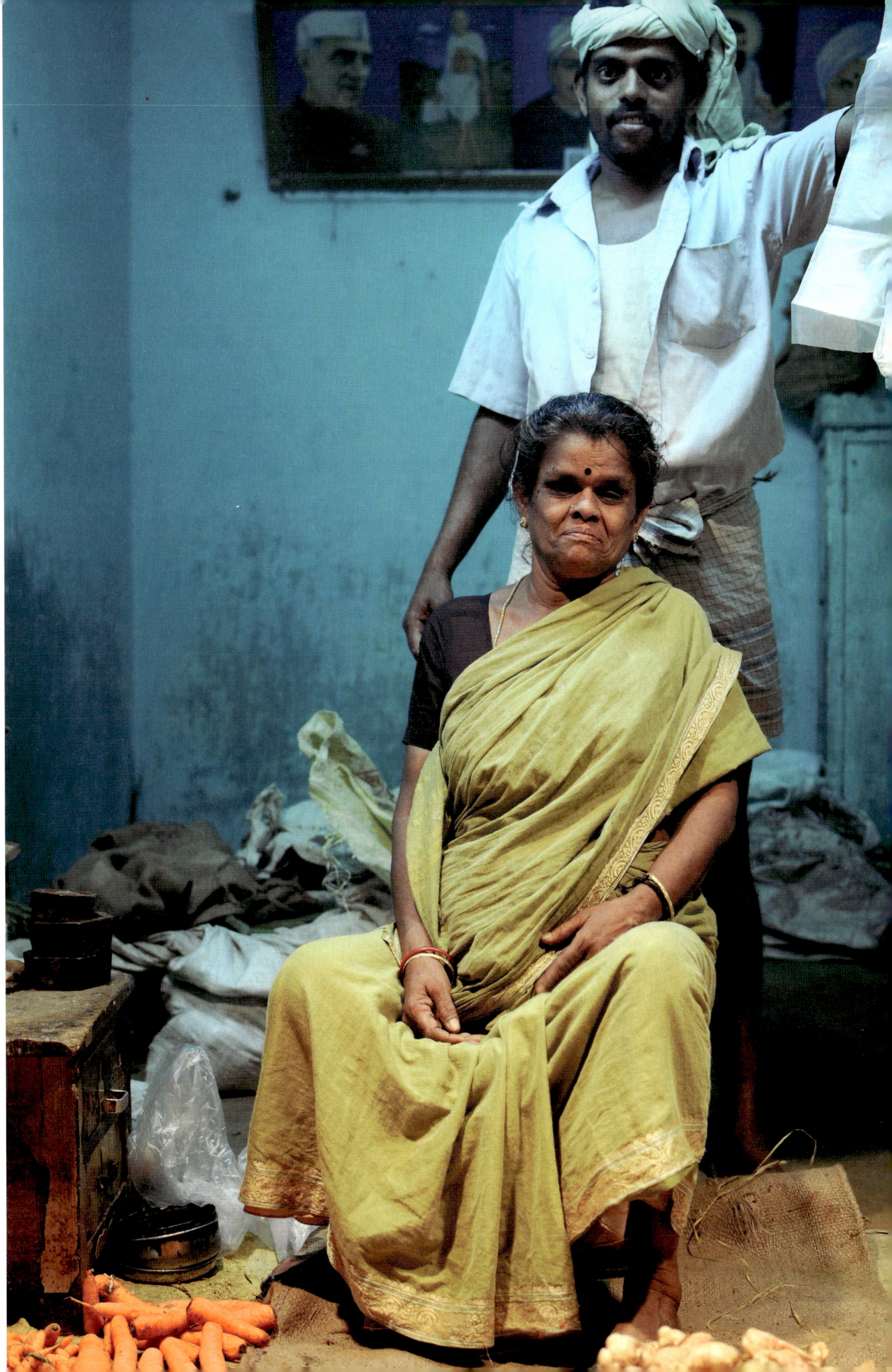

FRIED DUCK LIVER WITH MANGO, PINEAPPLE AND SWEET CURRY BROTH

ARTISTIC

TIP

The sweet broth is particularly suitable as a 'nage' for langoustines and lobster. Serve with a small spoonful of chutney.

FOR 4 PERSONS

CHUTNEY 80 g fresh pineapple, 80 g fresh mango, 1 red onion, 2 tablespoons peanut oil, 10 g sugar, juice of ½ lime, 2 cm ginger root, a pinch of sambhar masala

BROTH ½ litre water, 50 g sugar, 1 teaspoon coriander seeds, 1 teaspoon cummin seeds, a pinch of ginger powder, a pinch of cardamom powder, a pinch of chilli, a pinch of turmeric, 2 star anises, 3 apples, type Rennet, 3 passion fruits

MANGO PUREE 50 g flesh of a ripe mango, 50 g water

DUCK LIVER 4 slices of duck liver of 80 g each, sambhar masala, a pinch of coarse salt

PREPARATION

For the chutney cut the pineapple and the mango into pieces. Peel the onion and cut it up fine. Fry it in the oil. Add the pineapple and the sugar and let it caramelize. Deglaze with the lime juice. Peel the ginger root and grate it. Add the ginger and the sambhar masala to the pineapple and finally also the mango.

For the broth bring ½ litre water to the boil with the sugar. Add the cummin seeds, the caraway seeds, the ginger powder, the cardamom powder, the chilli, the turmeric and the star anise and let it simmer for half an hour.

Peel the apples, remove the core and cut them into pieces. Remove the flesh from the passion fruits and mix it with the apples. Pour the tepid broth over the fruit and leave it to infuse in a covered bowl in the refrigerator for at least 12 hours.

Strain the cooled broth and reheat it just before serving.

For the mango puree bring the mango to the boil in the water and mix to a puree in the blender.

Season the duck liver with sambhar masala. Fry it on both sides to a golden brown in a pan with non-stick coating.

Heat the chutney and put a little on a plate. Put a spoonful of mango puree and a piece of duck liver with it. Pour the hot broth over it.

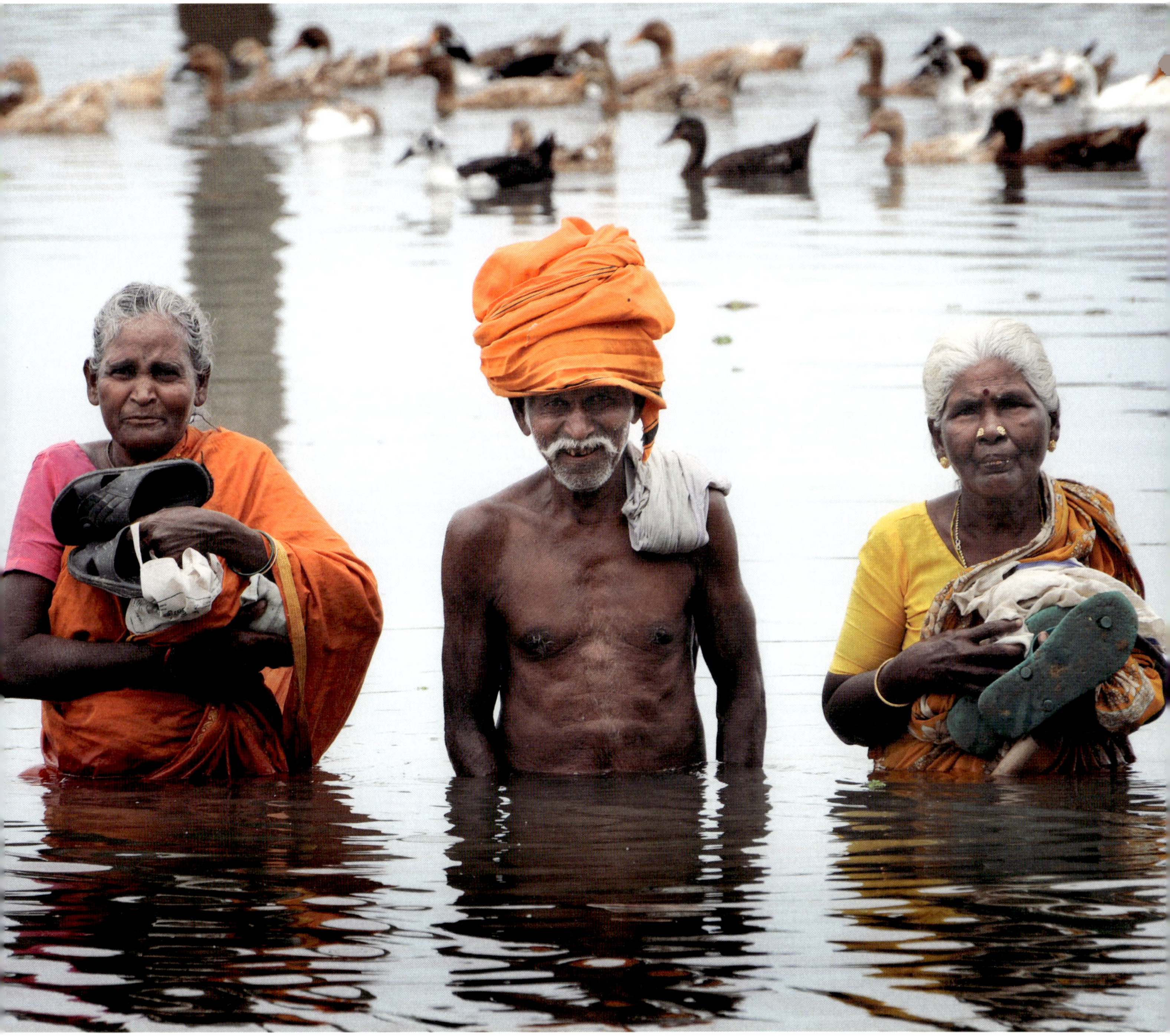

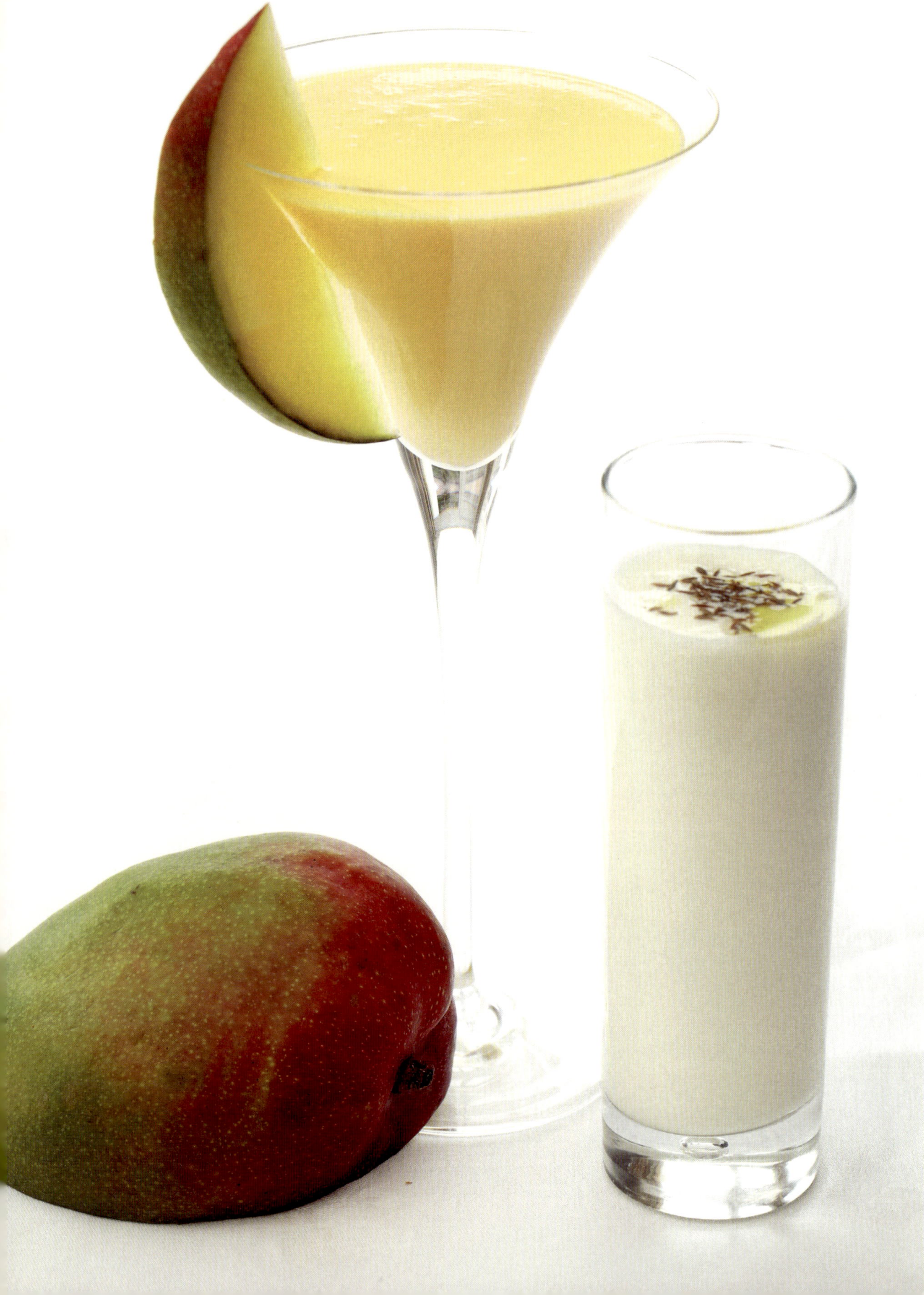

MANGO LASSI

CLASSIC

In India drinking lassi with a meal is as common as drinking wine with us. With curry the salt version of lassi is often drunk. The mild yoghurt taste, and the salty taste (which is unusual to us), are said to have a soothing and refreshing effect when eating highly spiced curries. We stick to the sweet mango lassi, a delicious yoghurt drink.

INGREDIENTS

500 g ripe flesh from mangos, salt, 2.5 dl full-cream milk, 2.5 dl full-cream (Greek) yoghurt

PREPARATION

Puree the mango in the blender with a pinch of salt and push it through a sieve so that there are no longer threads in it.
Beat the mango puree with the milk and the yoghurt. Serve ice-cold.

SALTED LASSI (OR CHAAS)

Salted lassi is much more popular in India than the sweet variant with mango. It is thinner because the milk is replaced by water. Chaas is a perfect thirst-quencher which helps to digest spicy and sometimes very rich curries.

INGREDIENTS

2 small green chilli peppers, 1 cm ginger root, ½ tablespoon fresh coriander, chopped, 1 teaspoon cummin seed, roasted, 2 teaspoons salt, 500 g full-cream yoghurt, ½ litre ice-cold water, oil, asafoetida (a typically Indian spice with a taste of onion and garlic)

PREPARATION

Cut the chilli peppers open lengthways, remove the seeds and chop them finely.
Peel the ginger root and grate it. Mix the chilli with the ginger, the coriander, the cummin seed and the salt.
Stir this mixture through the yoghurt with the water. Serve the lassi in glasses.
Heat a little oil and stir a little asafoetida into it. Dribble a little of this oil over the yoghurt for an extra touch.

KALAAN OF BANANA WITH MINCED MEAT AND CASHEW NUT BREAD

CLASSIC & WESTERN

Kalaan is a traditional Kerala dish with yoghurt and coconut, here with banana as an additional ingredient. Usually kaalan is served as part of a thali. In this recipe the hard-boiled egg has been replaced with a banana mix. I have also added cashew nuts to give the dish an extra crisp effect.

FOR 4 PERSONS

KALAAN 2 unripe bananas, 100 g sweet potatoes (or yam), a pinch of turmeric, a pinch of tikka masala, 4 tablespoon coconut oil, 1 teaspoon mustard seeds, 2 small red chilli peppers, 1 teaspoon cummin seeds, 100 g coconut, grated, 500 g full-cream (Greek) yoghurt, salt

MINCED MEAT LOAVES 1 tablespoon oil, 40 cashew nuts, 2 pinches tikka masala, salt, 750 g mixed minced meat, 1 egg, pepper, 2 egg yolks, 40 g flour, 40 g breadcrumbs, oil for deep-frying, broad-leafed parsley

PREPARATION

For the kaalan dip the bananas for 2 minutes in boiling water so that the peel bursts open. Peel the bananas, chop them into coarse pieces and put them in cold water.

Peel the sweet potatoes and cut them into large pieces.

Cook half the bananas with the sweet potato in ½ litre water, to which turmeric and tikka masala has been added, until they are done. Drain off the water.

Heat the oil in a pan and crisp the mustard seeds in it. Cut the chilli peppers in two lengthways, remove the seeds, and chop them fine. Fry the cummin seeds, the chilli and the coconut in the oil with them. Add the spiced coconut mixture to the bananas and the sweet potato. Pour in the yoghurt and heat it through well for another 2 minutes. Season to taste with salt.

Heat the oil for the minced meat loaves and fry the cashew nuts with a pinch of tikka masala and a pinch of salt in it. Chop them coarsely. Boil the remaining bananas in salted water until done.

Mix the minced meat with the egg and season that with pepper, salt, and a pinch of tikka masala. Divide it in four equal balls.

Press the balls flat and put some cooked bananas and cashew nuts in the middle. Pack everything inside the minced meat and let the minced meat loaves rest in the refrigerator.

Beat the egg yolks loose with a little water.
Pass each minced meat loaf through the flour, then through the egg yolks and finally through the breadcrumbs.
Deep-fry them two at the time in oil at 160 °C till they are golden brown.
Distribute the kaalan over the plates and put a minced meat loaf on top. Finish off with roasted cashew nuts and chopped parsley.

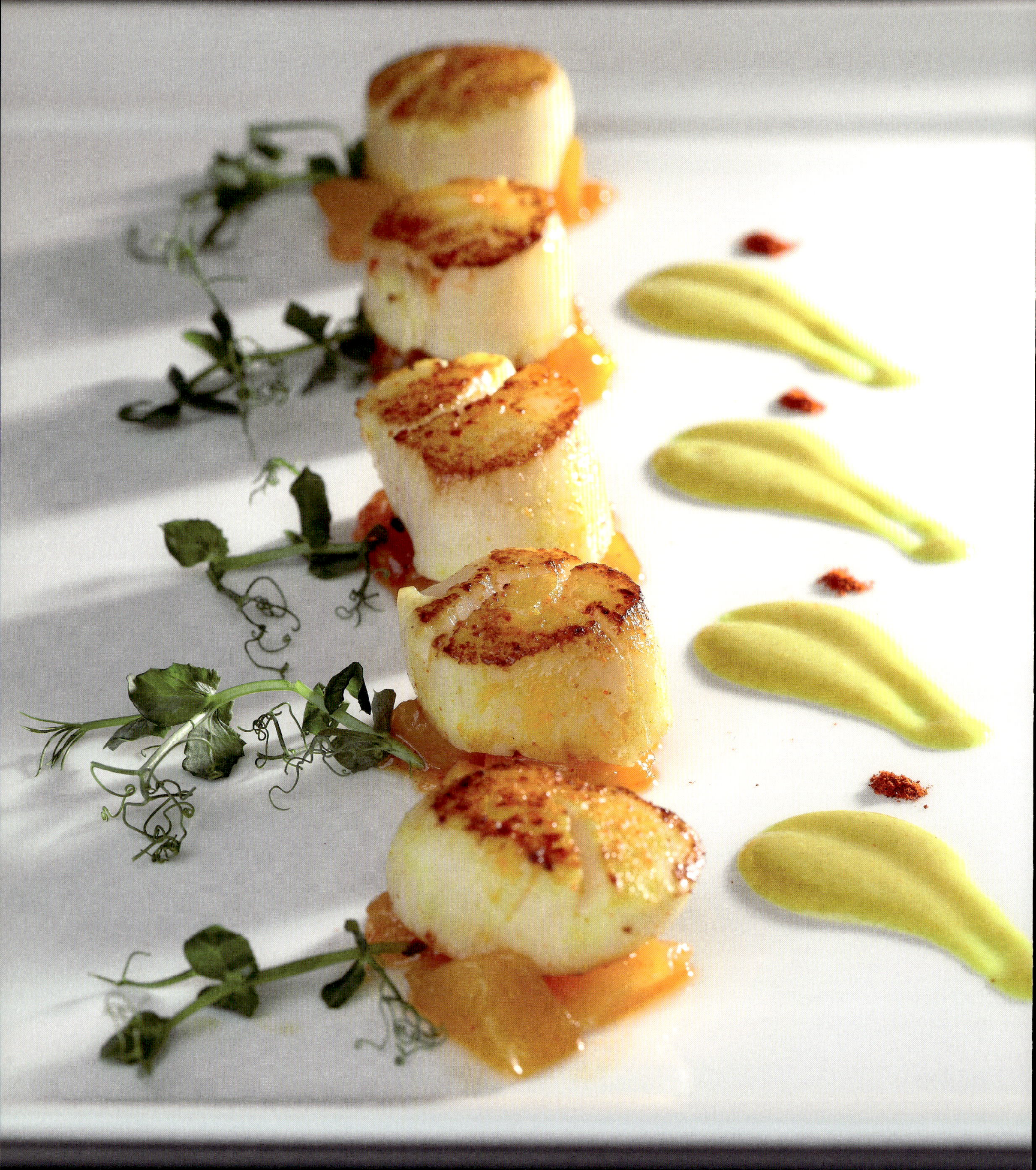

QUICK FRIED SCALLOPS ON A MANGO CHUTNEY WITH MANGO COCONUT CREAM

ARTISTIC

FOR 4 PERSONS

CHUTNEY *2 cloves of garlic, 2 cm ginger root, 3 tablespoons oil, 1 kg ripe flesh from a mango, 2 cinnamon sticks, 6 cloves, 100 g sugar, 1.5 dl vinegar, a pinch of Kashmir chilli*

SCALLOPS *16 large scallops, a pinch of turmeric, a pinch of vadouvan masala, oil, coarse salt*

MANGO-COCONUT CREAM *4 shallots, oil, 2 cm ginger root, 200 g ripe flesh from a mango, a pinch of vadouvan masala, a pinch of turmeric, 3 dl fish stock, 1 dl coconut cream, salt, a few pea shoots*

PREPARATION

For the chutney peel the garlic and the ginger root. Chop them finely and braise them in oil.

Add the mango, the cinnamon sticks, the cloves, the sugar and the vinegar and let the mango boil till soft. Bring to taste with Kashmir chilli. Remove the cinnamon sticks and the cloves. Let the chutney cool down.

Clean the scallops and rub them with a mix of turmeric and vadouvan masala. Fry them briefly on both sides in a little oil and season to taste with coarse salt.

For the mango-coconut cream, peel the shallots and chop them coarsely. Braise them in the oil. Peel the ginger and grate it. Add it to the shallots with the mango, the vadouvan masala and the turmeric. Add the fish stock and simmer until reduced to half the quantity. Add the coconut cream and cook until the desired thickness has been achieved. Strain the sauce and season it to taste with salt. Finish off the dish with a few pea shoots.

MUFFINS OF BANANA, GINGER AND LIME   CLASSIC

FOR 12 MUFFINS

1 lime, 300 g self-raising flour, 1 tablespoon ginger powder,
115 g soft brown sugar, 45 g preserved ginger, 60 g unsalted butter,
2 tablespoons acacia honey, 1.25 dl full-cream milk, 2 eggs,
3 large half-ripe bananas

PREPARATION

Scrub the lime clean and grate the green zest. Press the lime.
Mix the self-raising flour with the ginger powder in a large bowl.
Stir in the sugar and the preserved ginger which has been cut into pieces. Make it into a small heap with a little hole in the middle.
Melt the butter in a little saucepan and dissolve the honey in it.
Add the grated lime zest to it and leave to cool a little.
Beat the eggs loose with the milk. Peel the bananas, mash them with a fork, and mix them with the lime juice. Pour it all into the dip in the flour and stir it well. It does not matter if there are a few lumps in the batter.
Grease a muffin tray or fill it with paper moulds and fill them two-thirds full with the batter. Put it in a pre-heated oven at 210 °C for 20 minutes.
Take the muffins out of the oven, remove them carefully from the moulds and serve them warm.

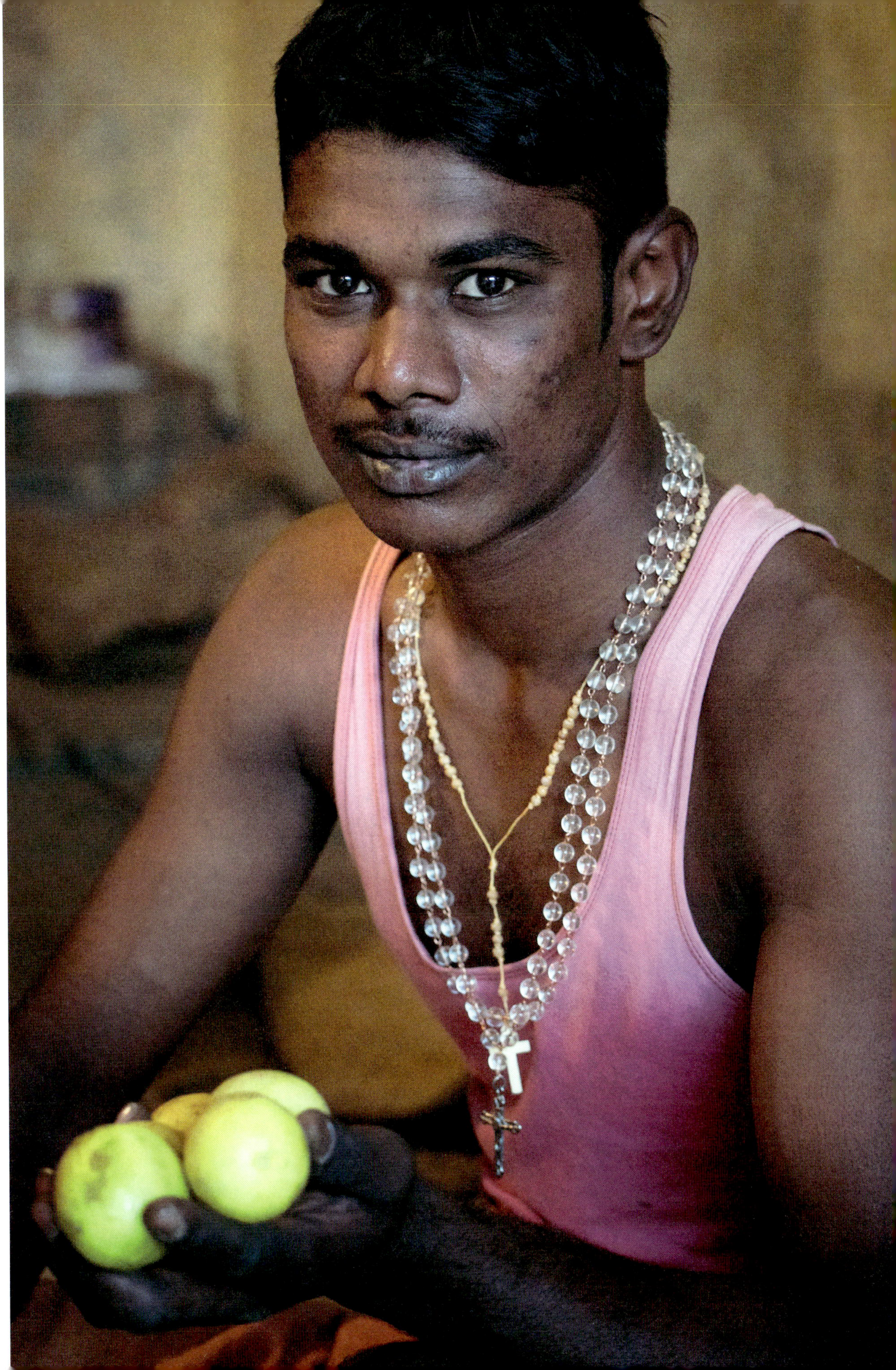

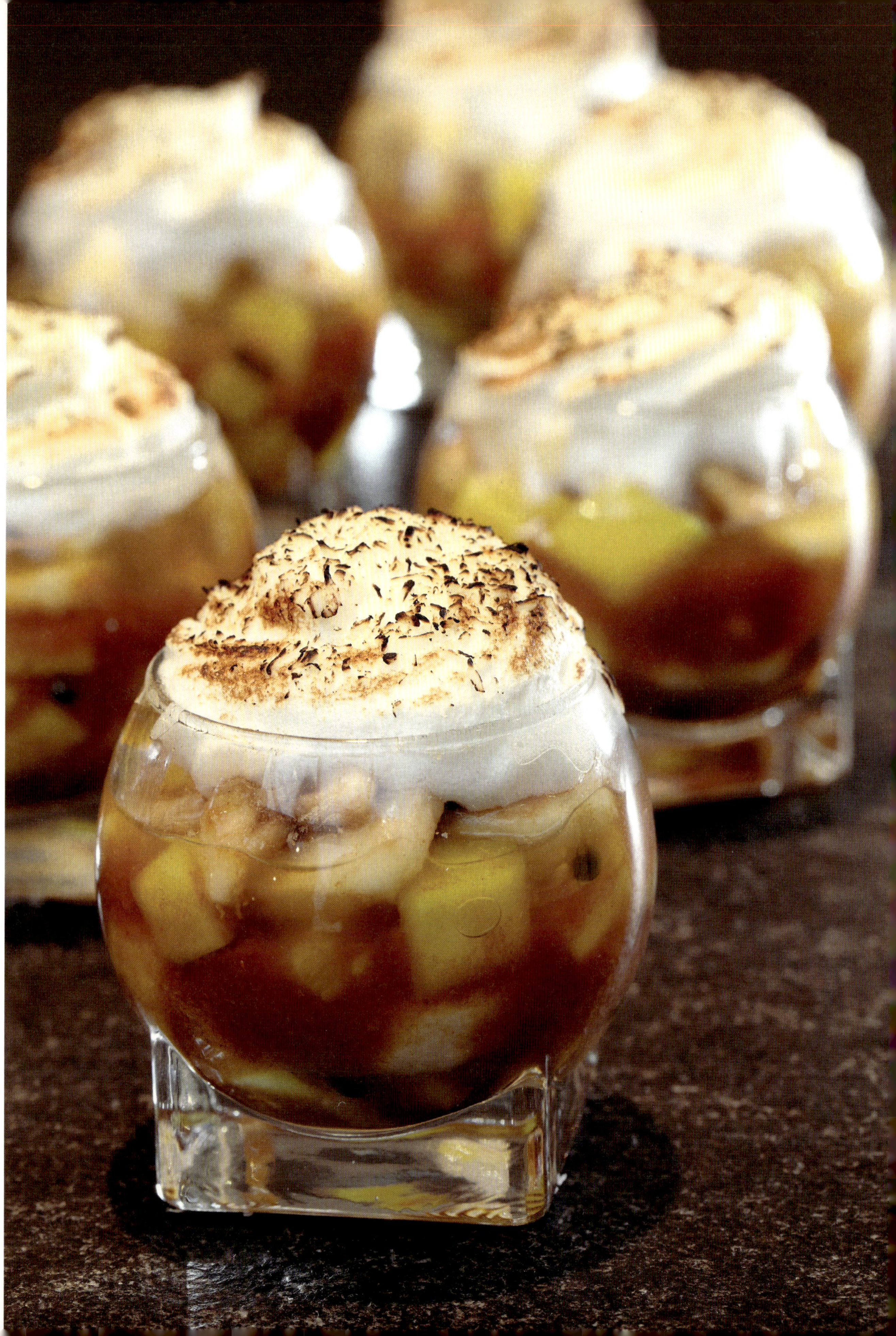

PICKLES OF SWEET FRUIT
WITH VADOUVAN MASALA AND MERINGUE   WESTERN

Chef Stephen of Malabar House is an expert in making pickles. Immediately noticeable when tasting them are the very strong spicy and sour tastes. These tastes are perhaps a little too pronounced for our European taste buds. Yet these pickles can't be left out here, they are too important in the Indian cuisine. For that reason we balance sweet fruit with mild spiciness. A dessert with a very generous taste experience.

FOR 8 SMALL GLASSES

PICKLES 1 mango, 1 banana, juice of 1 lime, ¼ pineapple, 1 dl cider vinegar, 3 passion fruits, 50 g caster sugar, 4 cloves, 1 cinnamon stick, a pinch of vadouvan masala

MERINGUE 2 egg whites, 30 g sugar, soft white sugar

PREPARATION

Peel the mango and cut the flesh into pieces. Peel the banana, cut it into slices and sprinkle them with a little lime juice. Peel the pineapple, remove the hard core and cut the fruit into cubes.

Put the pineapple in a pan and sprinkle it with the cider vinegar. Peel the passion fruits and add the flesh to the pineapple. Finally add the sugar, the cloves and the cinnamon stick. Bring it all to the boil and keep it boiling for 3 minutes.

Remove it from the heat and stir in the vadouvan masala, the mango, the banana and the remainder of the lime juice. Spoon them into small glasses and leave them to cool in the refrigerator.

For the meringue beat the egg whites very stiff and gradually add the sugar. Distribute this mixture over the glasses and finish off with soft white sugar. Burn the meringue a golden brown with a cook's blowtorch.

TIP

If the nuts are too spicy to your taste, adjust the quantity of vadouvan masala. The cashews are nicest when they are warm, but they will easily keep for some weeks in a tightly closed glass jar.

SPICED CASHEW NUTS

CLASSIC

The Portuguese brought Brazilian cajun nuts to Goa in India. From that point these nuts – meanwhile corrupted to cashew nuts – began their conquest of Asia. Sugared or spiced, they are still always a popular snack. Converted to a paste they are ideal to make curries a little milder.

INGREDIENTS

5 tablespoons oil, 400 g cashew nuts, 1 teaspoon cummin seeds, 1.5 tablespoon vadouvan masala, 1 teaspoon coarse salt, a pinch of turmeric

PREPARATION

Heat the oil on a moderate heat in a wok or karahi.
Stir-fry the nuts for 6 minutes in the oil until golden brown.
After 3 minutes add the cummin seeds to it.
Mix the vadouvan masala with the salt and the turmeric.
Sprinkle the mixture over the nuts.
Transfer the cashews to a baking tray, spread them out and leave them to cool a little.

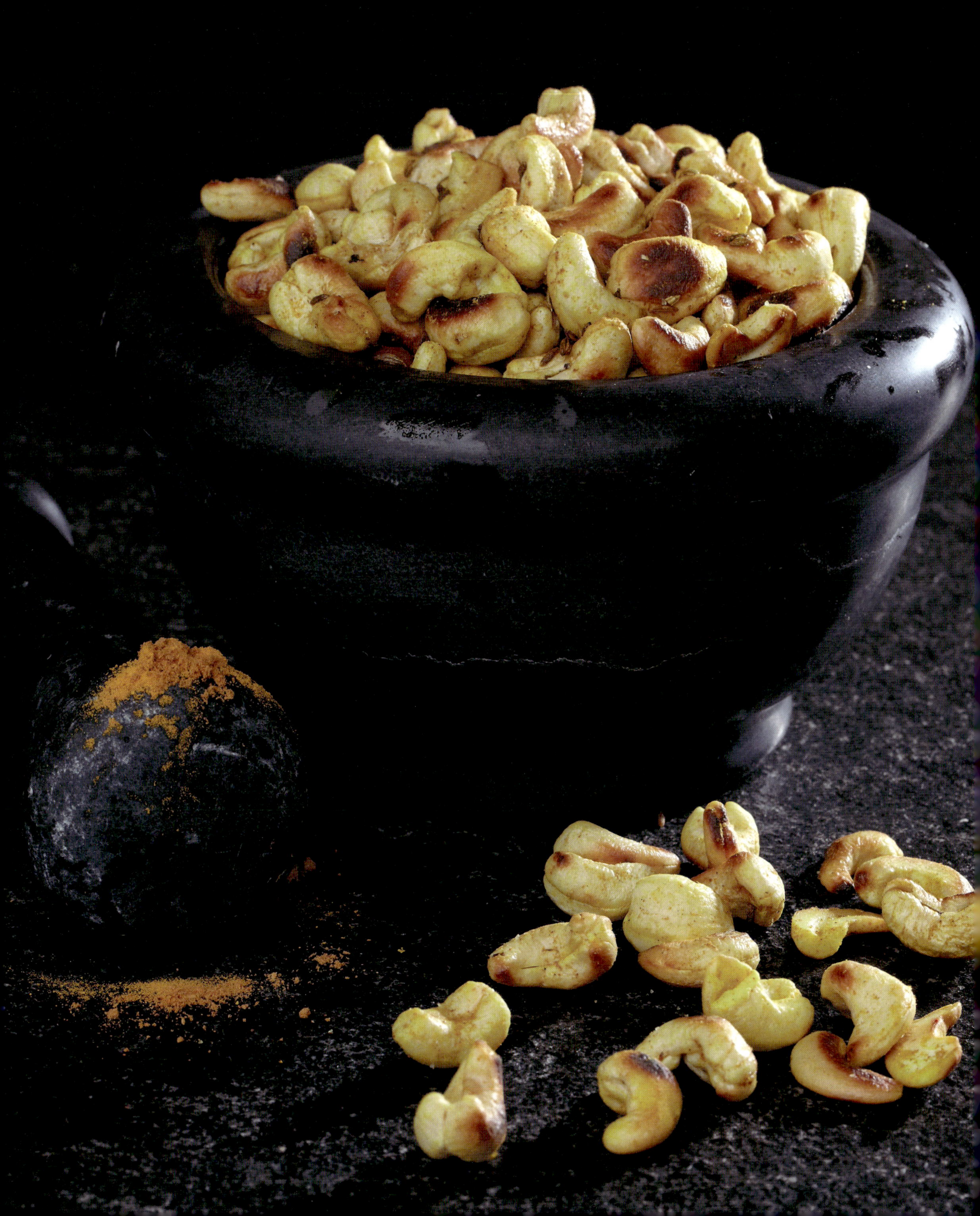

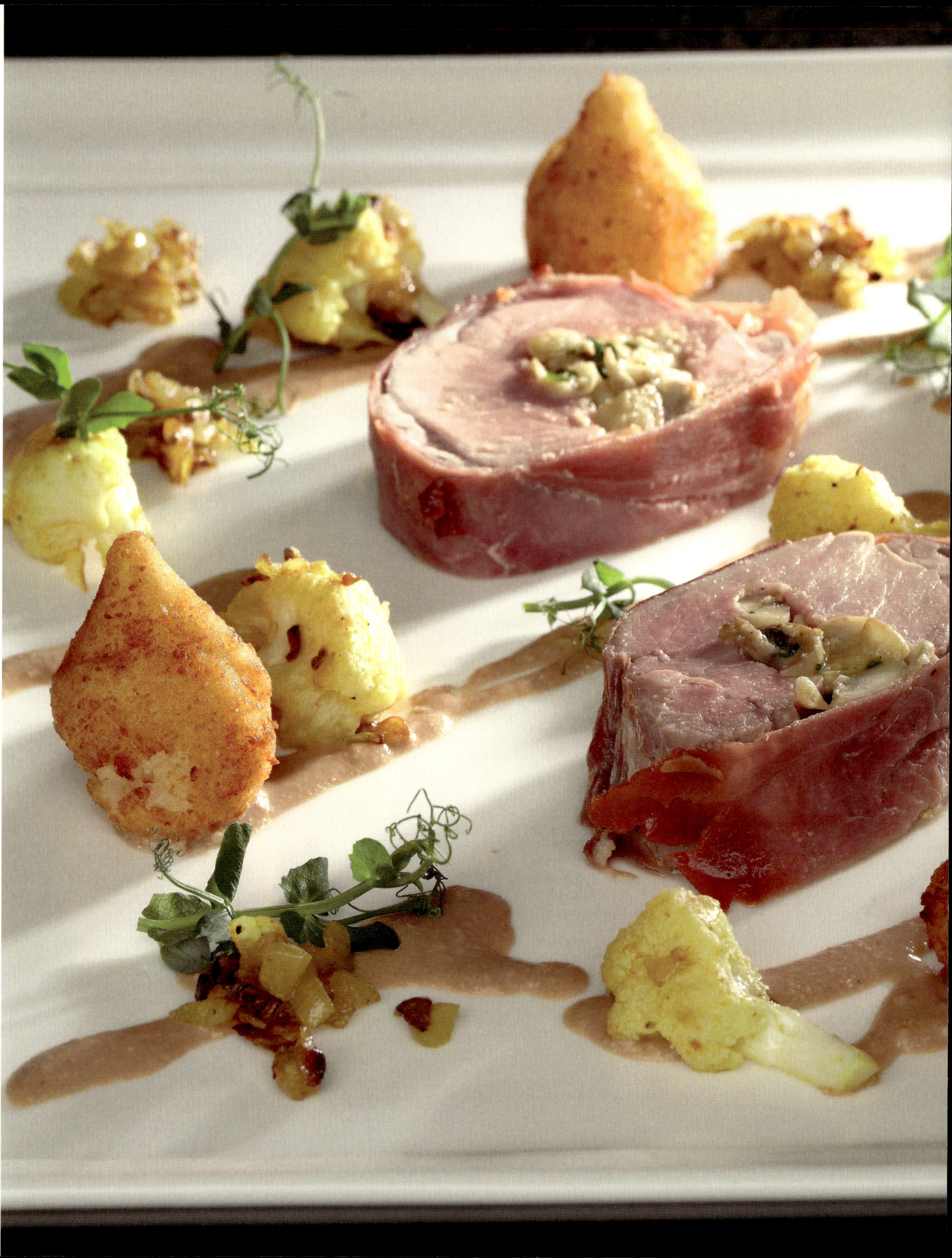

PORK TENDERLOIN FILLED WITH CASHEW NUTS, ALOO MASALA MASH CROQUETTES AND TURMERIC GOBI

ARTISTIC

FOR 4 PERSONS

200 g mushrooms, 1 dl clarified butter (or ghee), pepper,
¼ bundle of coriander, 50 g cashew nuts, a pinch of vadouvan masala,
salt, 2 egg yolks, 2 tablespoons cashew puree (see later),
2 pork tenderloins, 4 slices dried ham

PREPARATION

Cut the mushrooms into slices. Heat the butter in a pan, fry the mushrooms and season them with pepper. Chop the coriander finely and add to the mushrooms.

Roast the cashew nuts in a pan with non-stick coating and season them with vadouvan masala and salt. Chop them coarsely. Add the mushrooms and mix them with the egg yolks and the cashew puree. Cut the pork tenderloins lengthways without cutting through the bottom, and leave the ends intact. Fill the resulting pouch with the mushroom mixture and wrap the tenderloins in the dried ham. Heat the oil in a pan and sear the tenderloins with the closure downwards. Put them in an oven dish and cook them till done in 15 minutes in a pre-heated oven at 200 °C.

Carve the tenderloins into 6 thick slices.

CASHEW PUREE

INGREDIENTS

50 g cashew nuts, ½ dl water, 4 dl brown stock, pepper

PREPARATION

Mix the cashew nuts with the water in the blender.
For the sauce dilute the puree with a brown stock and season to taste with pepper.

ALOO MASALA MASH CROQUETTES

INGREDIENTS

500 g potatoes (aloo), salt, 1 egg, pepper, ½ onion, 2 tablespoons clarified butter (or ghee), 1 coffeespoon of cummin seed, 1 cm ginger root, a pinch of turmeric, 1 small green chilli pepper, 3 egg yolks, 50 g breadcrumbs, oil for deep-frying

PREPARATION

Peel the potatoes and cook them till done in salted water. Drain them and mash them to a puree with the egg. Season to taste with pepper and salt.

Chop the onion finely. Heat the butter in a pan and fry the onion with the cummin seed. Peel the ginger root and grate it finely. Add it with the turmeric to the onion.

Cut the chilli pepper lengthways, remove the seeds and chop it finely. Braise it with the onion.

Add the onion mixture to the puree and mix it well. Make little balls of about 3 cm diameter and put them in the refrigerator for a few hours.

Beat the egg yolks loose with a little water. Make teardrops of the little balls by flattening one end slightly. Roll them first through the egg yolk and then through the breadcrumbs. Do this again, so that the little balls get covered twice.

Deep-fry the croquettes to a golden brown in oil at 200 °C.

TURMERIC GOBI

INGREDIENTS

1 small cauliflower, 1 tablespoon coconut oil, 20 mustard seeds, 5 shallots, 2 cloves of garlic, 1 tablespoon turmeric, pepper, salt, 1 tablespoon mustard

PREPARATION

Clean the cauliflower and cook it *al dente*. Divide it into very small florets.

Heat the oil in a pan and crisp the mustard seeds.

Peel the shallots and cut them into rings. Peel the garlic and crush it. Add the shallots and the garlic to the mustard seeds and season it with turmeric, pepper and salt.

Add the cauliflower florets and let them colour. Finally add the mustard.*

---

* In India a paste is used made of mustard seeds, water and tamarind.

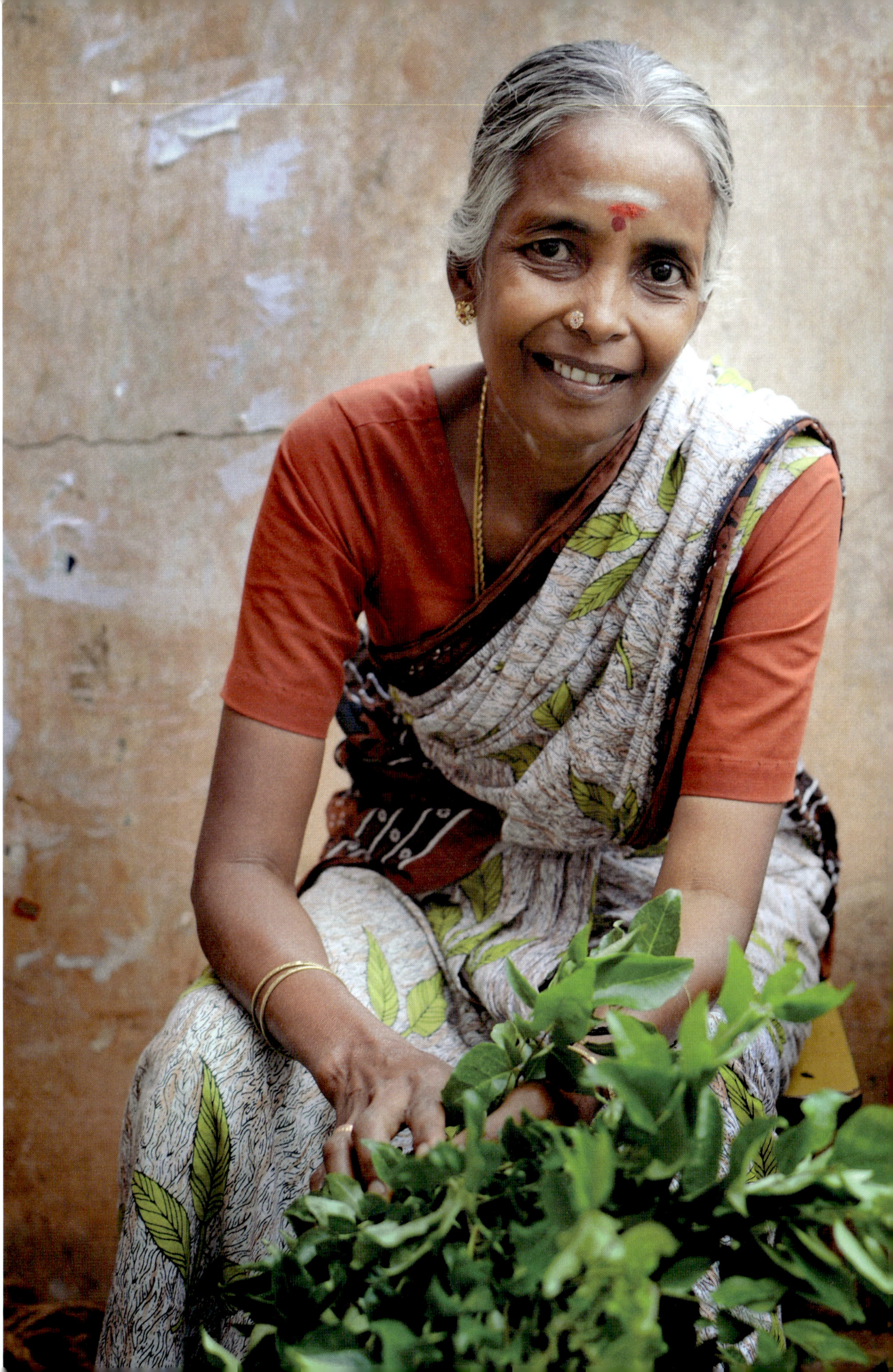

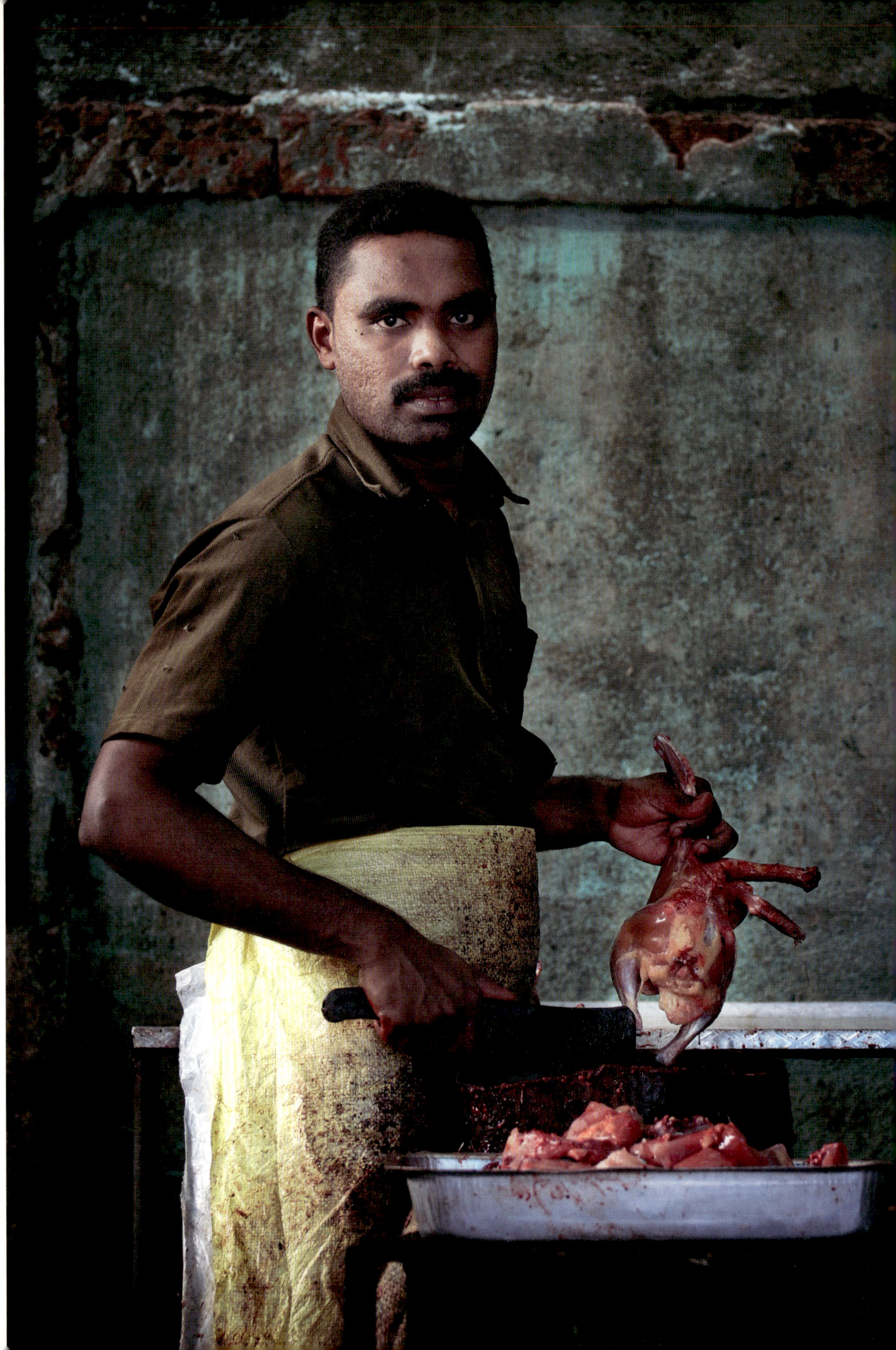

CHICKEN AND EGGS

THE FARMER AND THE ARTIST

With laughter in his eyes, the chef allows the chaos of activity in the market to embrace him. It does not worry him that this is happening in the early hours. On the contrary. He thoroughly enjoys every second he can wander unhindered through the narrow, untidy passages between the stalls. For him, these Indian early markets are rewarding places. Here he can satisfy his curiosity, his insatiable appetite for culinary know-how, with impunity. The true kings of this market are the farmers who have loaded their treasures onto carts in the depth of the night and have followed the stars from their distant villages. But they brought no gold, frankincense or myrrh. Their rough hands and shaggy looks betray the fact that their only riches are the fruits of their own hard work.

The market is above all an inspiration for the chef. Here is the beginning of it all; amidst the unlimited diversity of stalls, the ideas for his recipes will start gaining shape. Like the stallholders he knows that it is the freshness of the products which determines the outcome. So he quietly takes his time. He feels, he sniffs, he tastes. He lets the products slide through his hands and enjoys the approving muttering he hears when he makes clear how much he enjoys the taste of a juicy mango. The air smells of nutmeg. He can't withstand the invitation of piles of fresh coriander and mint. The many vegetables are still covered with the dew of the field and the bright colours of the fruit give life to the still early morning.

On the bloodied blades of the chopping block, sheep's eyes look defeated in his direction. The meat next to it looks fresh and appetizing. In his imagination, the chef can smell the biryani already. Unaware of danger the chickens cackle loudly and untroubled. With a swift cut of the razor-sharp knife, their lot is sealed by the tall poultry seller. Plucked and cleaned they disappear into the chef's bag...

> Only
> The love of cooking
> Can lead to
> The art of cooking

On the other side of the market chattering fisherman's wives noisily sell the last catch of the day. Their husbands have braved the turbulent waves of the Arabian Sea, set out their nets from rickety little boats according to local tradition to bring them in from the beach at dawn, chanting loudly. The chef walks through wet little passages of silt and brackish smelling fish water. Here it is teeming with cats, fighting for a dead fish head. But they will have to keep off the tiger prawns. Those are destined for a spicy starter.

Shopping has been done. Now the chef can withdraw to his own familiar habitat. Vegetables are washed and cut. Briskly and with a perfect elegance, he uses his knives. The steady rhythm of his hand betrays his skill.

The pestle and mortar are also brought in. Carefully, he starts on the composition of his magical spice mixture. Unlike no other, he knows the power of this Kerala gold and knows that he has to use it with care.

The fires are lit. Blueish-yellow flames grow and greedily lick at pans and casseroles. The smell of coconut oil immediately fills the kitchen. Vegetables, marinades and other preparations are waiting impatiently on the cooking island. Each one is given its own place by the chef in a few quick movements of his hands. In no time at all there is a happy concert of simmering, bubbling and crackling noises. Things are being stirred, shaken, meat is turned, something is tasted with a little spoon and the spicing adjusted. A dash of this and a pinch of something else. The chef knows how to protect his secrets.

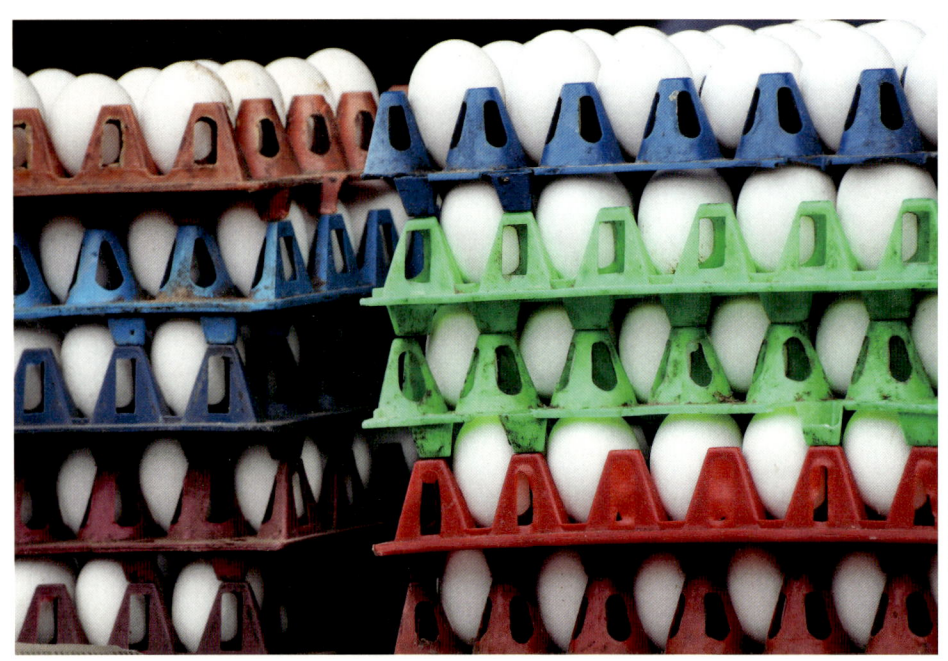

The pink 'parson's nose' of the chickens becomes a crisp brown and grey tiger prawns in their turn dress up in a pretty pink. Sauces assume a healthy colour and aromas fly in rich trails like exotic butterflies through the air. Like an accomplished tightrope walker, the chef manages perfectly to control the balance between his various fires. The chef is now completely focused and you feel that the peak of his efforts is close. Everything has to be perfect. Readiness, taste, and the insight to combine everything harmoniously. The chef now becomes an artist, someone who paints with his eye, nose and tongue.

    The plate can now be made up. The master is ready to put his signature to it. Like a red wax seal, this has to symbolize the alliance between farmer and artist. Another fine line of sauce, and then the plate can be taken to the dining room. Concerned as a proud mother who sends off her child to school with a last caress on his head, he looks on with satisfaction as it leaves his kitchen. Then he waits, until a little later the waiter comes in and calls out *'compliment au chef'*. The artist laughs...

Christophe

Next pages:
The famous Butterball in Mahabalipuram: the legend tells us how the English fruitlessly tried to pull down the rock from the slope with a whole horde of elephants.

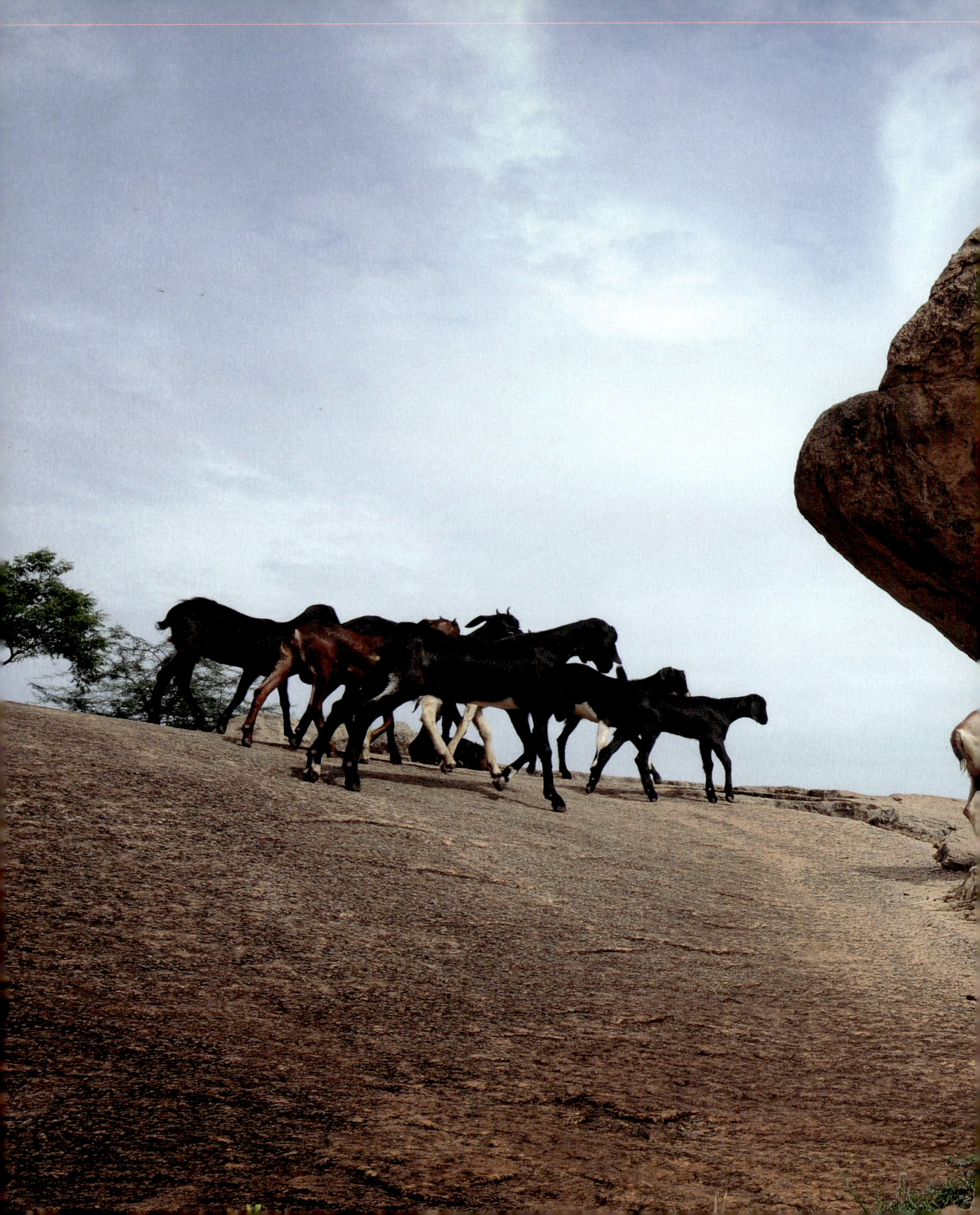

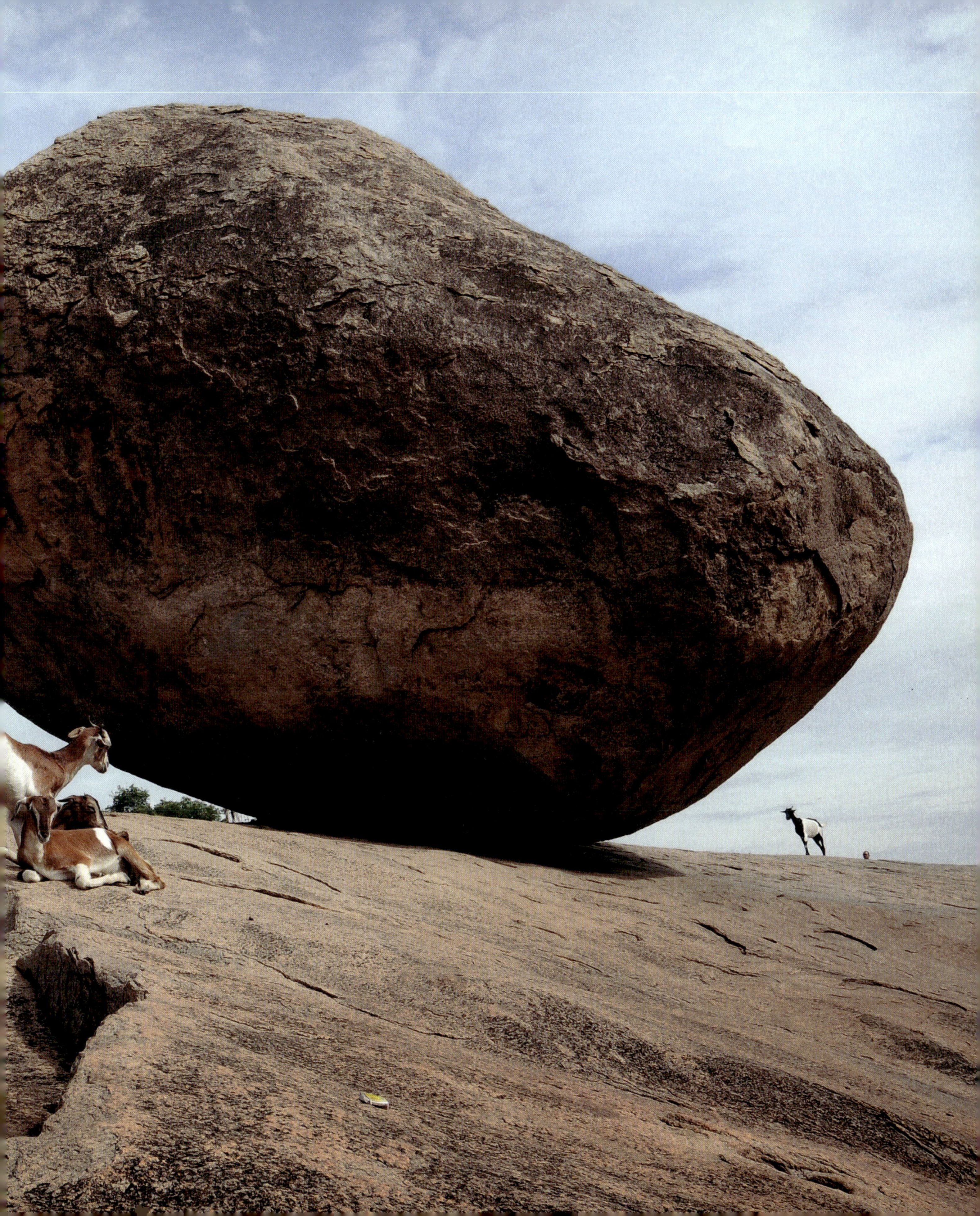

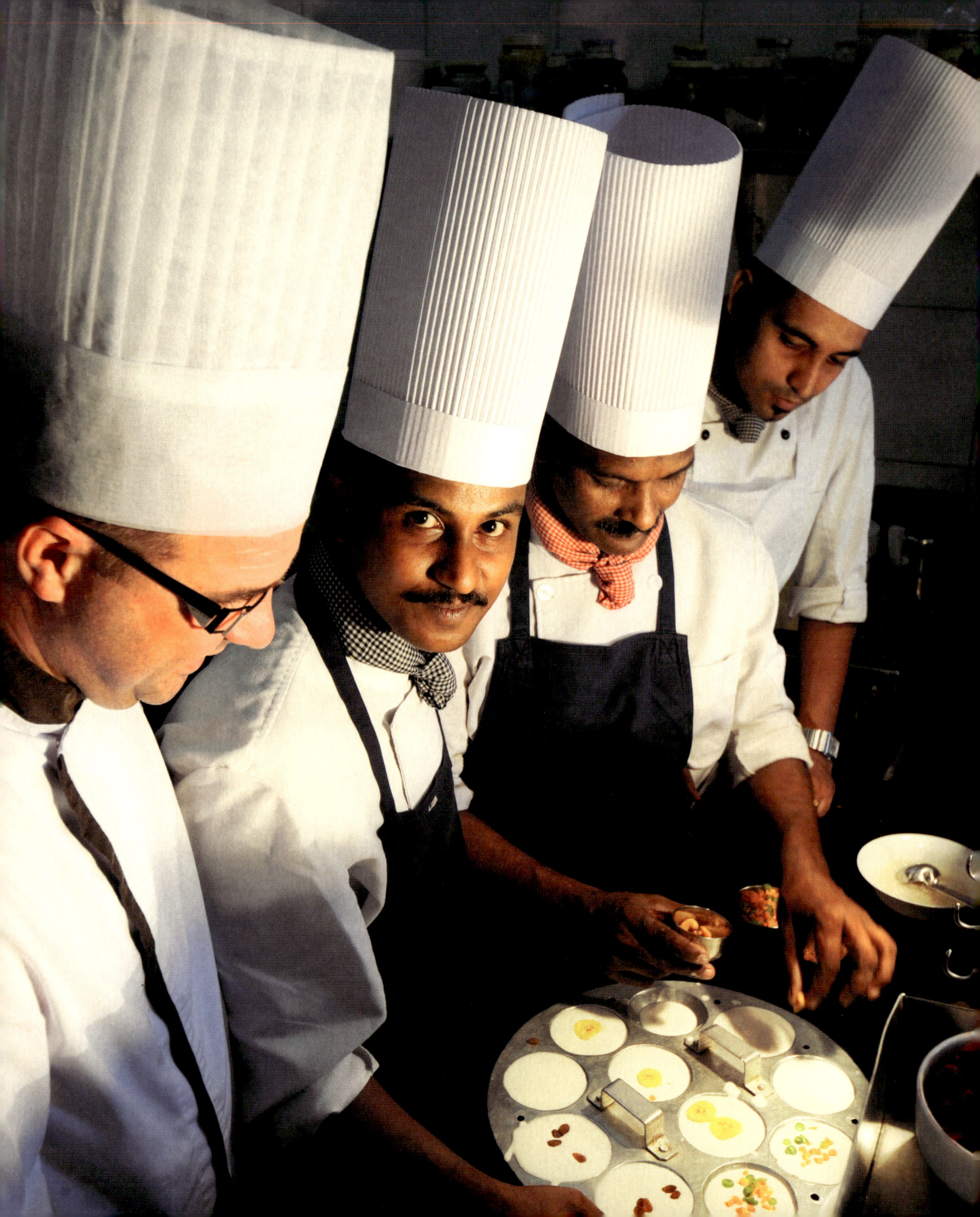

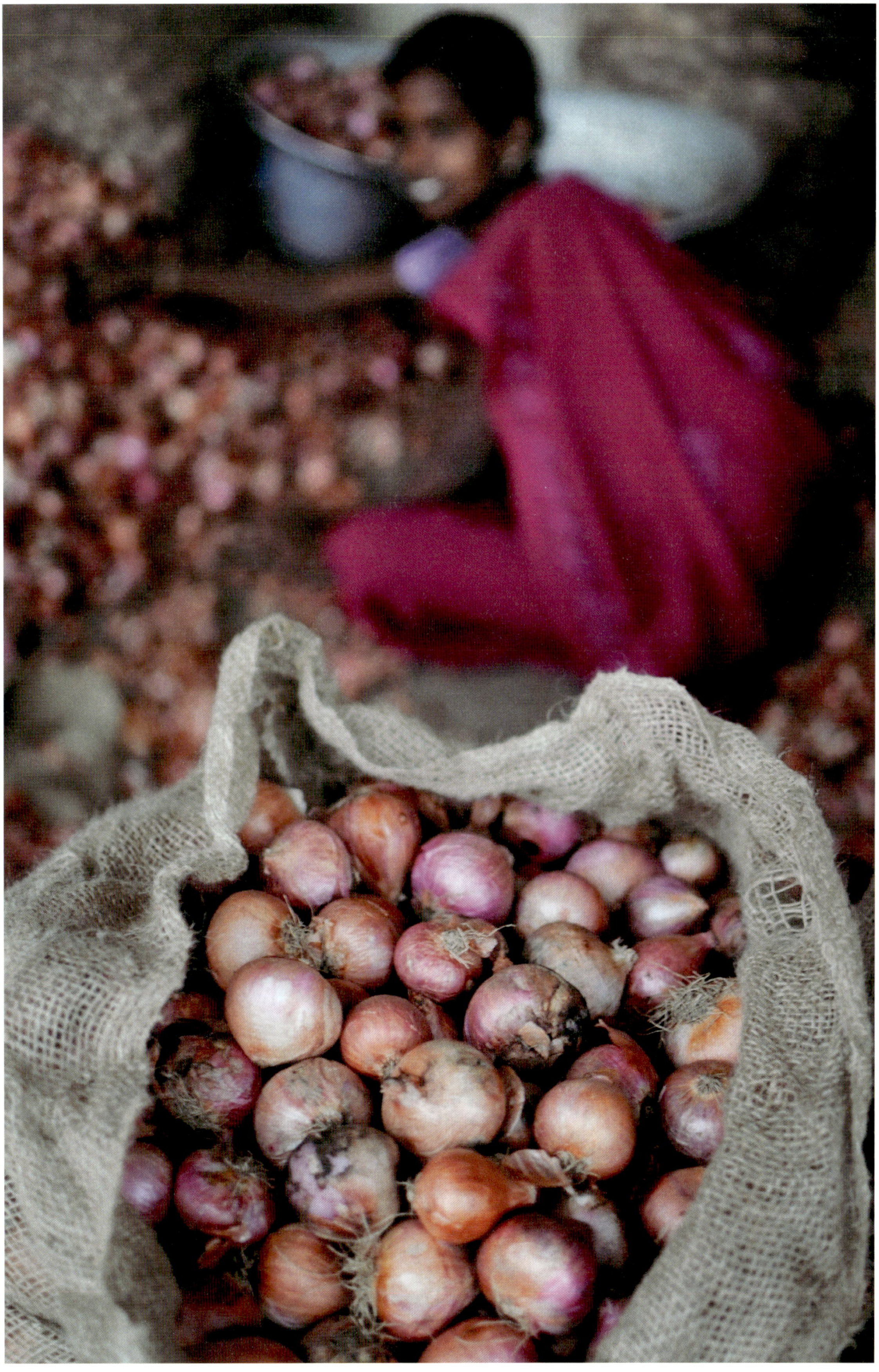

TIP

Serve this Indian waterzooi with naan instead of a baguette.

INDIAN CHICKEN CASSEROLE FLEMISH STYLE INDIAN

A genuine classic chicken casserole in the Flemish cuisine is called 'Waterzooi'. The word 'zooi' refers to the fact that several ingredients are cooked together. In India, too, you will discover this way of cooking. This is why this classic Flemish regional dish was given an Indian make-over by chef Biju.

INGREDIENTS

1 kg mixed vegetables such as carrots, leeks, celeriac and shallots and a few potatoes, 1 free-range chicken, 2 litres chicken stock, thyme, bay leaf, pepper, salt, nutmeg, 2 cm ginger root, 2 tablespoons vadouvan masala, 1 tablespoon cummin seeds, a few stalks of lemongrass, 3 egg yolks, 1.25 dl cream, 2 tablespoons cornflour, 0.25 dl coconut cream, parsley, coriander

PREPARATION

Clean all vegetables and the potatoes and divide them into two equal quantities.

Cut one half into cubes and set it aside. Put the other vegetables and potatoes whole in a large pan. Cut the chicken into large pieces and add them together with the carcass to the vegetables. Add the stock, bring it to the boil and let it cook on a low heat for half an hour till done. Skim the stock regularly and if necessary add some water to the chicken.

Take the chicken out of the pan and strain the stock. Skim off and remove the fat.

Add the cubed vegetables and potatoes to the stock. Start with the potatoes and carrots and after 10 minutes add the celeriac, the leeks and the shallots. Cool everything al dente and put the chicken back in again.

Season the chicken casserole with thyme, bay leaf, pepper, salt and a fair amount of grated nutmeg. Peel the ginger root and chop it fine. Add it with the vadouvan masala, the cummin seeds and the crushed lemongrass to the casserole.

Beat the egg yolks loose with the cream, the corn flour and the coconut cream. Take the pan off the heat and stir the mixture into the casserole. Make sure not to let it boil any longer.

Serve the casserole in soup plates and finish off with chopped parsley and coriander.

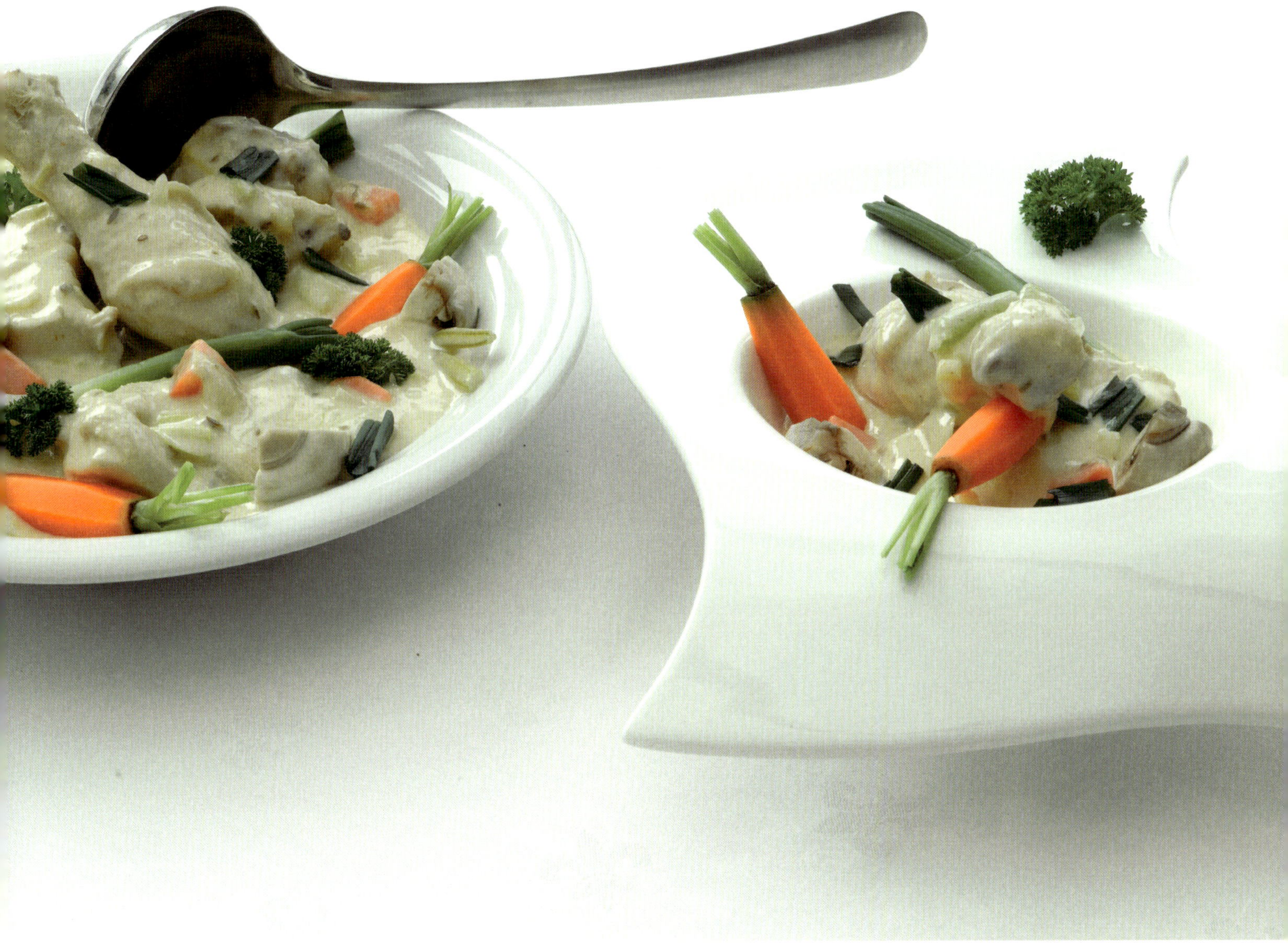

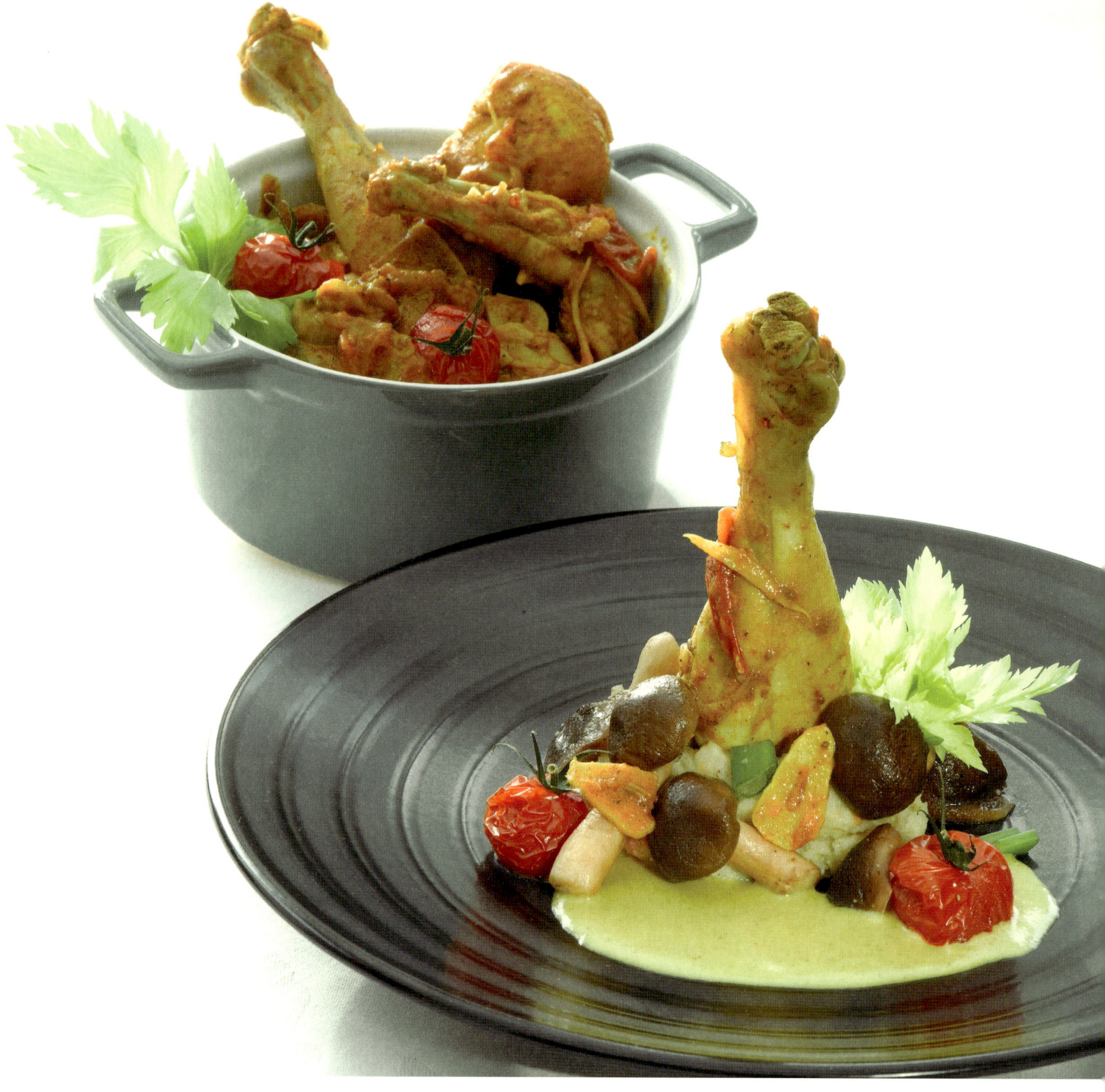

CHICKEN VINDALOO

WESTERN

TIP

For the adapted version of this dish we only use chicken legs. Remove the joints from the pan when they are done, and mix and strain the sauce. Serve with potato-garlic puree, mushrooms, finely cut spring onions and hot cherry tomatoes.

Vindaloo is derived from the Portuguese 'vinha de alhos', in which 'vinha' refers to wine or vinegar and 'alhos' to garlic. Originally it was a watery stew of pork, based on vinegar and garlic. When the Portuguese introduced this dish in India, it was completely adjusted to local tastes by the addition of herbs and spices and peppers. Over the years it has developed to one of the spiciest and most popular curries. Vindaloo is not as thick as korma and contains less gravy than other curries. It requires quite a lot of oil in its preparation and tastes, like so many stews, delicious a couple of days after its preparation, as the vinegar and other tastes will by then have largely blended in the dish. The pungency of the dish is mainly determined by the quantity of chilli powder. Make sure that the chilli does not dominate the subtle taste of the vinegar, which is a typical ingredient of the vindaloo. The dish can be prepared with pork, poultry, crustaceans and shellfish... and with vegetables such as brinjals (aubergine), potatoes, peas...

FOR 4 PERSONS

2 free-range chickens, 2 tablespoons garam masala, 1 tablespoon turmeric, a pinch of coriander powder, 1 teaspoon cummin seeds, 5 cardamom pods, 5 cloves, 1.5 dl white wine vinegar, 1 tablespoon balsamic vinegar or red wine vinegar, 2 large onions, 10 cloves of garlic, 2 cm ginger root, 3 large tomatoes, oil, ½ litre chicken stock, 1 tablespoon of soft brown sugar, salt, Kashmir chilli

PREPARATION

Cut the chicken into pieces and remove the carcass and the skin. Mix the garam masala with the turmeric, the coriander powder and the cummin seed. Crush the spices in a mortar with the cardamom pods and the cloves.

Mix the spices with the white wine vinegar and the balsamic vinegar. Rub the chicken pieces with this marinade and leave them to infuse for several hours in the refrigerator.

Peel the onions and cut them into rings. Peel the garlic and cut the garlic cloves into thin slices. Peel the ginger and cut it into small cubes (julienne). Chop the tomatoes coarsely. Braise all ingredients in a little oil.

Add the chicken to the tomatoes and fry them all round. Pour in the chicken stock and add the remaining pulp of the marinade and the brown sugar. Let it simmer until the chicken is done and season to taste with salt. Season to taste with Kashmir chilli.

LACQUERED PINCHOS OF CHICKEN WITH TAMARIND

ARTISTIC

FOR 4 PERSONS

300 g dried prunes, 1 tablespoon tamarind puree, 100 g honey, 50 g ginger syrup, 50 g preserved ginger, 25 g soya sauce, 1 dl old sherry vinegar, 1 teaspoon garam masala, 120 g grape seed oil, 1 kg chicken legs

PREPARATION

Bring the prunes with the tamarind puree, the honey, the ginger syrup, the preserved ginger, the soy sauce and 1 dl water to the boil. Add the garam masala to it and mix the marinade. Pour it through a sieve and finish with the grape seed oil.

Cut the meat of the chicken legs into cubes and string them onto bamboo sticks. Rub the marinade onto the sticks and roast these in a preheated oven at 200°C until the lacquer-like coat caramelizes.

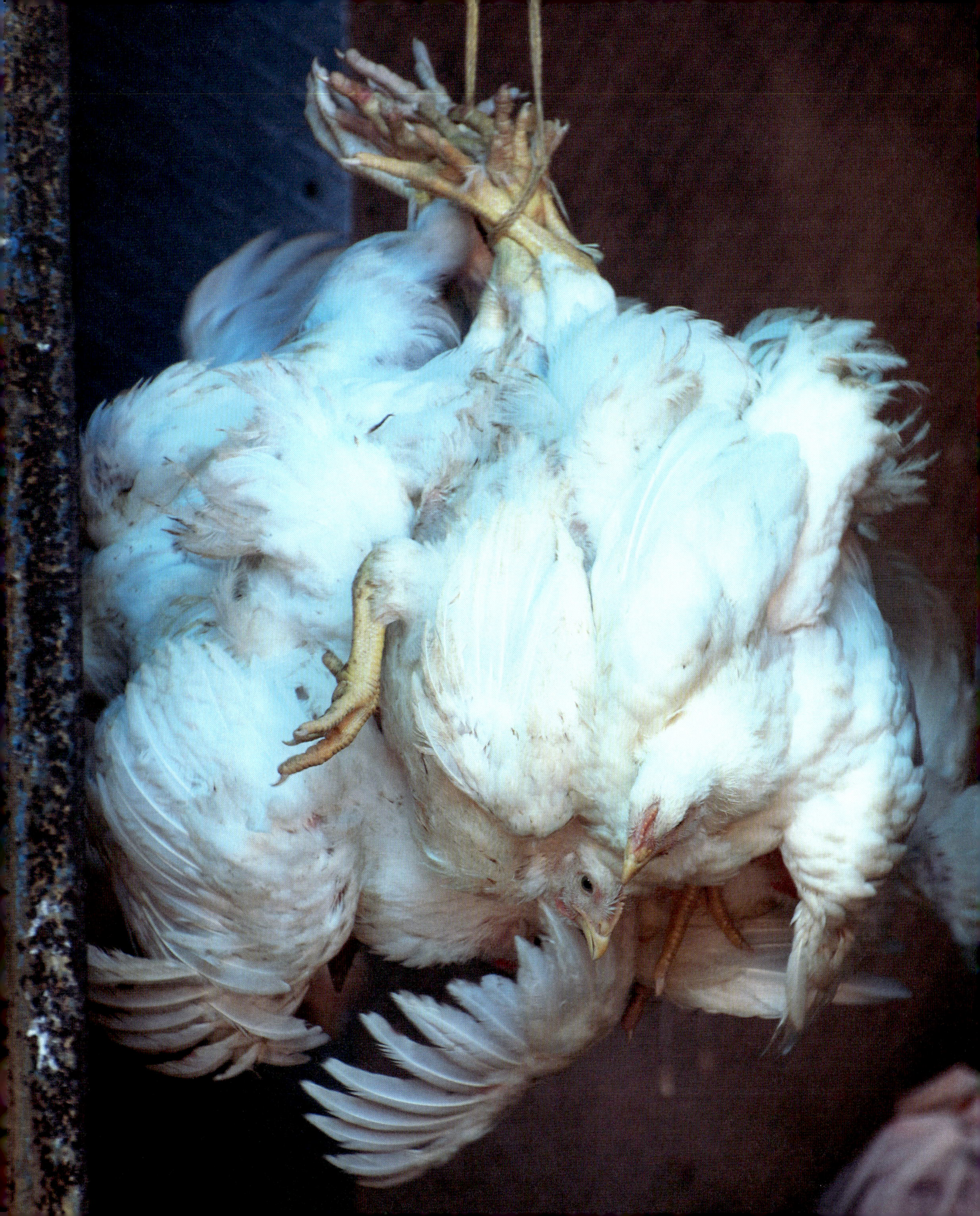

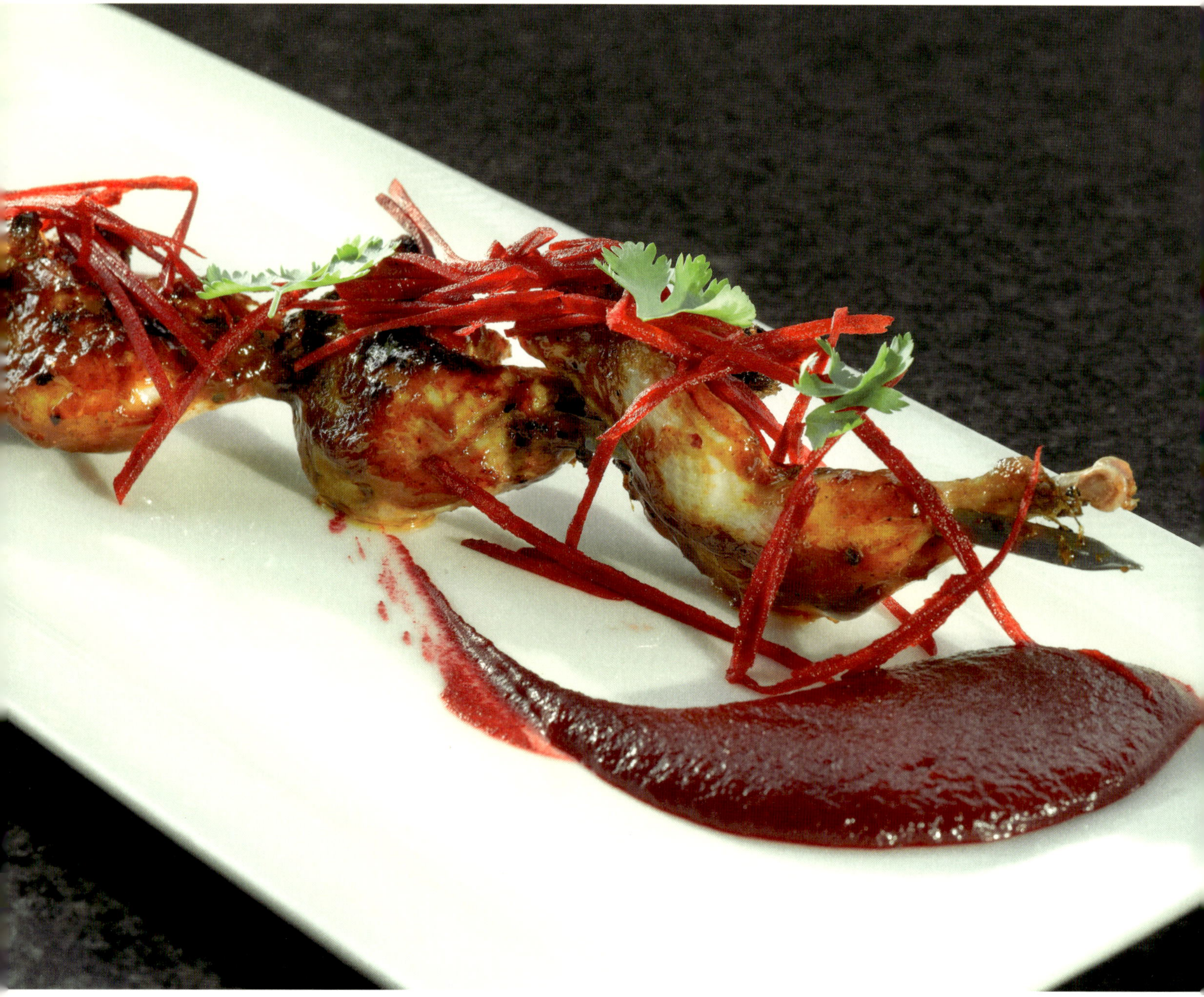

FRIED SPRING CHICKEN WITH A PACHADI OF BEETROOT — WESTERN

On my culinary journeys of discovery in India I ate pachadis in all possible colours. The principle of a pachadi is simple. In most cases fresh root vegetables are mashed and seasoned very hot and spicy. Pachadi of beetroot, carrots, potatoes and bitter pumpkins form a richly coloured bouquet. In Tamil Nadu and Kerala pachadi is always seasoned with peppers and mustard seeds, and prepared with grated coconut.

FOR 4 PERSONS

PACHADI PUREE 100 g beetroot, a pinch of sambhar masala, a pinch of turmeric, salt, 20 large raisins, 4 shallots, 1 small red chilli pepper, 1 tablespoon oil, 20 mustard seeds, 2 tablespoons coconut, grated, 8 curry leaves

PACHADI JULIENNE 100 g beetroot, a pinch of sambhar masala, a pinch of turmeric, salt, 20 large raisins, 4 shallots, 1 small red chilli pepper, 1 tablespoon oil, 20 mustard seeds, 2 tablespoons coconut, grated, 8 curry leaves – 4 spring chickens, butter, a pinch of sambhar masala, a pinch of turmeric, salt, 2 tablespoons coconut, grated, sugar, salt, 20 coriander leaves

PREPARATION

Peel the beetroots and cook them till done with the sambhar masala, turmeric, salt and raisins. Drain and mix to a smooth puree.

Peel the shallots and chop them fine. Cut the chilli pepper open lengthways, remove the seeds and chop it very fine.

For the puree, heat the oil in a pan, crisp the mustard seeds and add the shallots, the chilli pepper, the grated coconut, and the curry leaves. Add the beetroot puree and simmer it for a moment more.

For the julienne peel the beetroot and cut it into strips. Cook them till done in the same way as for the puree, drain them, but don't puree them. Prepare the rest of the recipe in the same way as the puree, but at the end fry the beetroot julienne with the rest.

Separate the spring chickens into fillets and parson's noses. Season the meat with sambhar masala and turmeric. Fry the meat all round in butter. Leave it on a low heat till it is done.

Add some grated coconut, a pinch of sugar and a little salt to the meat.

Put the chicken on plates, add some of the julienne and sprinkle coriander leaves over them. Serve it with the pachadi puree.

THEEYAL OF MECHELEN ASPARAGUS AND FREE-RANGE EGG

INDIAN

Alain: 'One day I asked chef Biju to prepare an Indian variant of our famous 'asparagus Flemish-style'. I explained the recipe and the method of preparing it to him. I hadn't finished speaking when he interrupted me. This would have to be a theeyal…'

A theeyal is a very traditional South-Indian dish with a characteristic taste of burnt coconut and tamarind. By adding eggs this became the perfect companion for asparagus.

INGREDIENTS

2 bundles of white asparagus, 1 stalk of leeks, salt, a pinch of turmeric

THEEYAL 5 eggs, 100 g coconut, grated, 1 small red chilli pepper, 10 shallots, 2 cloves of garlic, oil, a pinch of turmeric, a pinch of Kashmir chilli, 30 g tamarind, ½ bundle parsley

PREPARATION

Peel the asparagus with a peeler. Clean the leek and cut it into pieces.

Cook the asparagus and the leek in salted water for 10 to 15 minutes till done. In the last 5 minutes add a pinch of turmeric to it.

For the theeyal boil the eggs hard and peel them. Slice one egg and chop the rest into coarse pieces.

Colour the coconut in a pan with non-stick coating. Cut the chilli pepper open lengthways, remove the seeds and chop it finely.

Peel the shallots and chop half of it coarsely. Add the chilli and the shallots to the coconut and simmer it together. Mix in the blender to a smooth paste.

Cut the rest of the shallots and the cloves of garlic into fine slices and braise them in a little oil with turmeric and a pinch of Kashmir chilli. Soak the tamarind in 1 dl water. Pour through a sieve and keep the water. Add the tamarind water to the shallots together with the coconut paste. Add 2 dl water to it and let it thicken. Add the coarsely chopped eggs to it.

Arrange the asparagus on a plate and spoon some theeyal over the ends. Sprinkle chopped parsley over it and finish with a slice of egg.

TIP

A traditional theeyal is vegetarian and can be prepared with almost any vegetable.

Colour grated coconut in a pan with non-stick coating and add a finely chopped red chilli pepper, coriander seeds, and 5 finely chopped shallots to it. Mix to a smooth paste. Cut 5 shallots and 2 cloves of garlic into thin slices and braise them in oil with turmeric and a pinch of Kashmir chilli.

Cut vegetables such as aubergines, courgettes and potatoes into cubes and add them to the shallots. Soak 30 g tamarind in 1 dl water, pour it through a sieve and add the water to the vegetables, together with the coconut paste. Add ½ litre water and cook the vegetables till done.

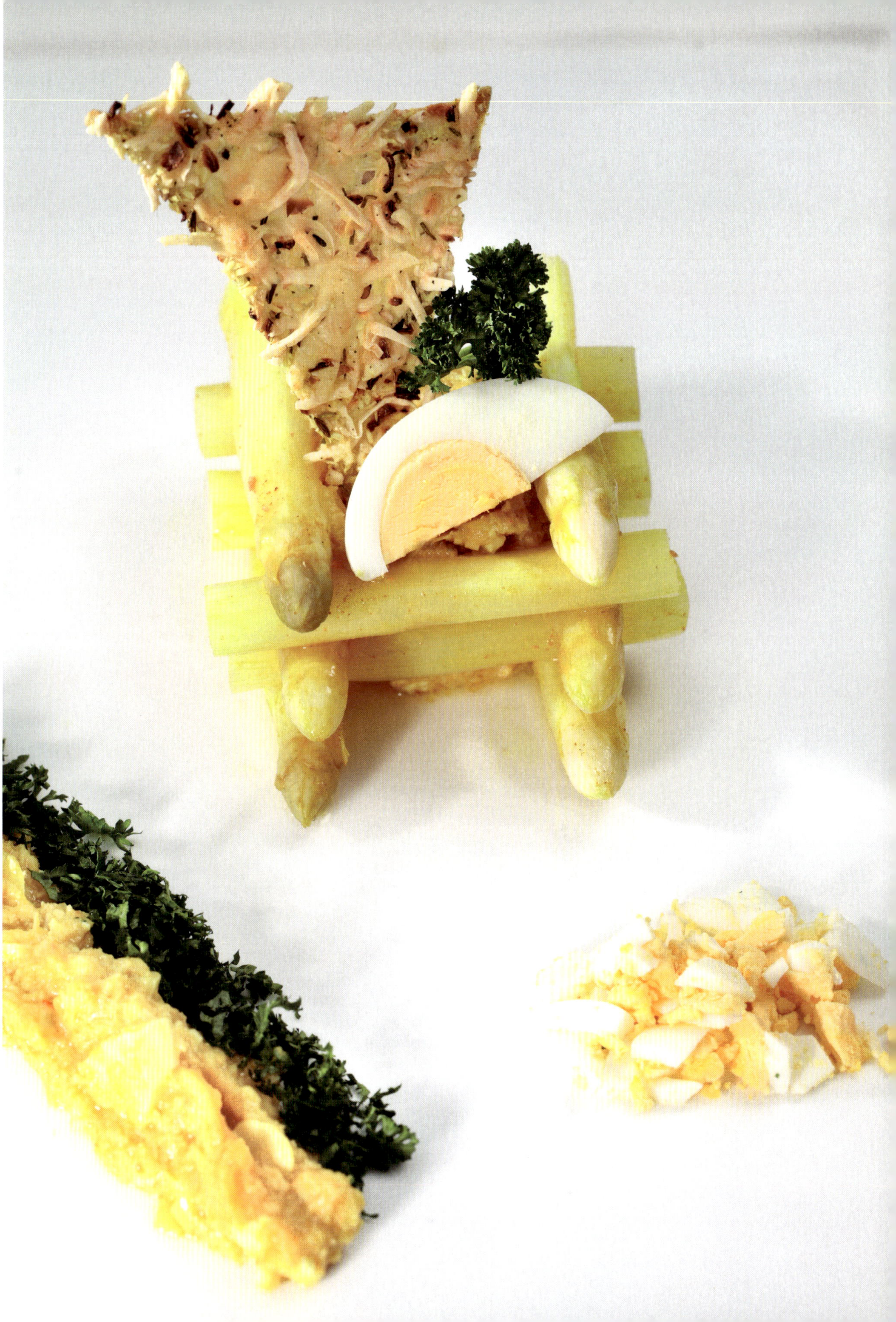

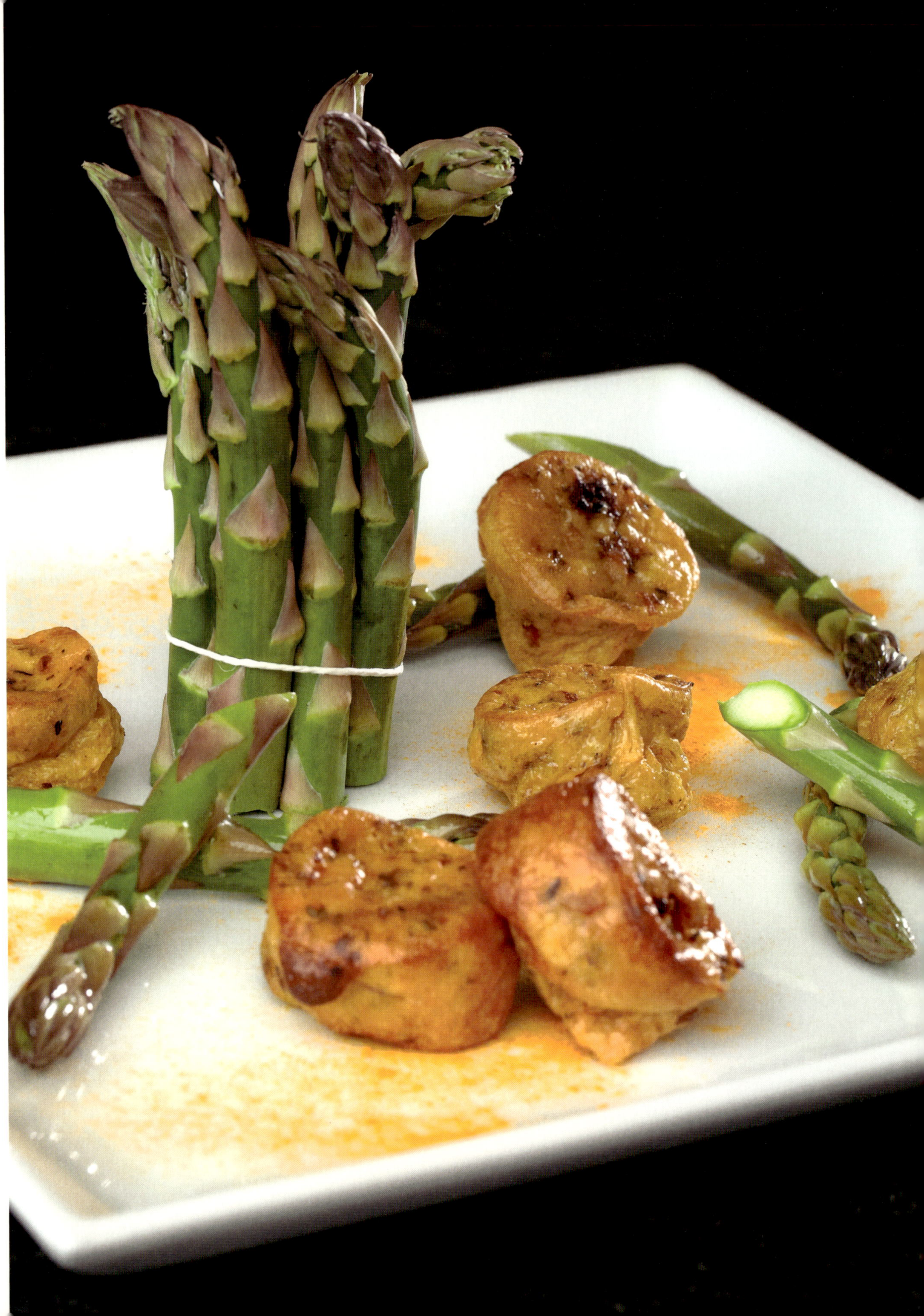

SPICED MINI-CLAFOUTIS OF CHICKEN AND GREEN ASPARAGUS CURRY

WESTERN

Clafoutis has not yet found its way to India, but it forms an amusing common dish, because qua taste this version is really typically Indian. Other vegetables can also be added to the curry.

FOR 4 PERSONS

ASPARAGUS CURRY *1 bundle green asparagus, 2 stalks of leeks, 1 chicken breast, oil, a pinch of tikka masala, pepper, salt*

CLAFOUTIS *3 eggs, 125 g flour, 250 g milk, ¼ tablespoon tikka masala, ¼ tablespoon turmeric*

PREPARATION

Peel the asparagus with a peeler and cut it into 1 cm pieces. Cut the leek fine and cut the chicken into cubes.

Heat the oil in a pan and allow the tikka masala to colour. Fry the chicken until half done and then add the leeks and the asparagus to it. Fry the asparagus al dente. Season with pepper and salt and let it cool.

Beat the eggs loose and add the flour, the milk, the tikka masala and the turmeric. Beat it to a smooth batter.

Spoon a little asparagus curry into clafouti moulds, pour a little of the batter over it and bake them golden brown in the oven at 180 °C.

TIP

The clafoutis in small moulds are ideal to accompany the aperitif. Clafoutis also make an amusing main dish. In that case cut all the vegetables larger and cover them in a large bowl with the clafoutis mix. It can also be made with pieces of pre-cooked fish to replace the chicken.

NARGISI KOFTA WITH THAKKALI CURRY — INDIAN

Eggs are very popular in India. They are sold in small stalls in the towns – freshly cooked, peeled and with a spoonful of chutney. For this traditional Indian version Chef Biju made 'small meatballs (kofta) in tomato sauce' into bird's nests, because according to him meatballs needed an egg.

FOR 4 PERSONS

500 g mince (preferably lamb), 5 small eggs, 2 pinches of garam masala, a pinch of salt, a pinch of turmeric, 2 cloves of garlic, 2 egg yolks, a few tablespoons of flour, a few tablespoons of bread crumbs, oil for deep-frying

THAKKALI CURRY 2 cloves of garlic, 8 shallots, 3 small red chilli peppers, 3 cm ginger root, 5 tablespoons coconut oil, a pinch of sambhar masala, a pinch of turmeric, salt, 1 tablespoon cummin seeds, 8 ripe tomatoes, ½ litre vegetable stock, ¼ bundle coriander

PREPARATION

Mix the minced meat with 1 beaten egg and season it with garam masala, salt and turmeric.

Crush the garlic and add it to the mince.

Boil the remaining eggs soft in 4 minutes, leave them to cool in cold water and peel them.

Divide the mince mixture into four and push each part flat. Put an egg on each section of mince and fold the meat carefully round it.

Leave to rest for half an hour in the refrigerator.

Beat the egg yolks loose with a little water. Mix a little garam masala through the breadcrumbs. Pull the kofta through the flour, the egg yolks and the breadcrumbs. Deep-fry in oil to a golden brown at 180 °C.

Peel the garlic for the curry and cut it into fine slices. Peel the shallots and chop them finely. Cut the chilli peppers open lengthways, remove the seeds, and chop the chillies finely. Peel and grate the ginger root.

Heat the oil and braise the garlic, the shallots, the chilli and the ginger root. Season with sambhar masala, turmeric, salt and cummin seed until all the aromas are released.

Cut the tomatoes coarsely and add them to the spices. Deglaze with vegetable stock and simmer until reduced to a thick sauce. Chop the coriander finely and add it just before serving.

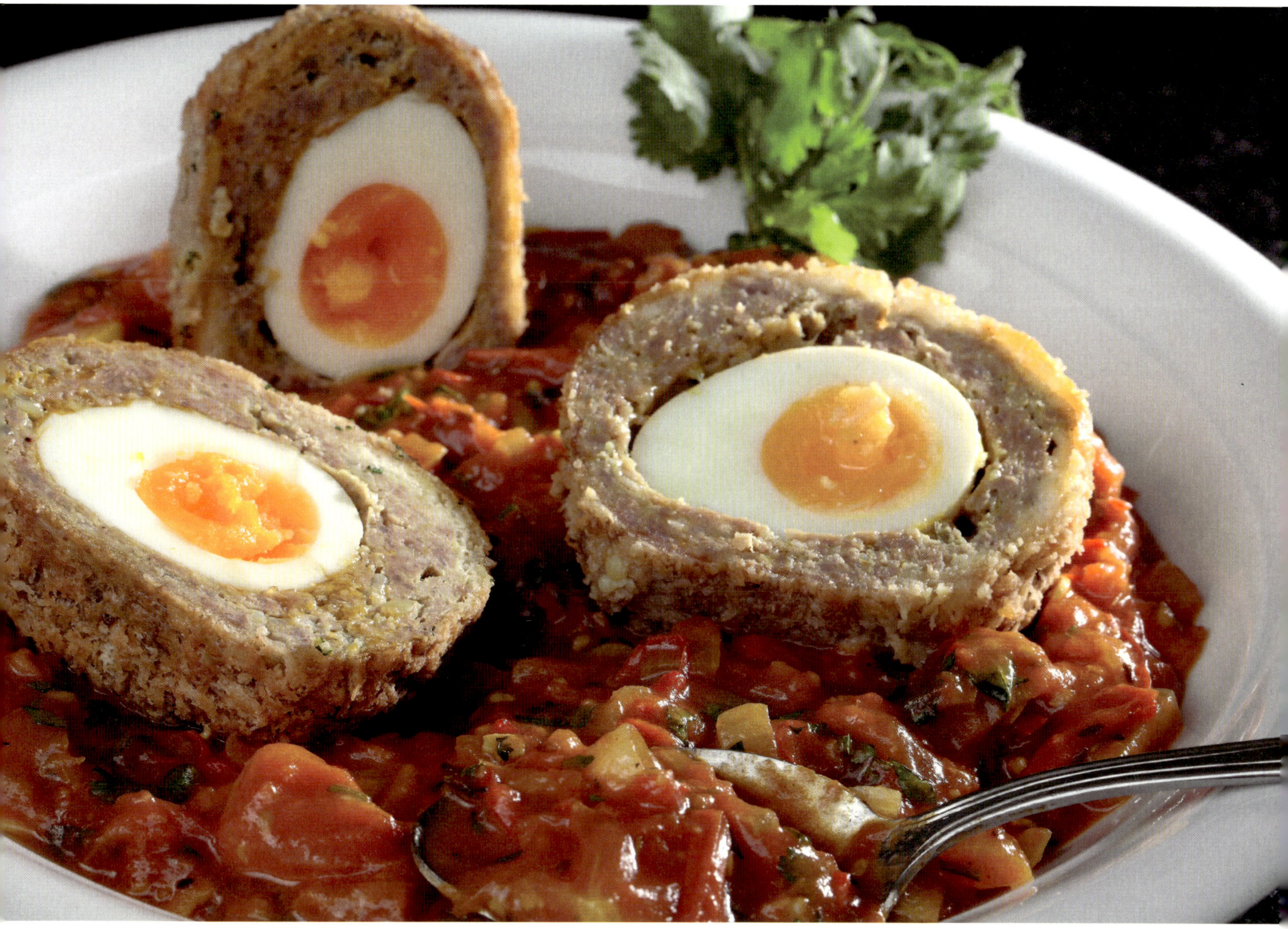

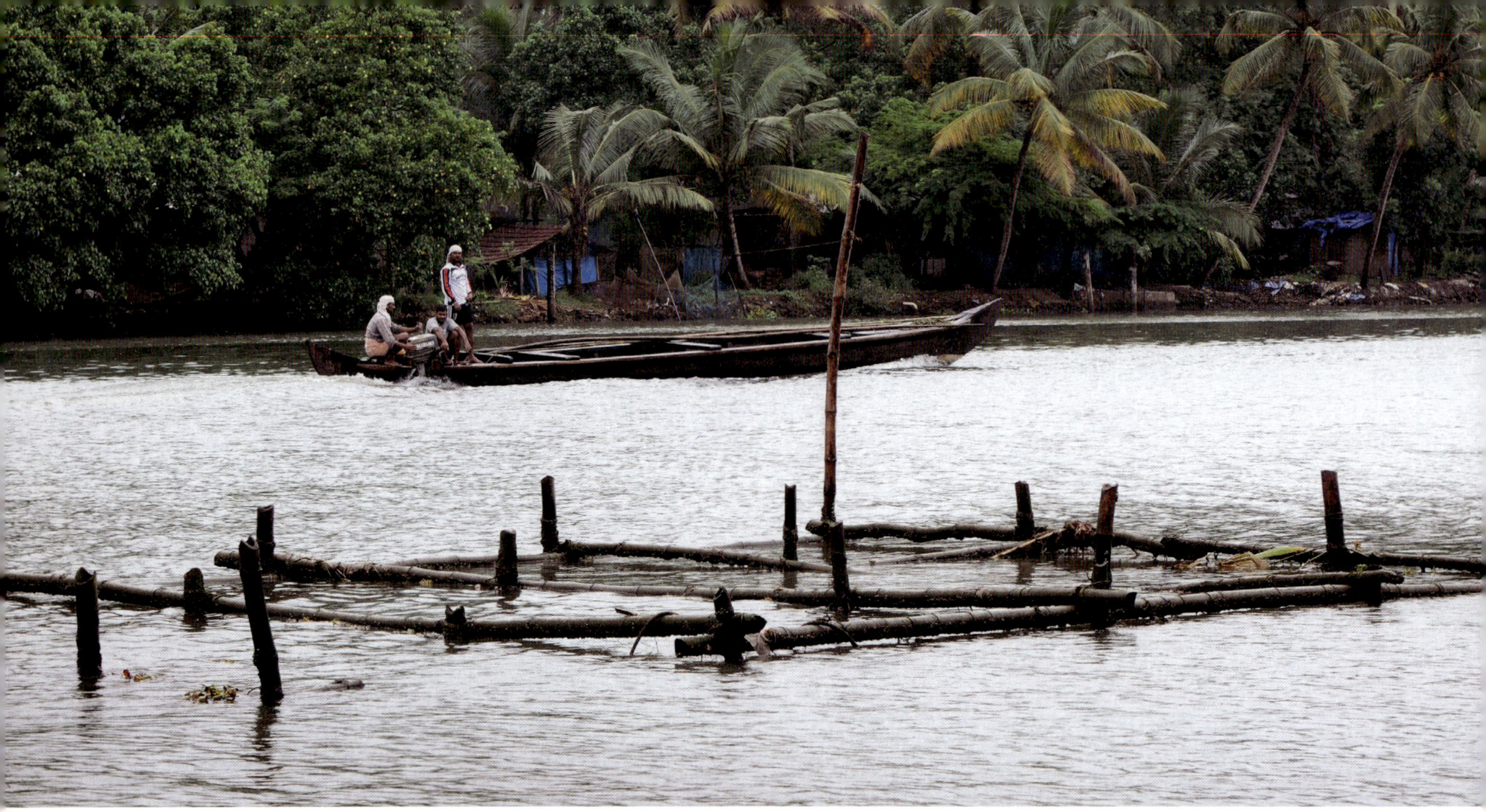

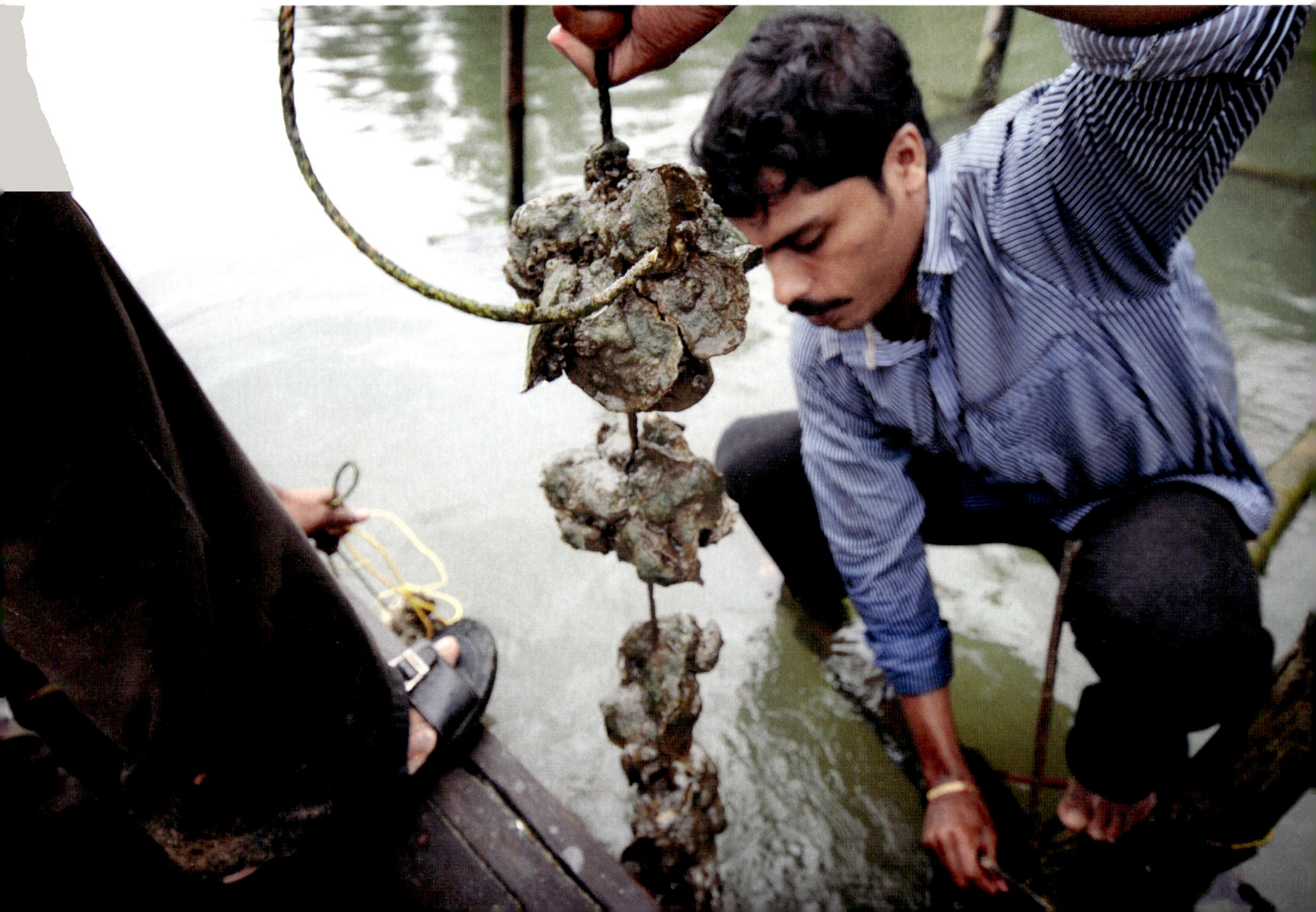

CRUSTACEANS AND SHELLFISH

LOUNGING THE BACKWATERS

'At the third bridge, on the other side of the water', that's where we have arranged to meet. We walk with Txuku through the drizzling rain in the direction of the ferry. At Fort Cochin this way of travelling is very popular, dirt-cheap and moreover it's a good way of saving time. Obviously you have to make sure at the mooring that you will be able to carry on with public transport or, in our case, that there is a car waiting for you. Txuku has carefully figured everything out beforehand. Her driver has left a few hours earlier to travel overland the distance we now comfortably do across the water. He has driven towards us in a wide loop via a whole range of bridges. With an umbrella in his hand, he now accompanies us to the car. Then we set off for the place of our meeting.

Our conclusion that the density of traffic has increased enormously in the past few years can't be denied. With all its bridges and viaducts Cochin and its surroundings increasingly resemble a spider's web, in which the growing number of cars, buses, lorries and bicycles get caught with increasing ease. So we are very relieved when we can leave this hectic tangle behind us and the roads in the direction of the temple town of Guruvayur get narrower. There is a beautiful temple in the heart of the town. Pilgrims come to it from far and near. But for foreign visitors the long trip results in a rather disenchanting outcome, because this holy place is only accessible to Hindus. A visit to the hostel for elephants just outside town has to make up for it a little. Although here the question arises whether these splendid animals would and should feel more at home in the woods.

    However, today we leave the main road a fair distance before Guruvayur. Via narrow roads, weaving between land and water, we travel through small villages where tranquility still typifies the daily life. In this magical setting of waterways and evergreen roofs of foliage, I am again reminded how beautiful

Kerala is. Even on dull days like this, the South-Indian state does not have any difficulty in honouring its epithet of God's own country. We reach the banks of one of the many dozens of sea arms, which throw themselves into the inland waterways like the tentacles of an octopus. The inland waterways form one of the great touristic attractions of Kerala. A network of rivers, small lakes, lagoons and canals have spread themselves around the gigantic Lake Vembanad. A pearl of nature, so beautiful that it seems like a mirage of land which merges with water. Each year more and more tourists go on the characteristic, graceful Kerala houseboats to admire this spectacle and seek the peace and quiet of the water.

We have come to the end of the car ride. From this point we can only continue on foot. A very narrow path, slippery after the rain, looking like a dark pencil line through this idyllic landscape, leads our company to a large rowing boat. We get on board and leave the bank in the direction of the oyster banks. Raindrops the size of pearls are now falling from the grey sky. The mussel gatherers on their narrow prahus rock gently back and forth with the movement of the rippling river. A little further on we see figures with hands outstretched coming almost soundlessly from under the surface of the water. They are shell fishers. They are clearly quite undisturbed by the rather extreme circumstances. For a moment they take time to get their breath back. Then, as nimble as cormorants, they dive back again to the dark river bed.

A post boat full of passengers causes the waves around our sloop to rise up a little. We have just reached the oyster bed. Time for the *moment suprême*. A knife is brought up, the live harvest from the sea is released from its shell and savoured and enjoyed. On a dancing boat, with tears of happiness from heaven. Alain and Biju can appreciate it.

Christophe

WOMEN IN POWER

The oyster is and will always be a strange creature. Loved by many, but found to be in bad taste by others. In the course of time it has developed in Europe from something commonplace to a delicacy. The fact is that it is consumed nearly everywhere in the world. Although from time immemorial fish has been in plentiful supply, in watery Kerala oyster production has only been a significant part of the market since the early 1990s. That is when the authorities started a programme to promote oysters to a wider public. Before that time it was mainly confined to a small number of local customers.

Nowadays the culture of oysters is established in almost every Kerala family. And not least among the women. Many among them have formed 'self-help groups' who farm oysters and receive financial support from the Kerala authorities.

We decided to seek out one of these self-help groups and set off to find out more about the oyster farm on Vypin Island, near Cochin. Dr Mohamed, founder of this farm, talks to us together with two of his female colleagues.

Dr Mohamed: 'In the months of December and March we allow the larvae to attach themselves. Nowadays we deliberately farm two crops a year with the aim of being able to offer oysters continually. Some 15 to 20 oysters will easily attach themselves to a single shell, dependent on the height. If too many assemble round one and the same shell, some will be taken away regularly so that new oysters can continue to grow there. After an average of 6 to 8 months they are gathered by the women. This happens in the period from November to February, and it is no accident that it happens to coincide with the peak season for tourism, when the demand is at its peak.

First the oysters are washed and scrubbed well, then they are left in boiling hot water to remove the sludge. A good five minutes later the shell will open and the oyster meat is removed. This is frozen before it is put on the market. So far there has been no tradition of eating them raw. As the oysters are currently still farmed in clusters, it is difficult to open them manually. With a kind of sickle we try to break open the flat side of the oysters. There is, of course, some hidden danger that you will then get splinters from the shell in the oyster. These will then have to be washed out, but then you lose its natural moisture, which is exactly what you all are so fond of... (laughs)

Another way of farming oysters is with the help of roof tiles to which a layer of lime powder has been attached. The roof tiles are then put in the

The Vembanad Lake

water, so that the larvae can settle on them individually. These oysters are suitable to be eaten raw, as is a normal custom in Europe. This method is obviously more labour intensive. At the moment we still have to wait to see how the demand for this method will evolve and whether a similar tradition will develop here as in your country.

The most usual kind of oyster in Kerala is the *Crassostrea Madrasensis*, known to us as the *Kadal Muringa*. You will find the largest farm in this region near Kollam, in the Ashtamudi Lake.

This specific oyster farm is mainly managed by female self-help groups, known as *Sthree Sakthee*, meaning *Women Power*. We are very pleased with the development of these women's organizations. They prove their value daily. In this way the local economy has been improved, more and better oysters have been farmed, and the available water reserves in Kerala are increasingly being used to support the local development. Not to mention the extra income generated for the many poorer members of the population. The success of this formula in India shows that, if the federal and local authorities work together, quite considerable progress can be achieved in a short time. So we are also quite convinced that other developing countries with similar water reserves could devise a plan for an oyster culture in the interest of their rural communities. With emphasis on the involvement of women, of course!'

Sam

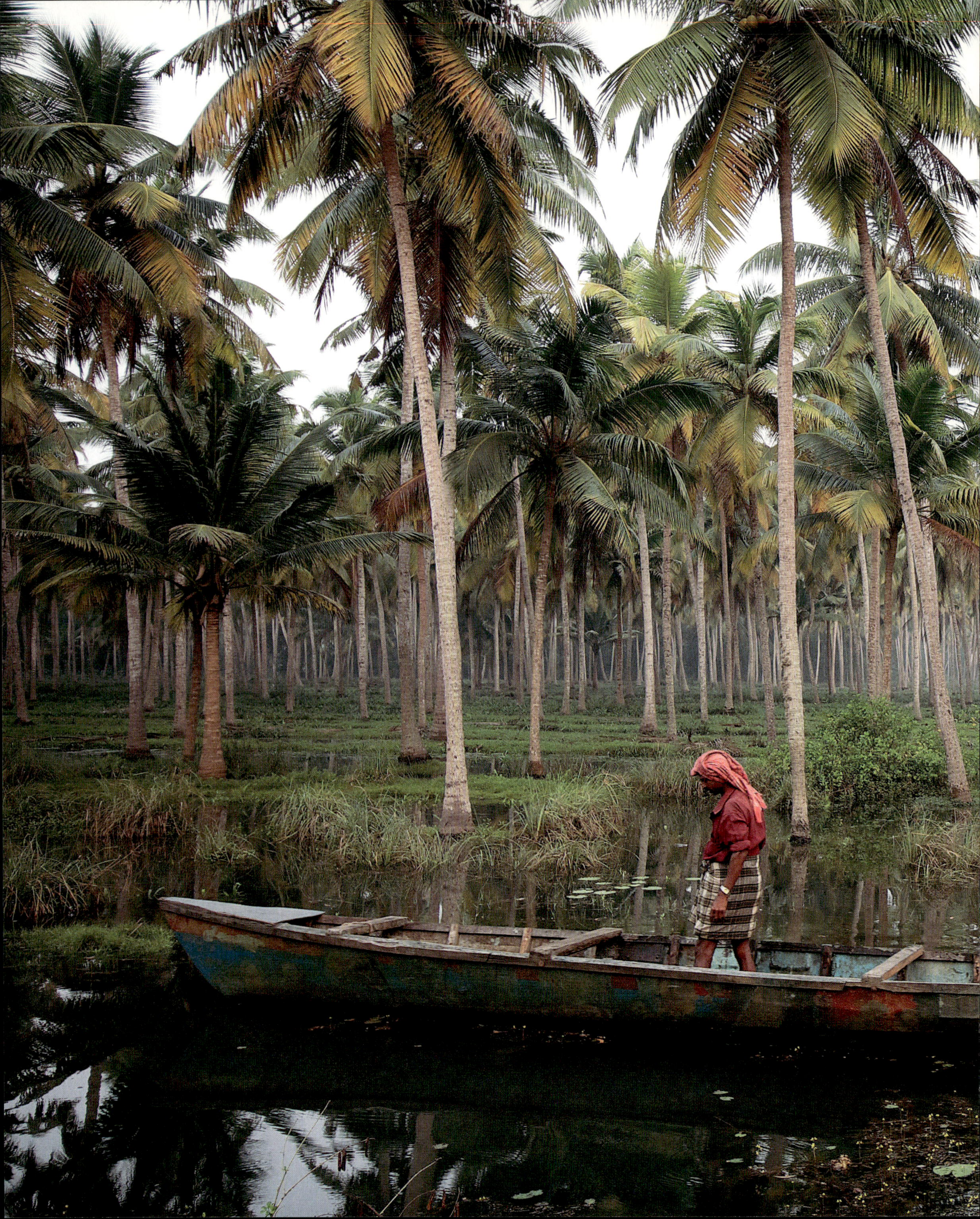

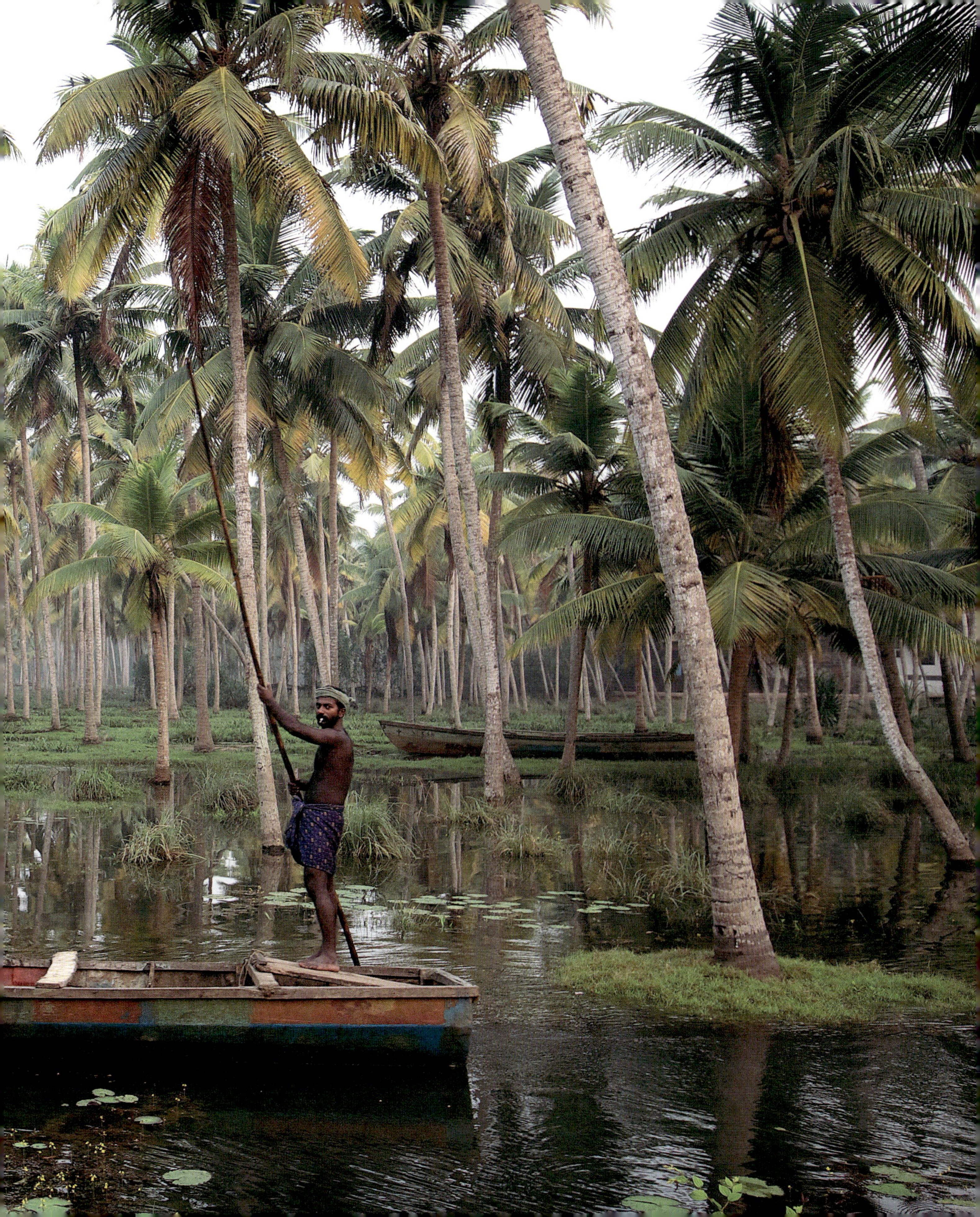

MARINATED TIGER PRAWNS IN A NUT AND SAFFRON SAUCE

ARTISTIC

FOR 4 PERSONS

100 g almonds, chopped, 100 g cashew nuts, chopped, 4 shallots, 2 cardemom pods, 2 cm ginger root, 1 small green chilli pepper, 4 tablespoons clarified butter (or ghee), turmeric, 5 dl fish stock, salt, sugar, garam masala, 2 dl cream (40% fat content), 100 g garlic, 75 g ginger root, pepper, 20 tiger prawns (or scampi 8/12), oil, 100 g full-cream yoghurt, 50 g cream, saffron, 20 cummin seeds, 2 stalks of leeks

PREPARATION

Cook 75 g almonds and 75 g cashew nuts in 1 dl water until they are soft. Mix in the blender to a smooth paste.
Peel the shallots and chop them finely. Remove the pits from the cardamom and chop them finely. Peel the ginger and chop it finely.
Cut open the chilli pepper, remove the seeds and chop the chilli finely.
Heat the butter in a pan and briefly sweat the shallots, cardamom, ginger and chilly. Add the turmeric and the largest part of the nut paste.
Add the fish stock to the shallots and let it simmer to reduce a little on low heat. Season to taste with a pinch of salt, sugar and garam masala.
Add the cream, leave it to thicken and pour it through a sieve.
Peel the garlic and the ginger root. Mix them in the blender with a little water. Season with salt, pepper and a pinch of turmeric.
Peel the tiger prawns, but leave the tails. Remove the intestines.
Mix the spice paste with the prawns and let this rest for 10 minutes.
Fry them briefly in a little oil.
Mix the yoghurt with the cream, saffron, salt and cummin seeds.
Add the tiger prawns to this.
Bake the prawns for 5 minutes on a baking tray in a preheated oven at 200 °C.
Clean the leek, cut it in rings and steam it till done. Make a little turret per person and finish off with nut paste and the remainder of the chopped nuts.
Finish the sauce with a good helping of saffron. Distribute this over the plates, and add the tiger prawns and a little turret of leeks.
Finish off with some green herbs.

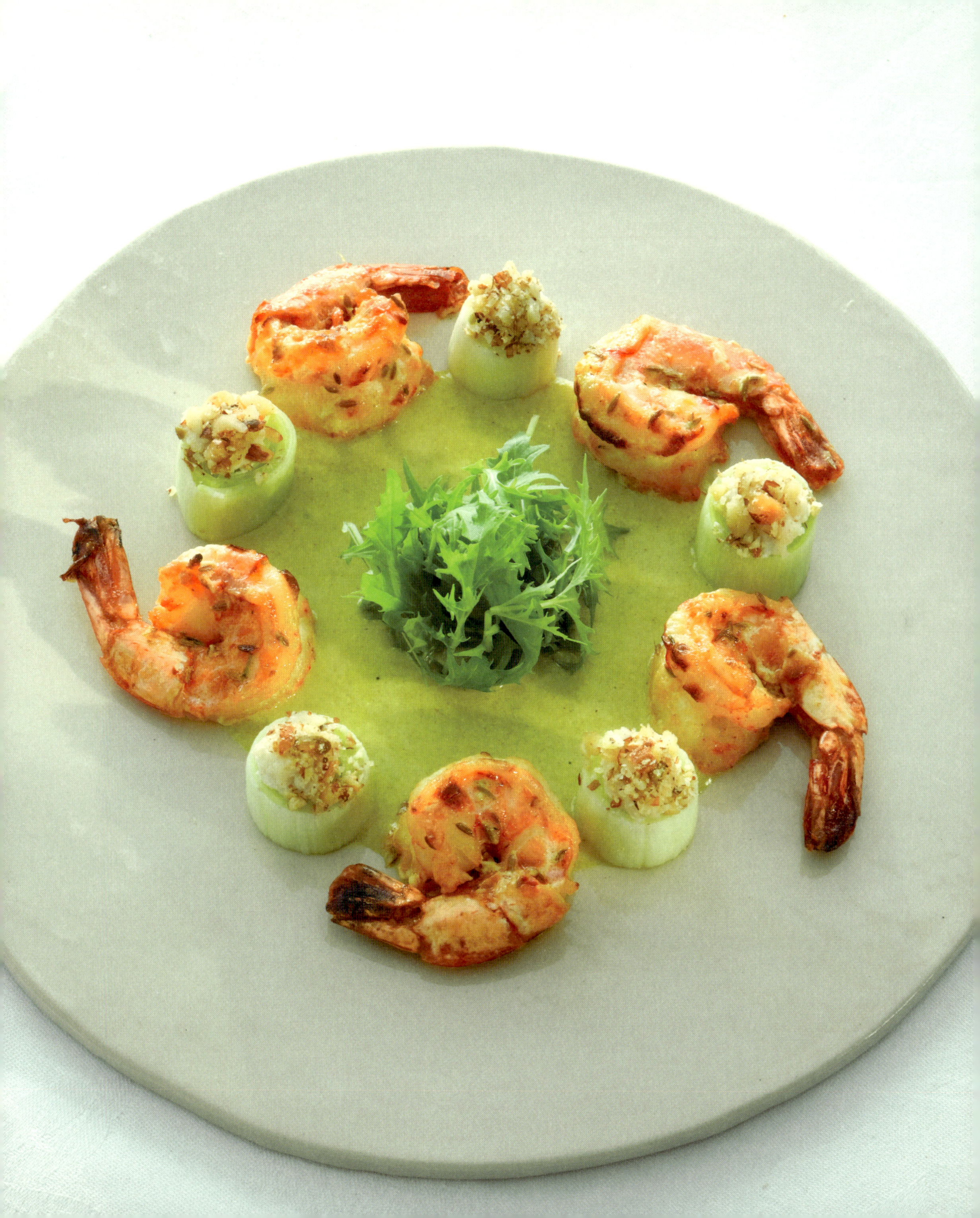

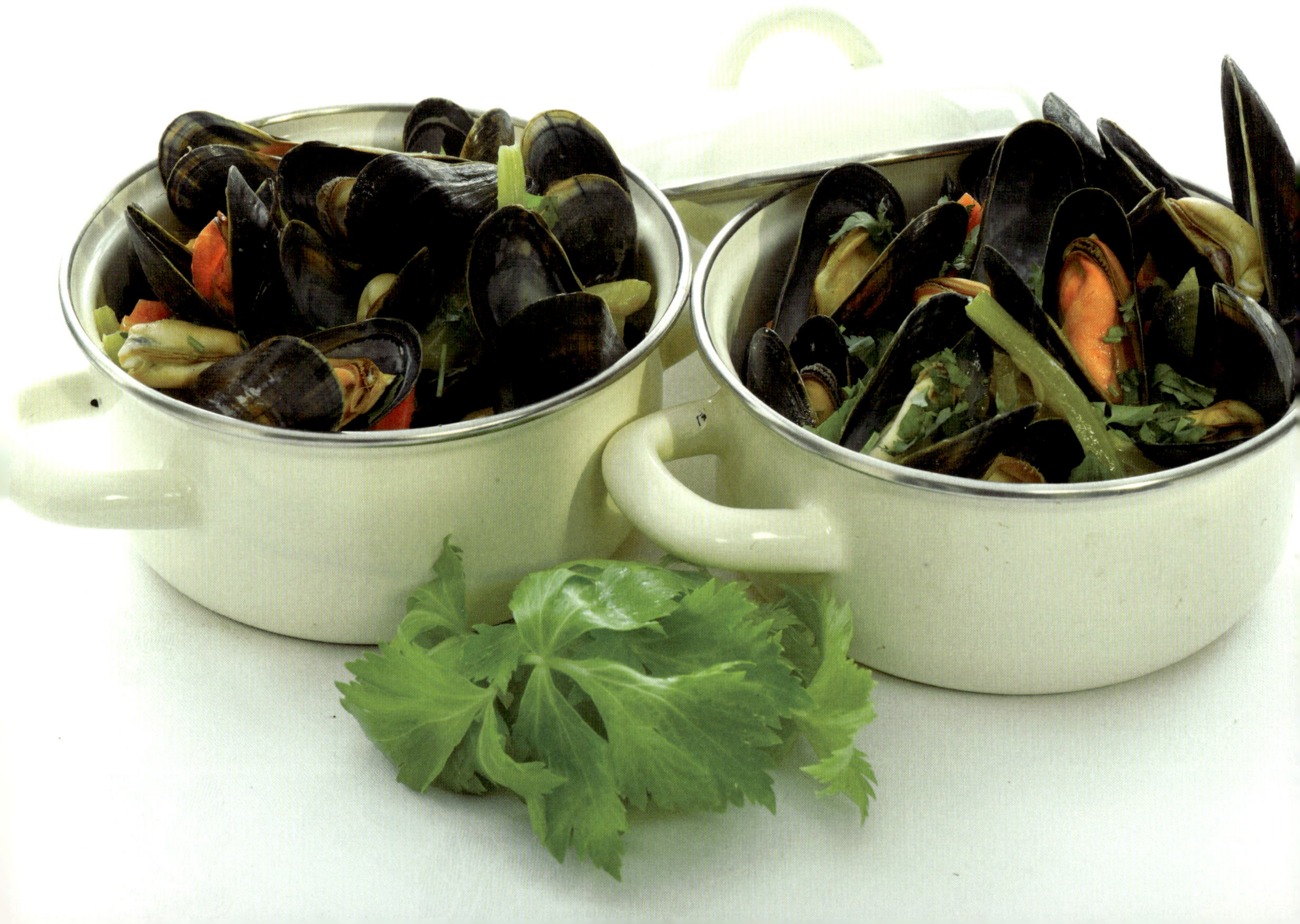

MULLIGATAWNY OF MUSSELS   INDIAN

In Tamil Nadu, in the south of India, they make a thin soup: rasam (see Rasam on page 61). The British colonial rulers renamed this rasam mulligatawny, a classic in hotel school training. Millagu means 'pepper' in Tamil and thanni means 'water', which literally gave mulligatawny the nickname 'peppered water'.

This mulligatawny is a splendid, simple dish. Quickly made and easy to prepare well in advance. Just at the last moment add the mussels and it's done... The suitable answer from chef Biju to our 'mussels nature' and 'mussels in white wine'.

FOR 4 PERSONS

2 onions, 4 cloves of garlic, 2 large carrots, 3 sticks celery, 15 g clarified butter (or ghee), a pinch of vadouvan masala, a pinch of turmeric, a pinch of ginger powder, 2 tablespoons flour, 1 tablespoon tomato puree, 1 l fish stock, 6 kg mussels (Jumbo's), 1 dl white wine, pepper, 10 curry leaves, 12 cherry tomatoes, chilli powder, 1 apple

PREPARATION

Peel the onion and the garlic and chop them fine. Clean the carrots and the celery and cut them in long strands. Keep the leaf of the celery. Braise the vegetables in clarified butter and season them with a pinch of vadouvan masala, turmeric and ginger powder. Sprinkle flour over it and add the tomato puree.

Pour the fish stock over the vegetables and leave them to simmer until the vegetables are done al dente.

Rinse the mussels thoroughly in cold water and put them in a pan with the wine. Spice with pepper, turmeric and curry leaves.

Add the mulligatawny soup to the mussels when they are half open and let them simmer until the mussels have opened completely. Divide over individual cooking pots.

Halve the cherry tomatoes and add them to the mussels. Cut the green leaf of the celery fine and scatter it over the mussels. Finish off with a little turmeric and – for added piquancy – with chilli.

Cut the apple into matchsticks and arrange them on the mussels.

TIP

Scatter breadcrumbs over the mussels for a crisp crust.

The butter can be kept well in the freezer. Divide it into smaller pieces for this.

MUSSELS AU GRATIN WITH INDIAN HERB BUTTER

WESTERN

Indian herb butter is delicious with grilled chicken, jacket potatoes, or scampi. It fits in perfectly with most barbecue and grilled meat dishes. In this recipe it is used to gratinate mussels.

FOR 4 PERSONS

HERB BUTTER *2 g cummin seed, 2 g coriander seed, 4 g fennel seed, 2 teaspoon vadouvan masala, 2 teaspoon turmeric, 6 shallots, 2 cloves of garlic, 1 small red chilli pepper, 1 small green chilli pepper, 1 lemon, 2 cm ginger root, 500 g salted farmhouse butter – 1 large onion, 2 stalks of celery, butter, 1.25 kg mussels, 1 tablespoon turmeric, pepper, 2.5 dl white wine*

PREPARATION

Heat the seeds in a pan with non-stick coating until the aromas are released. Crush them fine in a mortar and add the vadouvan masala and the turmeric.

Peel the shallots and the garlic. Cut the peppers open lengthways and remove the seeds. Chop everything very fine.

Peel the lemon with a parer and cut some of the yellow skin (zest) very fine. Peel the ginger root and grate it. Add the zest, the ginger and the remainder of the herbs to the butter and mix carefully.

Wrap the butter in foil and make a long roll. Leave to stiffen in the refrigerator.

Peel the onions. Cut the onions and the celery coarsely and braise them in a little butter.

Rinse the mussels carefully and add them to the vegetables. Season with turmeric and pepper and add the white wine. Bring to the boil and take from the heat as soon as the mussels have opened.

Loosen the mussels, but leave them in their shells. Put them in an oven dish and put a small slice of Indian herb butter on each mussel. Let them turn a golden brown under the grill.

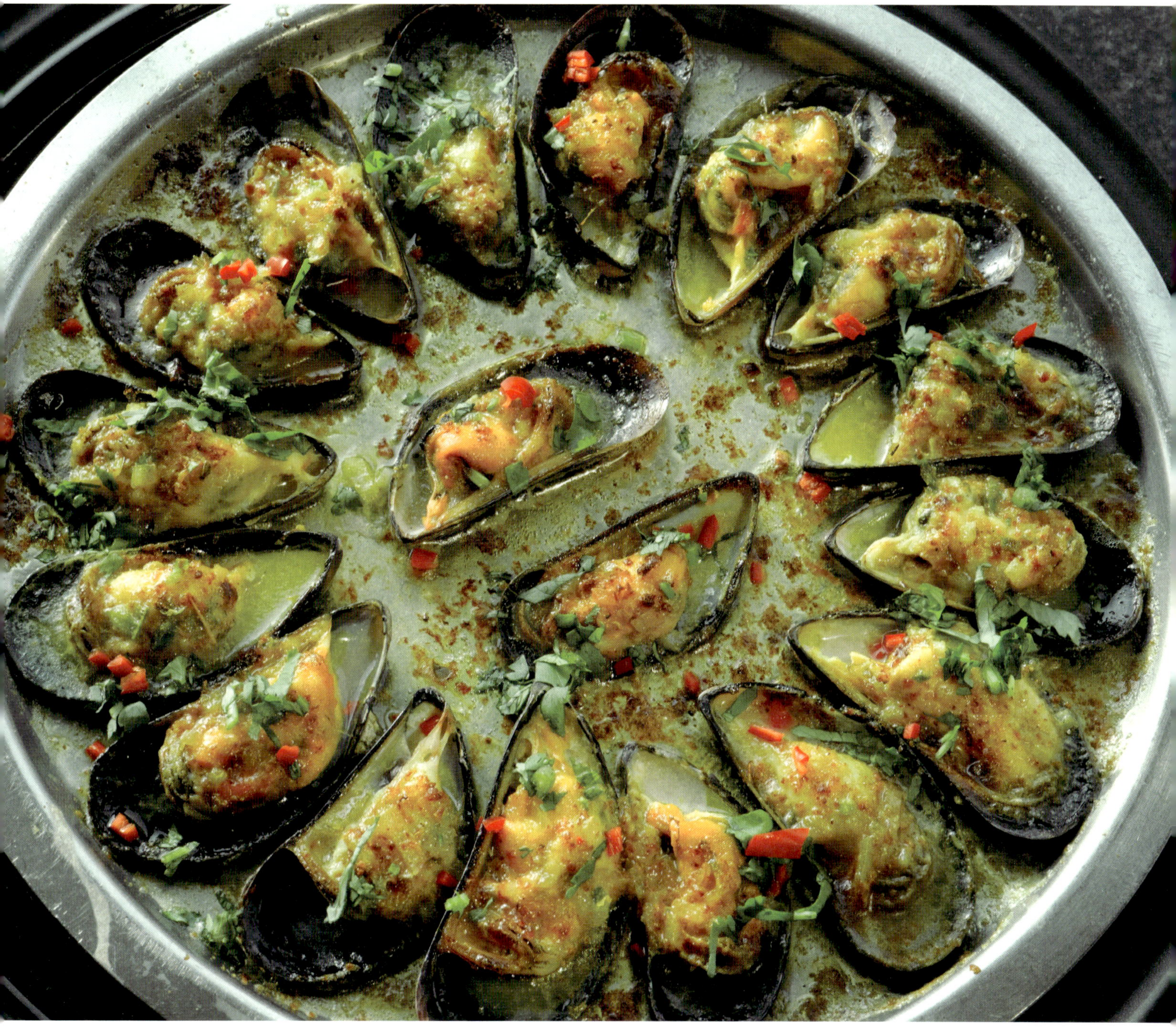

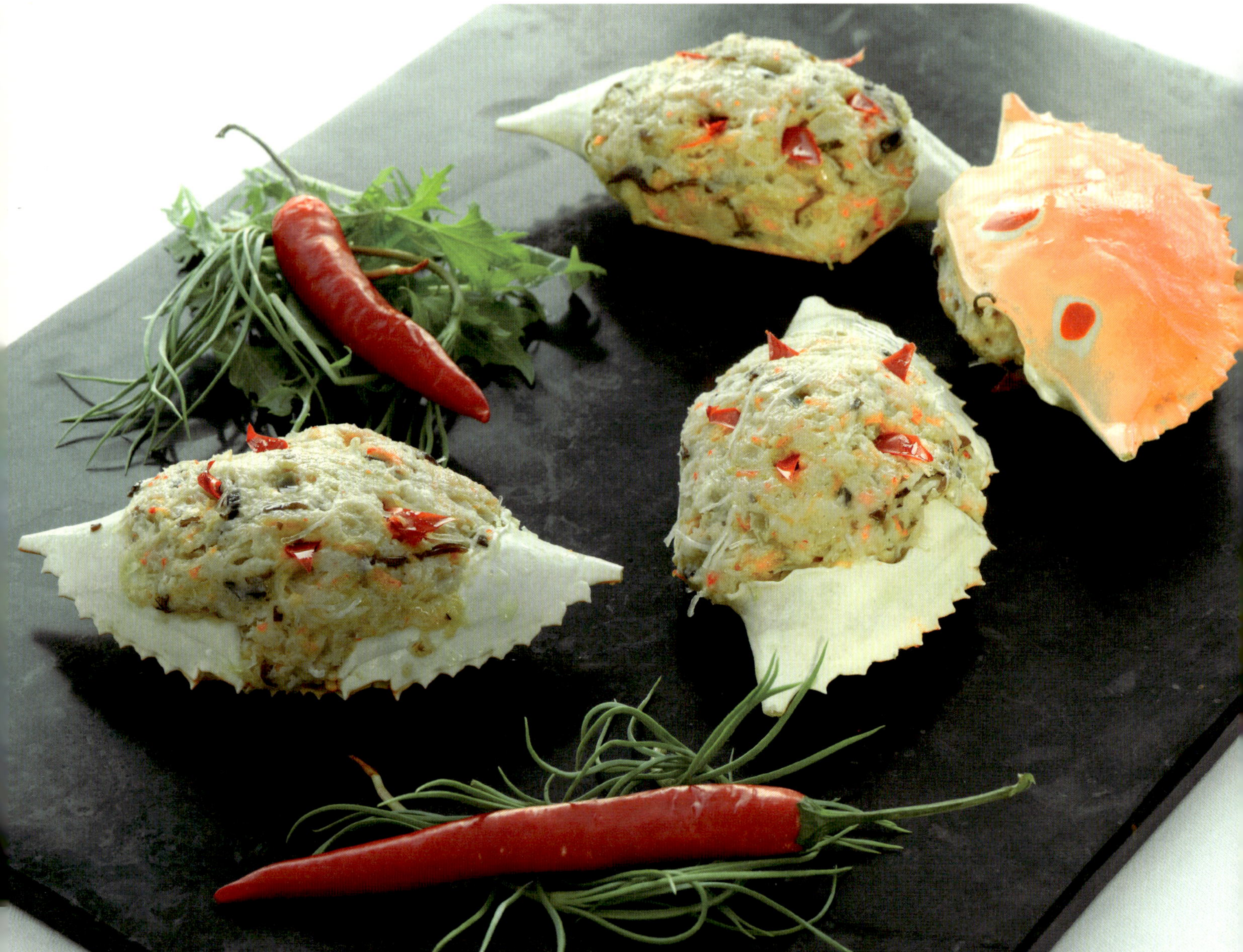

GOAN CRAB CAKE

CLASSIC

Alain: 'Chef Sinaj prepared this fantastic crab cake during our last visit. Delicious, but perhaps slightly too spicy for our tastes, so that the subtle taste of crab is lost. I have tried to merge the mild taste of crab and the essential spiciness into a tasty dish which is more suited to our taste buds.

FOR 4 PERSONS

50 g basmati rice, salt, 500 g crab meat (legs of king crab or tinned crab), 1 small green chilli pepper, 1 small red chilli pepper, 10 shallots, 2 cloves of garlic, oil, 1 tablespoon cummin seeds, ¼ bundle coriander, 1 tablespoon tikka masala, 50 g breadcrumbs, 1 egg

PREPARATION

Cook the basmati rice in salted water until done, drain and leave to cool.

Crack the king crab legs, take out the meat and chop it coarsely. Cut the peppers open lengthways and remove the seeds (or leave them in if you want to make the crab cake extra spicy). Chop them finely. Peel the shallots and the garlic and chop them finely.

Heat some oil in a pan and braise the shallot with the garlic and the chilli peppers. Add the cummin seeds to it.

Chop the coriander finely. Add the crab meat and the coriander to the shallots and add the tikka masala.

Finally add the rice, the breadcrumbs and the egg to the crab. Let it cool down for a moment and form the mixture into large balls. Flatten them a little.

Fry the crab cakes golden brown on both sides in a little oil.

TIP

Fill the cleaned crab shells with the mixture, coat it with a little beaten egg yolk and sprinkle with breadcrumbs. Leave it till done in a preheated oven at 180 °C and finally put it under a heated grill for a moment.

Small crab cakes are perfect as appetizers.
Serve the crab cakes with a chutney of mango.

OYSTERS IN A JELLY OF CUCUMBER WITH CHUTNEY

ARTISTIC

TIP

Don't cook the oysters too much; they will keep their salty taste that way. The fresh cucumber jelly and the rather warming chutney complement each other well in this dish.

FOR 4 PERSONS

24 oysters, Creuses II

CHUTNEY 1 cucumber, 2 cloves of garlic, 2 cm ginger root, 2 tablespoons honey, juice of 1 lime, 3 tablespoons sushi vinegar

JELLY 1 cucumber, 4 leaves of gelatine, 1 tablespoon sushi vinegar, juice of 1 lime, pepper, salt, ½ lemon

PREPARATION

Rinse the oysters clean in plenty of water and put them in a large pan at a high heat. Let them cook a little in their own sap until the oysters have opened up.
Take the oysters out of the pan and strain the cooking liquid. Take the half-done oysters out of their shells. Keep half of the shells for filling.
Peel the cucumber for the chutney and cut it into thick strips.
Peel the garlic and the ginger root. Chop them into a very fine brunoise.
Heat the oil in a small saucepan and add the lime juice and the sushi vinegar to it. Add the garlic and the ginger root and let it briefly caramelize without browning. Simmer the cucumber strips in this for the chutney.
Pulverize the cucumber for the jelly in the liquidizer.
Soak the gelatine in cold water. Heat 1 dl of the oyster liquid and dissolve the squeezed out gelatine in it. Mix the liquid with 2 dl cucumber juice, the sushi vinegar and the lime juice.
Season to taste with pepper and salt and leave it to cool.
Put a teaspoon of chutney in each oyster shell. Put an oyster on it and pour some of the cooled jelly over it. Leave it to set in the refrigerator.
Cut the zest of ½ lemon into fine strips.
Serve with an extra spoonful of chutney and a little lemon zest.

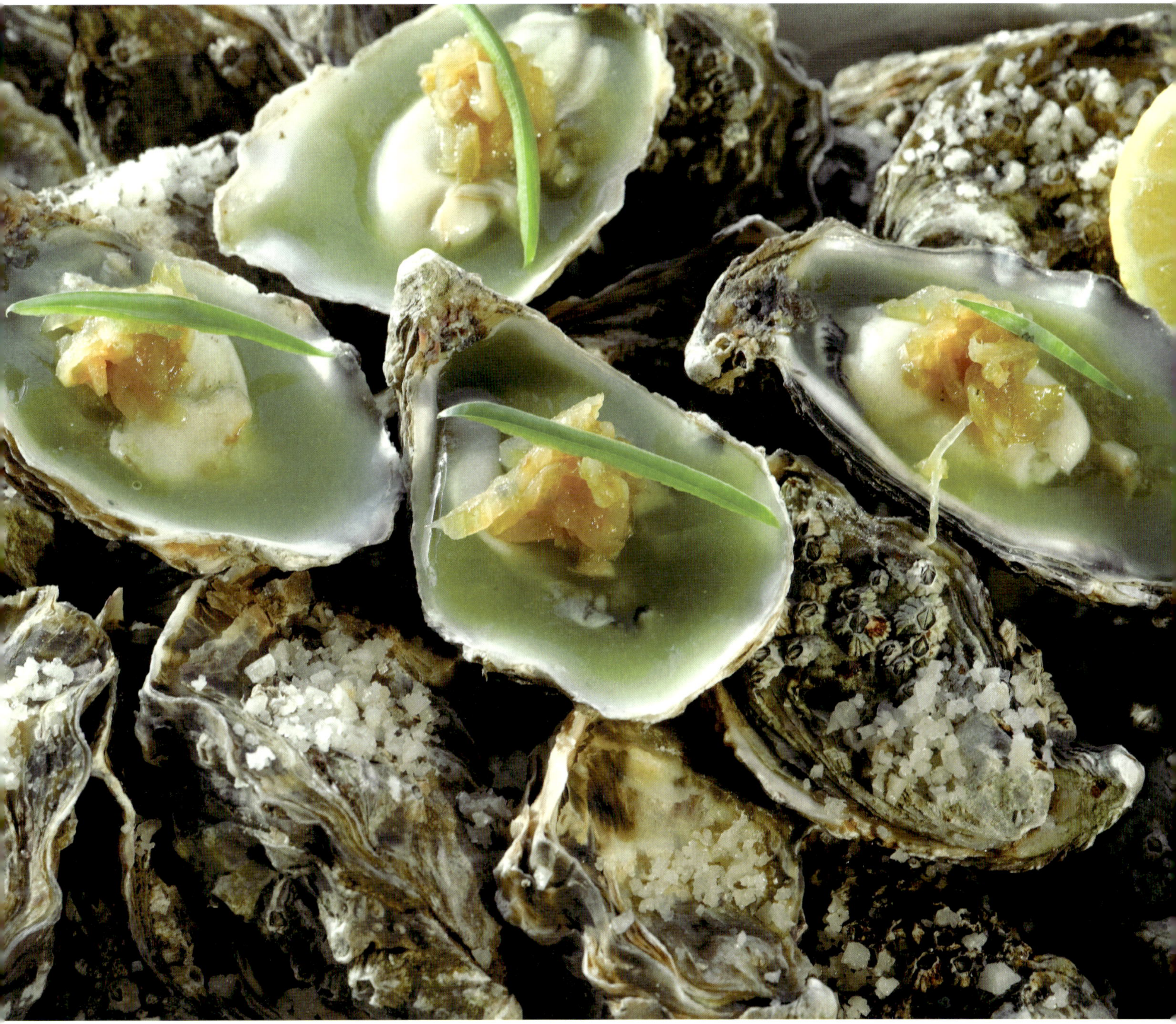

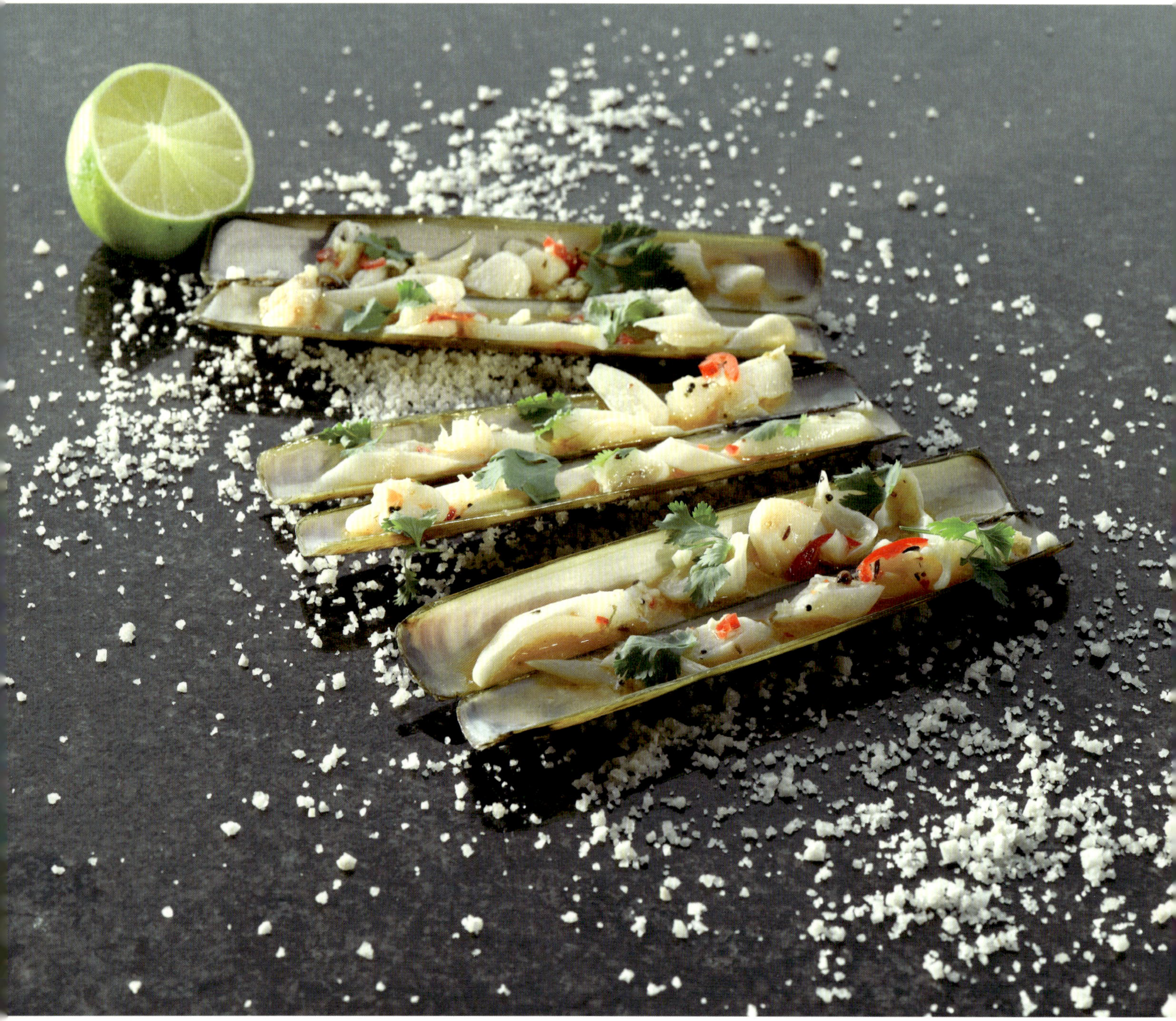

RAZOR SHELLS
IN LIME-AND-CORIANDER MARINADE — ARTISTIC

FOR 4 PERSONS

12 large razor shells, 1 teaspoon mustard seeds, 1 teaspoon cummin seeds, 1 teaspoon fennel seeds, 1 teaspoon coriander seeds, 5 tablespoons peanut oil, 3 cm ginger root, 1 clove of garlic, 1 small red chilli pepper, 2 spring onions, 10 chives, ⅛ bundle coriander, juice of 1 lime, a pinch of salt

PREPARATION

Rinse the razor shells thoroughly, put them in a pan and let them open up on high heat. Take the meat out of the shells and cut it into pieces. Set the cooking liquid aside. Fill the shells with the meat. Colour the mustard, cummin, fennel and coriander seeds in 2 tablespoons of oil until the aromas have been released. Let them cool and then crush them in a mortar.
Peel the ginger and the garlic. Cut the chilli pepper lengthways in two and remove the seeds. Grate the ginger, and chop the garlic and the chilli pepper fine.
Chop the spring onions, the chives and the coriander fine.
Mix the spices, the ginger, the garlic, the chilli, the spring onions, the chives and the coriander with 3 tablespoons of oil, a pinch of salt and the juice of the blanched razor shells.
Let the marinade cool down and then pour it over the shells.
Finish off with chopped green herbs.

TIP

Serve them with a glass of ice-cooled rasam (see Rasam on page 61)

BAINGAN OF AUBERGINES WITH TIGER PRAWNS AND TOMATO CHUTNEY

WESTERN

A baingan is a kind of curry dish or stew. By serving it in an aubergine with tiger prawns it becomes a dish in its own right.

FOR 4 PERSONS

BAINGAN 4 aubergines, 2 large ripe tomatoes, 2 onions, 3 cloves of garlic, 50 g cashew nuts, ¼ bundle coriander, 4 tablespoons coconut oil, 1 tablespoon garam masala, a pinch of chilli powder, 2 pinches of salt

CHUTNEY 4 large tomatoes, 1 large onion, 2 cm ginger root, 1 small red chilli pepper, 3 cloves of garlic, 80 g caster sugar, 1.2 dl white wine vinegar

TIGER PRAWNS 1 tomato, 3 shallots, 10 tablespoons coconut oil, 2 teaspoons vadouvan masala, juice of 1 lemon, 2 tablespoons salt, 20 tiger prawns, oil for frying, a few twigs of coriander

PREPARATION

Cut two aubergines and the tomatoes into cubes. Peel the onions and the garlic and cut them up fine. Grind the cashew nuts and the coriander to a powder.

Heat the oil and fry the onions with the garlic and the aubergine cubes. Add the tomatoes and season with garam masala and chilli powder. Add the powdered nuts and season to taste with salt.

Pour 2 dl water on the vegetables and let them simmer until nearly all liquid has disappeared.

Halve the two remaining aubergines and rub them with a little coconut oil and the crushed garlic. Leave them in an oven at 180 °C for 5 minutes till done. Scoop them out a little and fill them up with the baingan.

For the chutney peel the tomatoes and take the pips out. Peel the onion and chop it fine. Peel the ginger root and grate it. Cut the chilli pepper open lengthways and remove the seeds. Crush the garlic. Braise the tomatoes with the onion, the sugar, the ginger root, the vinegar, the chilli pepper and the garlic. Let it all simmer into a chutney for 20 minutes.

Peel the tomato, remove the pips and cut the flesh very fine. Peel the shallots and chop them fine. Mix them with the coconut oil and season with vadouvan masala, lemon juice and salt.

Peel the tiger prawns and remove the intestines. Rub them with the marinade and leave them to infuse for an hour. Fry the prawns in a little oil.

Serve the stuffed aubergines with the prawns, rice and tomato chutney and sprinkle some chopped coriander over it.

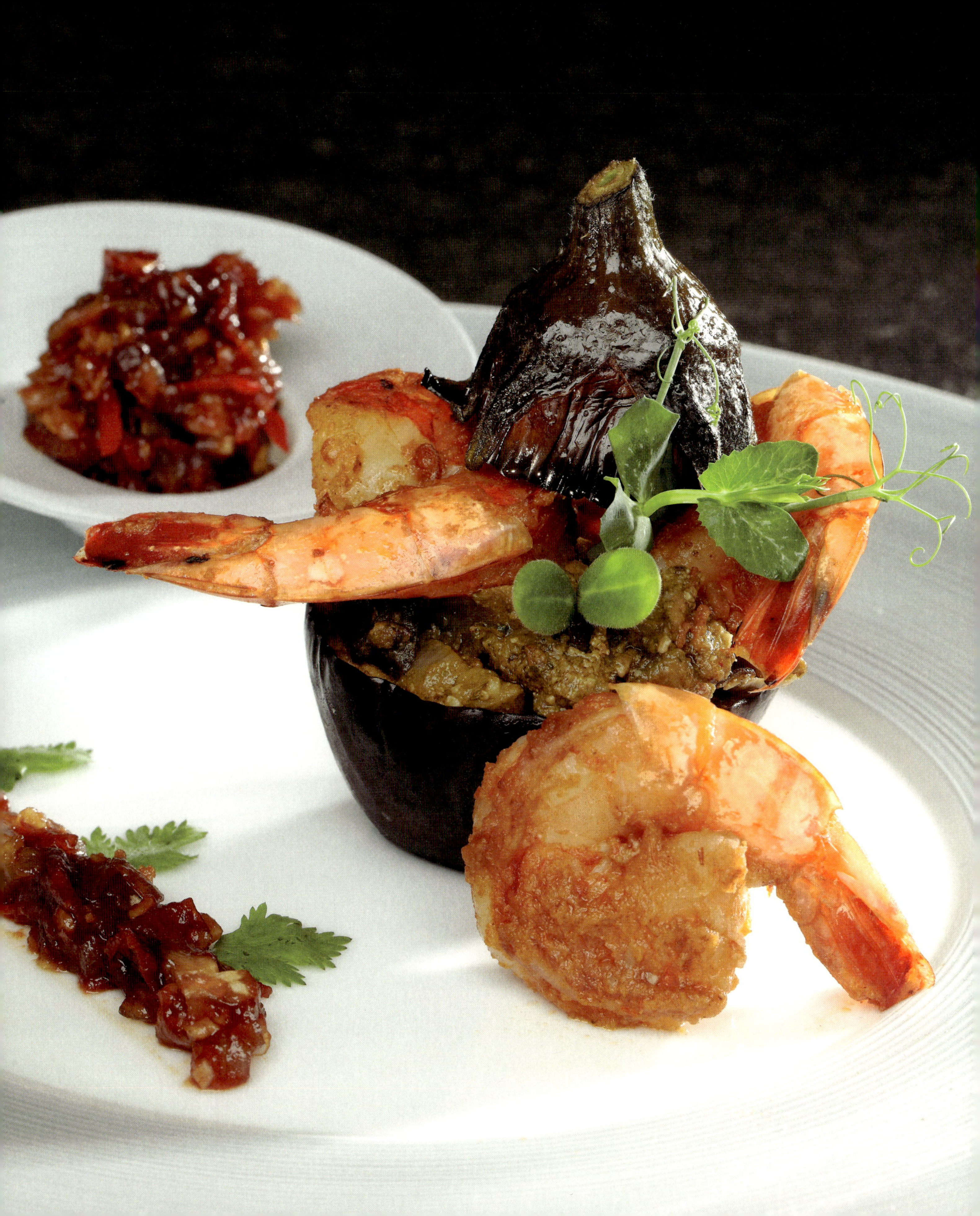

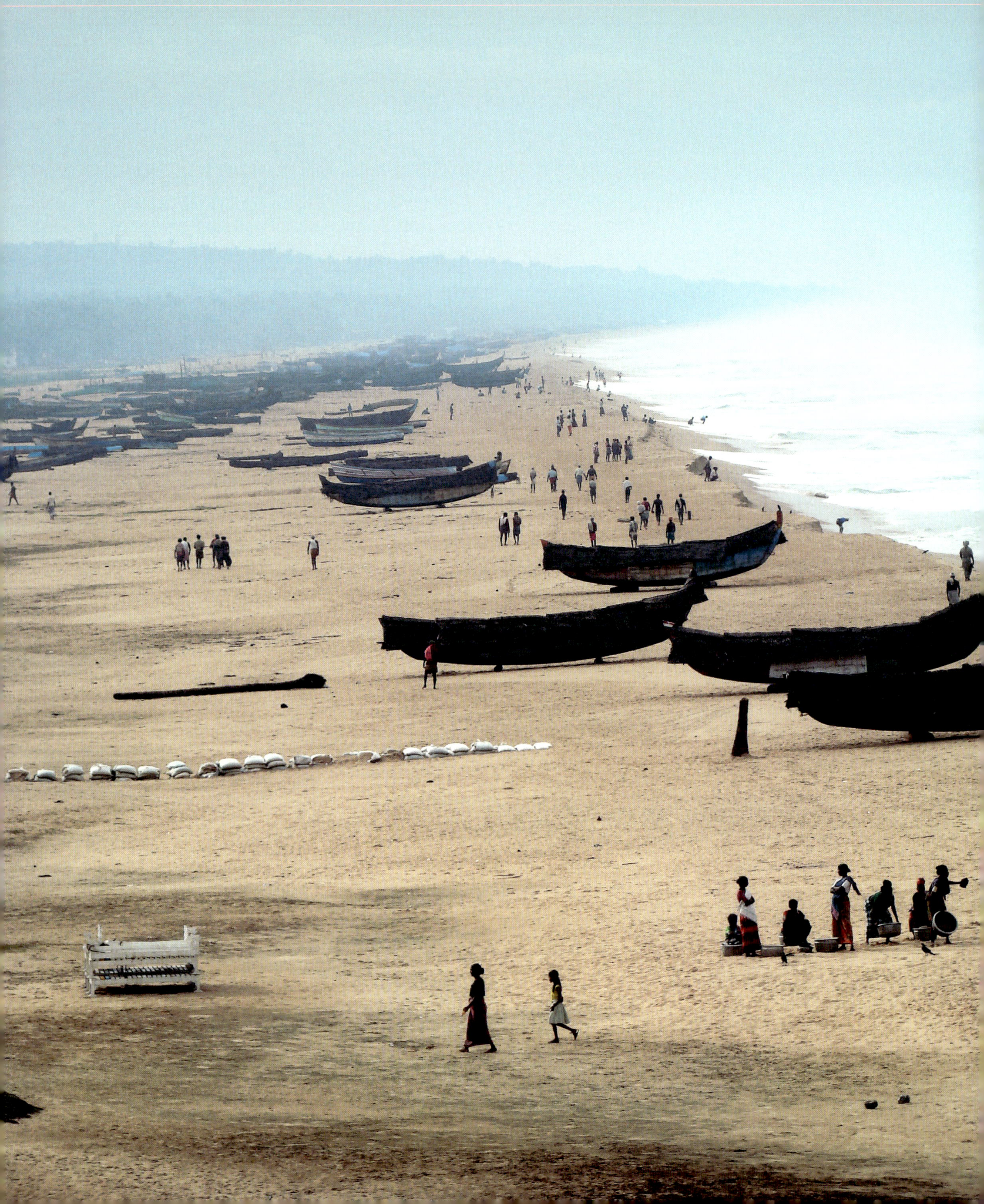

KERALA FISH

"I WILL EAT ANY FISH THAT DOES NOT BITE ME IN RETURN!"

A houseboat trip on the backwaters of Kerala is at the top of every tourist's wish list. The labyrinth of lakes, rivers and canals is a revelation, time and time again. The longest lake in India and the largest in Kerala, the Vembanad Lake in Allepey, looking like a still-life, welcomes every visitor. Only too willingly it offers its shallow waters in the service of the many tourist boats and the canoes of local fishermen.

In the shadow of the heavenly 'Purity Lake Resort', lives the 69-year-old fisherman N.K. Ramanan together with his wife, Bhavapsiya. In his spare time he takes tourists around on the lake. But what he still enjoys most is fishing, day-dreaming about his time at sea…

N.K.Ramanan: "Fishing is, as with so many people here, a family tradition. I followed in my father's footsteps when I was 22 years old. After a year's training, I soon went to sea on board a fishing boat. My son has embarked on a different course, he works in an office. All three of my daughters have married fishermen, so they remain closely linked with the fishing fraternity. The youngest is very successful in her studies and can count on a promising future. That fills my heart with great pride.

I have experience of fishing at sea as well as in the backwaters. The greatest difference is obviously that at sea it can sometimes be very rough. The lake here is almost always quiet. As far as the fish is concerned, it is particularly the size which is remarkable. On average four kilograms per fish in the lakes and quite quickly fifteen kilograms at sea. The most common sorts are swordfish, snappers, bream, mackerel, kingfish, trout and several kinds of prawns. From little ones which can be used in curries to the tiger prawns and jumbo prawns. I don't have any preference myself, as long as they are served well-spiced. I actually like any fish that does not bite me in return! (laughs)

It is possible that you find the same fish in both territories, but usually it is then a case of migrants. In the area between the sea and the backwaters there are dams that regulate the salt-water content and there are always some that slip through the holes in the net then. During the summer, from March to June, the salt content is at its highest in the lake and then the best fish can be found there.

In the backwaters fishing is mainly for freshwater mussels, small prawns and what we call 'Karimeen'. That is the only fish that lives in fresh water alone, and the Kerali really are mad about them! It is a flat, oval-shaped fish, it looks a little like a bream. We usually prepare them with a sauce, folded inside banana leaves, and call them 'Karimeen Pollichathu'. The thing about this fish is that it feeds on the waste of people.

In the backwaters overfishing is not an issue, there are plenty of fish around and motorized fishing boats are not allowed in. At sea there are also certain restrictions, For instance, during the breeding season in June and July the sea is a prohibited zone for the seagoing fishing fleet. Moreover, the local population eats mainly sardines and there are more than enough of them in the sea.

Most of the time we left before dawn had broken and only came back after sunset. There were some six of us on board: four fishermen, a captain and a mechanic. Unfortunately I had never been able to sail with my father, because when I started he was no longer able to do the hard labour. I ended my seafaring activities 27 years ago. Since then I have been taking out my own little boat with two men every day. In theory I could have retired nine years ago, but it's just in my blood. To look at the horizon without being able to sail towards it isn't something I would wish even my enemy to suffer. And all those adventures I would be missing...

I will never forget how one day, fifteen years ago, we were on our way back from a long day on the lake. We had just got to that little island over there when a heavy thunderstorm burst out. Our canoe capsized and all three of us landed in the water. I managed to get them back to the canoe and brought them safely home. I am still very proud of that and they are still grateful that I saved their lives. Or there was the time when I jumped into the sea to rescue some expensive floats. Everyone said I was mad, but I succeeded in bringing them back on board, after swimming around in the sea for ten minutes. My superior thanked me at length, although he considered it too big a risk. In those days I knew no fear. Now I am not quite so brave. But nothing, of course, can compare to the marvellous appearance of the fish themselves. A school of dolphins to accompany you, or the moment I was confronted by a kind of whale, as big as an elephant. Every day I still thank my Maker for that, that He showed me such a wonderful sight!"

Sam

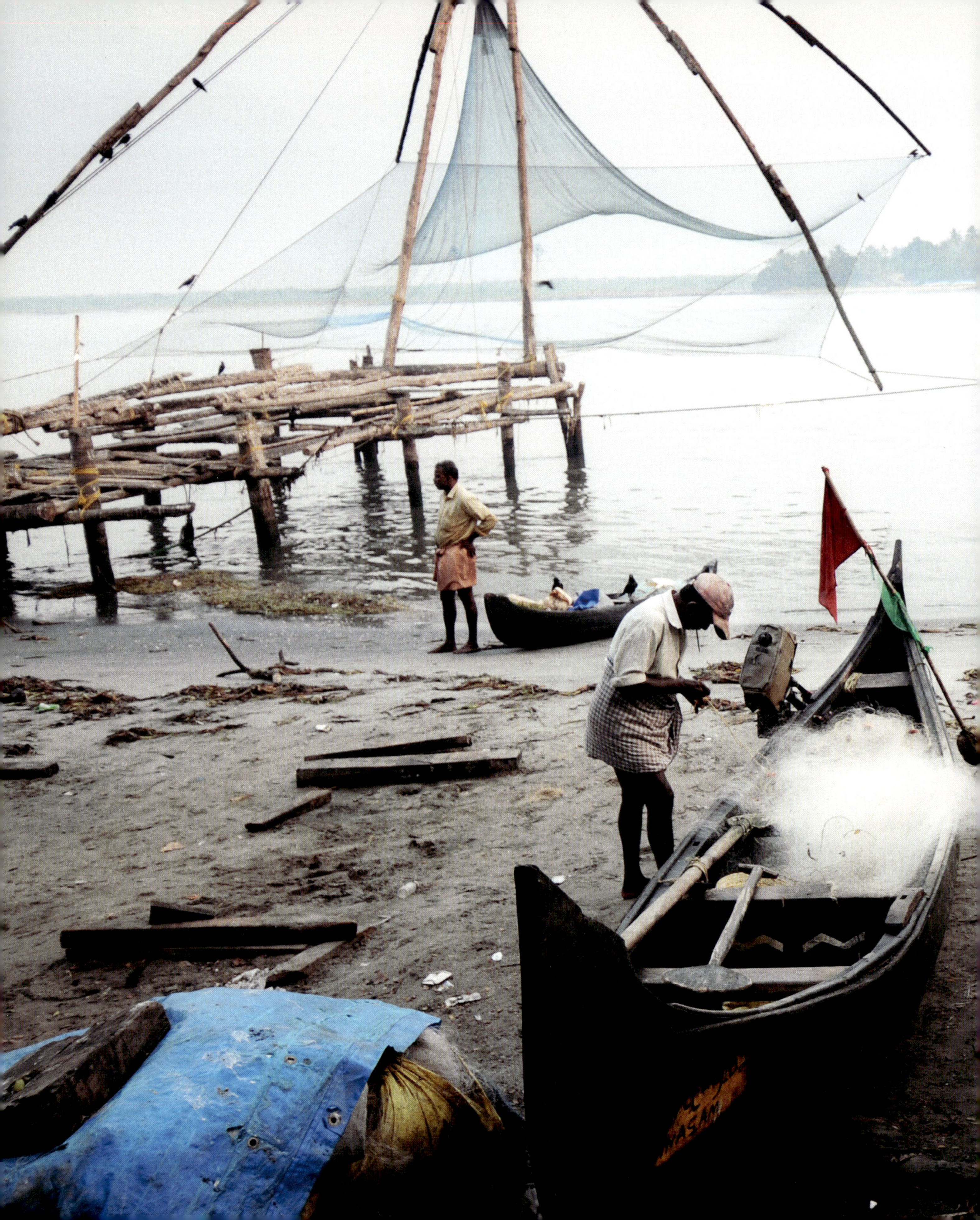

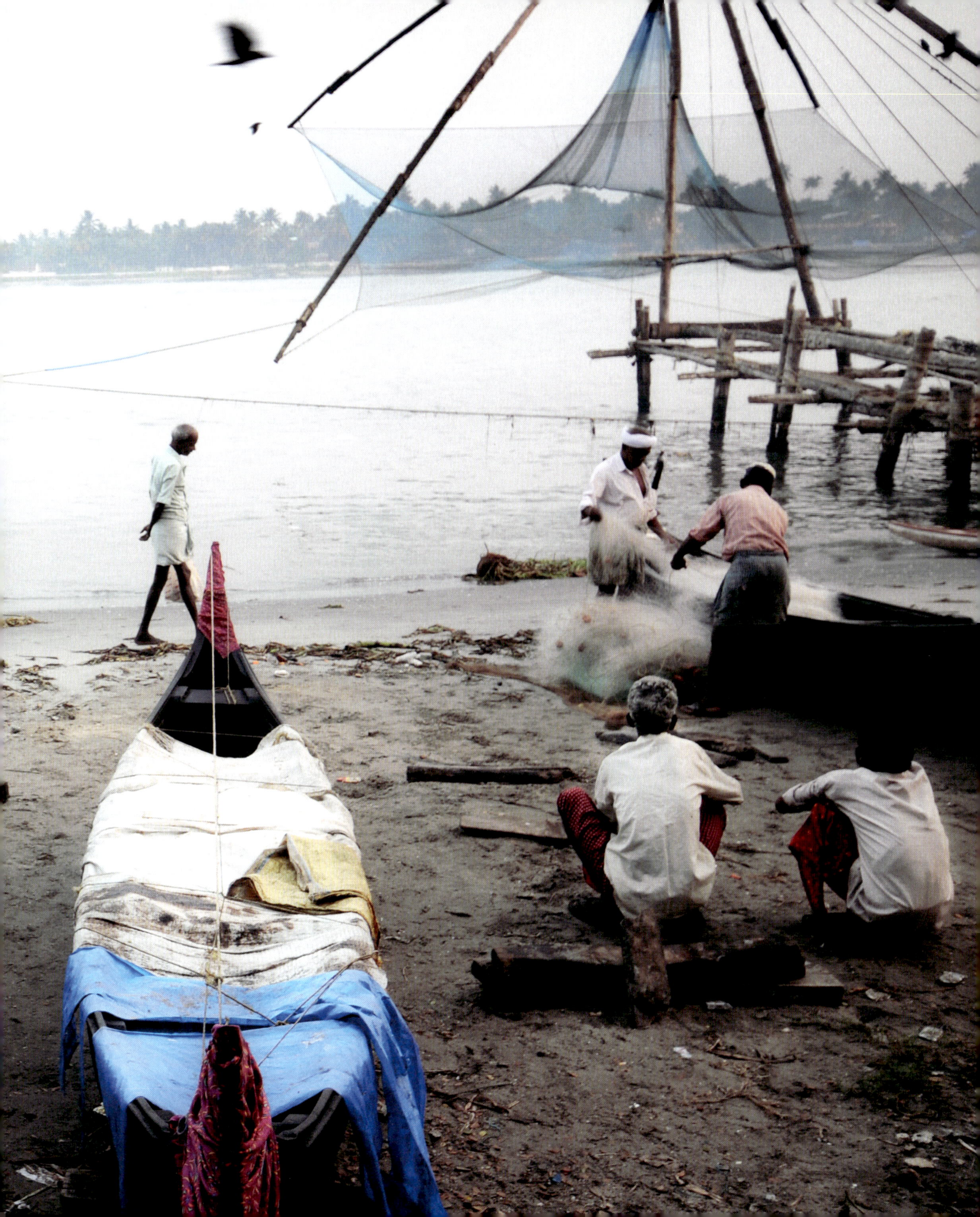

| TIP | # EEL RAS CHAWAL | INDIAN |

TIP

If you like coconut, you can add some coconut cream to the sauce and scatter a little freshly grated coconut over the eel.

EEL RAS CHAWAL

Alain: 'At a small eating booth near the temples of Trichy I tasted ras chawal, a green fish curry, for the first time. It was a very mild curry with fish, but one which in Tamil Nadu is also regularly prepared with chicken. The dish had a very subtle lemon taste and was moderately spiced by the use of small seedless green chilli peppers. While I thoroughly enjoyed my tasty meal, I began to remember how my late grandmother was able to make the best stewed eel in chervil sauce when eels were still gathered in bucketfuls from the canals. So I asked Biju to make an Indian version based on my eel recipe, with this dish as a result.'

FOR 4 PERSONS

1 kg eels, cleaned and cut into pieces, a few tablespoons flour, a pinch of vadouvan masala, butter, 4 shallots, 2 cloves of garlic, 1 small green chilli pepper, 3 dl fish stock, 3 stalks of lemongrass, 1 bundle parsley, 1 bundle coriander, 1 bundle basil, ½ bundle mint, ½ bundle lemon balm, 200 g spinach, 10 sorrel leaves, 1 bundle watercress, 5 green cardamom pods, peeled, salt, 1 tablespoon green curry paste, pepper, lime

PREPARATION

Clean the eel thoroughly and pat it dry.
Mix the flour with the vadouvan masala and dip the eel in it.
Fry the eel in a little butter.
Peel the shallots and the garlic and chop them fine. Cut the chilli pepper open lengthways and remove the seeds. Add the shallots, the garlic and the chilli pepper to the eel and deglaze with the fish stock. Flatten the lemongrass with a large knife and add it to the eel. Heat to just below boiling point for 20 minutes till done.
Clean the parsley, the coriander, the basil, the mint, the lemon grass, the spinach, the sorrel and the watercress and cook it with the cardamom pods for 5 minutes in salted water. Drain, cool at once in iced water. Mix everything in the blender with 1 dl water and the curry paste.
Add the green mixture to the eel and season to taste with pepper and salt. Serve with slices of lime and a few bits of green herbs.

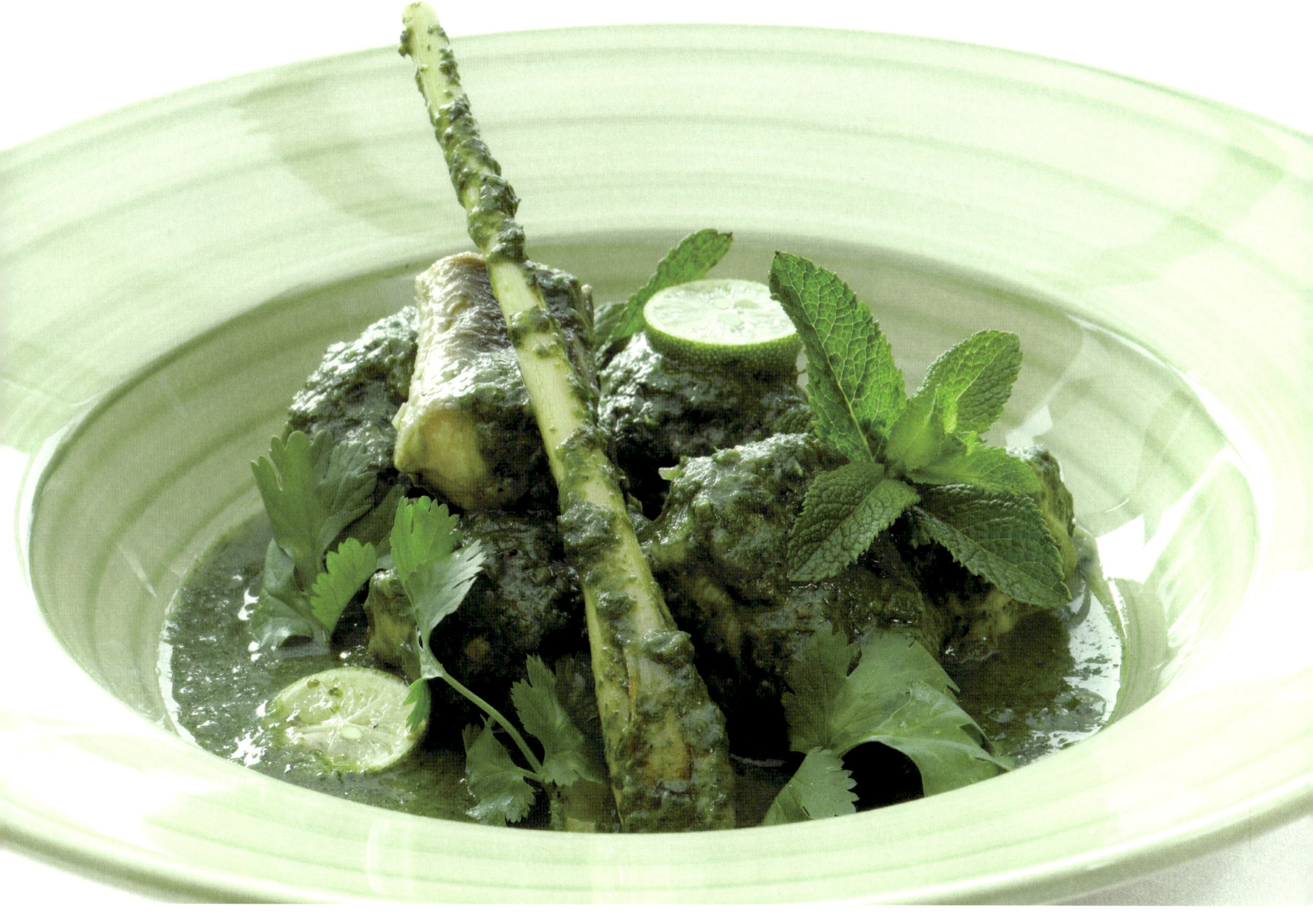

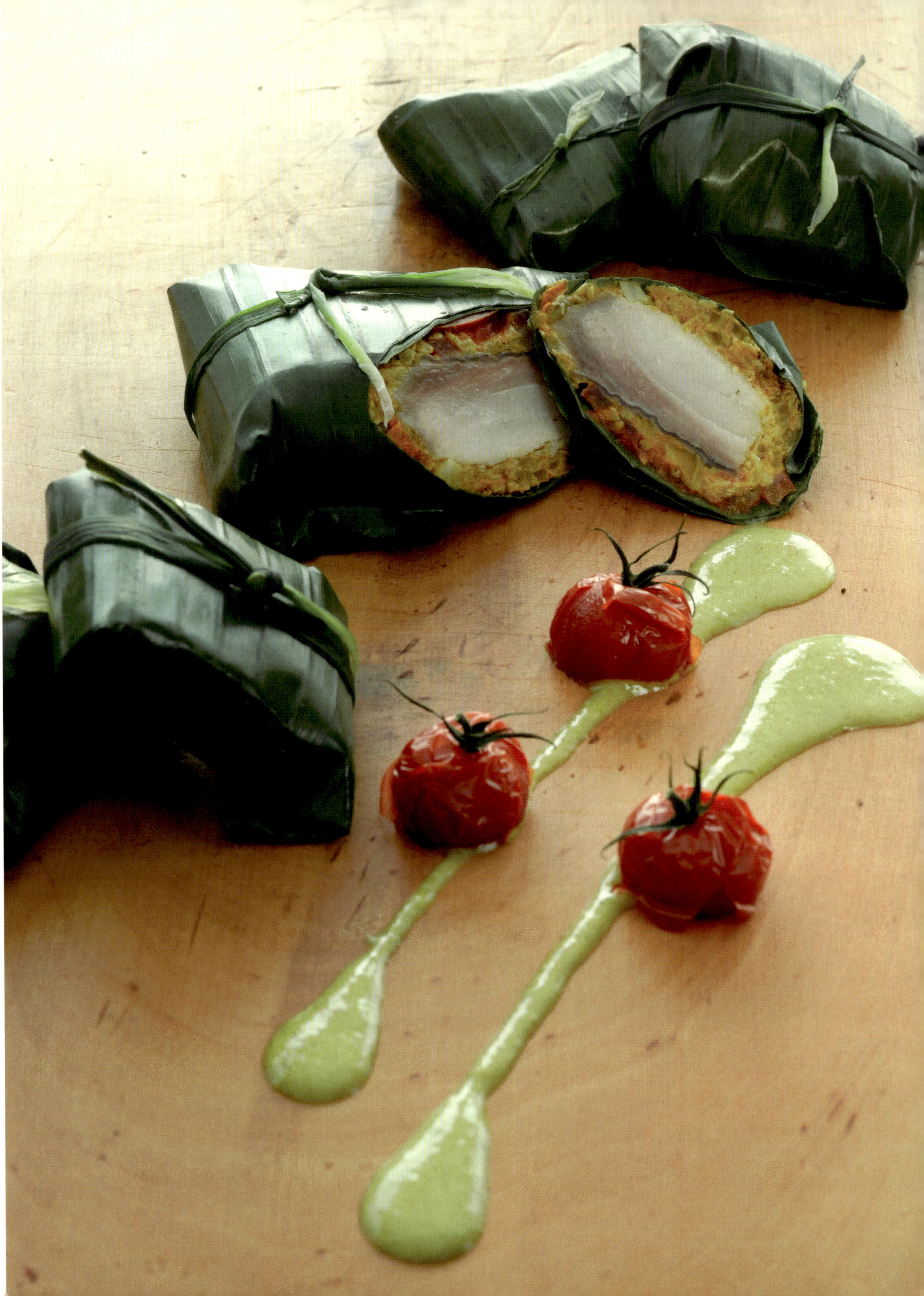

POLLICHATHU OF SWORDFISH   CLASSIC

Alain: 'In Privacy, the splendid charming hotel at the Vembanad Lake, we were treated to a boat trip on board the wonderful Discovery. For our lunch we were given pollichathu. The taste was quite amazing. A sublime combination of sweet, salt, sour and spice, wrapped in a papillote of a banana leaf. The perfect degree of readiness of the swordfish (because for this dish a solid kind of fish has to be selected) and the well-balanced tomato curry made this dish into a real experience.'

FOR 4 PERSONS

TOMATO CURRY, 3 teaspoons tamarind puree, 1 small red chilli pepper, 20 shallots, 2 tablespoons coconut oil, 25 mustard seeds, 2 cm ginger root, 4 cloves of garlic, a pinch of chilly, a pinch of turmeric, salt, a pinch of garam masala, 4 dl coconut milk, 6 tomatoes, 2 tablespoons of grated coconut

MARINATED FISH, 500 g swordfish fillet, a pinch of vadouvan masala, a pinch of turmeric, salt, 2 tablespoons coconut oil, juice of 2 limes

PAPILLOTE
1 large banana leaf, 2 tomatoes (type roma), oil for frying

PREPARATION

For the tomato curry let the tamarind puree soak in a cup of warm water.
Cut the chilli pepper lengthways, remove the seeds and chop it fine. Peel the shallots. Chop one half fine and cut the other half in slices.
Heat the coconut oil and crisp the mustard seeds. Peel the ginger and grate it.
Crush the cloves of garlic. Add the ginger and the garlic to the mustard seeds and then fry the shallots in it. Season with the chopped chilli, turmeric, salt and garam masala.
Add the tamarind water and the coconut milk to the shallots. Add the tomatoes which have been cut into pieces and leave it all to simmer for 20 minutes on a low heat.
Finally add the grated coconut to it.
Cut the fish into fillets of about 120 g and beat them flat so that they will not be too thick.
Make a little pap of the vadouvan masala, the turmeric, the salt, the coconut oil and the lime juice. Rub the fish fillets with this marinade.
Make the banana leaf supple by turning it quickly round in a pan with a non-stick coating or over a gas flame. Spoon a little tomato curry in the middle of the leaf. Next put a fish fillet on it and another little layer of curry.
Cut the roma tomatoes into thin slices and put them overlapping each other on the fish with the curry. Fold the banana leaf shut and tie it with some kitchen string or raffia.
Bake the papillote for about 10 minutes in a little oil in a pan with non-stick coating. Turn it over regularly.

MOLEE FISH CURRY OF MACKEREL CLASSIC

Molee is a refined fish stew which is particularly popular in Southern India and on the west coast of India. The mackerel can be replaced by rolls of sole or monkfish fillet. Moreover, almost all sea food tastes well with it.

FOR 4 PERSONS

4 mackerel fillets of 120 g, a pinch of turmeric, salt, 3 tablespoons of coconut oil, 25 mustard seeds, 1 large onion, 3 cm ginger root, 4 green chilli peppers, 4 cloves garlic, 2 large tomatoes, 2.5 dl fish stock, juice of 1 lime, 2.5 dl coconut cream, 1 tablespoon tomato puree, 3 cardamom pods, 10 curry leaves

PREPARATION

Rinse the mackerel fillets and pat them dry. Rub them with turmeric and salt and put them in the refrigerator for 15 minutes.
Heat a little coconut oil in a pan and fry the mackerel fillets on both sides.
Take them out of the pan, add a little extra oil and crisp the mustard seeds.
Peel the onion and cut it into rings. Peel the ginger root and cut it into long strips.
Cut the chilli peppers lengthways and remove the seeds. Peel the garlic.
Chop the chilli and the garlic finely.
Fry the onion, the ginger, the garlic and the chilli in the oil. Cut the tomatoes into thick slices and add them to the pan.
Deglaze with fish stock, lime juice and coconut cream and season to taste with cloves, cardamom and curry leaves.
Put the fish on the molee curry and leave it for another 3 minutes till done.
Take the whole spices out of the pan and serve the curry at once.

VARIANT

The molee from this recipe is particularly tasty, but for guests we thought up a contemporary fusion version while keeping its characteristics and taste. With this presentation we come close to the philosophy of Ranjit Mathrani, chairman of the event Masala World in London: 'Indian chefs are craftsmen; Belgian chefs are artists. Combine those two and you will have perfect fusion cuisine.'

Strain the molee curry and set aside the liquid. Mix the pulp with a puree of three boiled potatoes.
Allow the liquid to reduce to the desired thickness for the sauce.
Cut a tomato into thin slices and put them in a circle on a plate. Put a little puree in the centre, put the cooked mackerel fillet on it and spoon some sauce around it.
Finish off with sea fennel and young shoots.

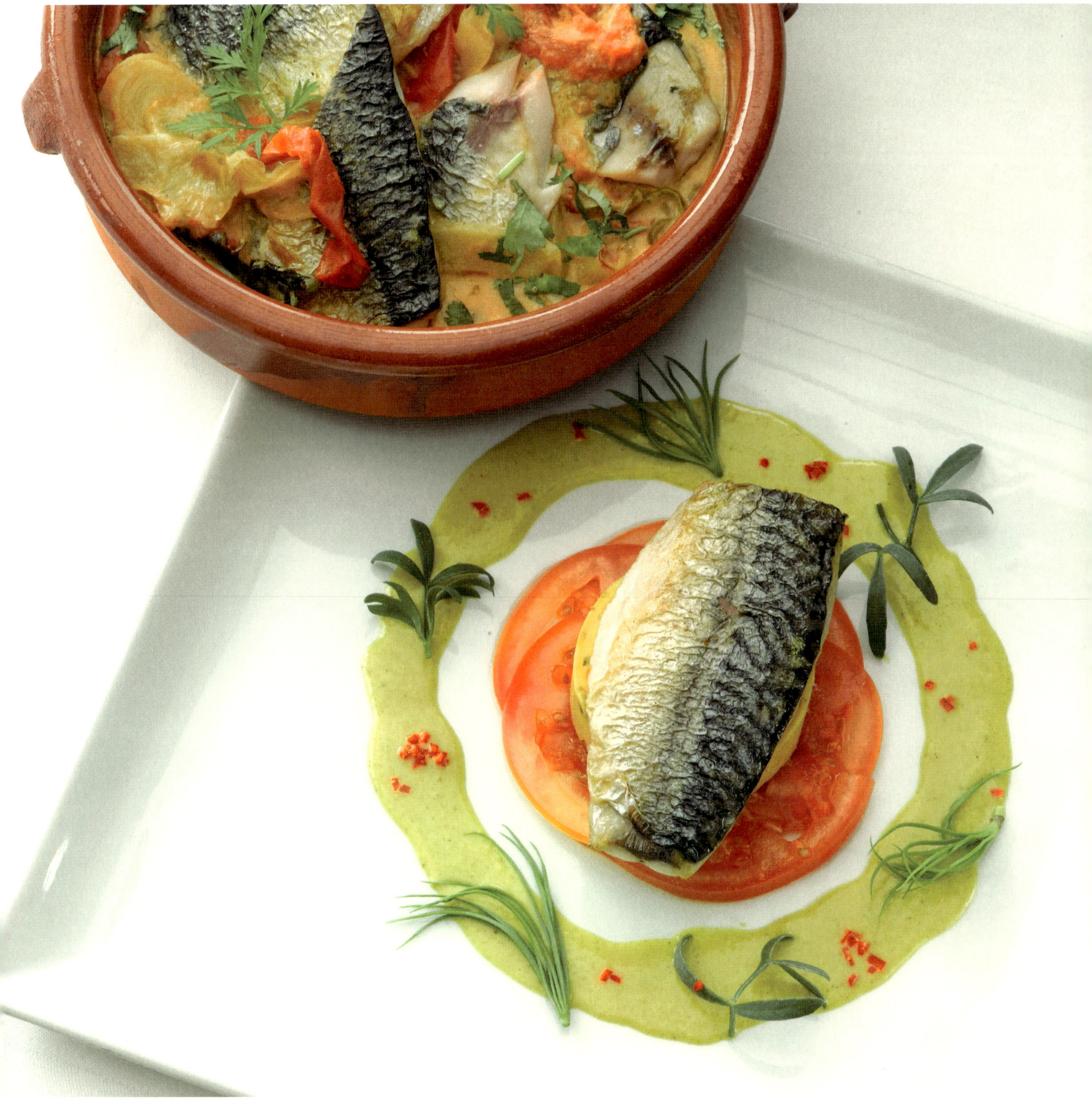

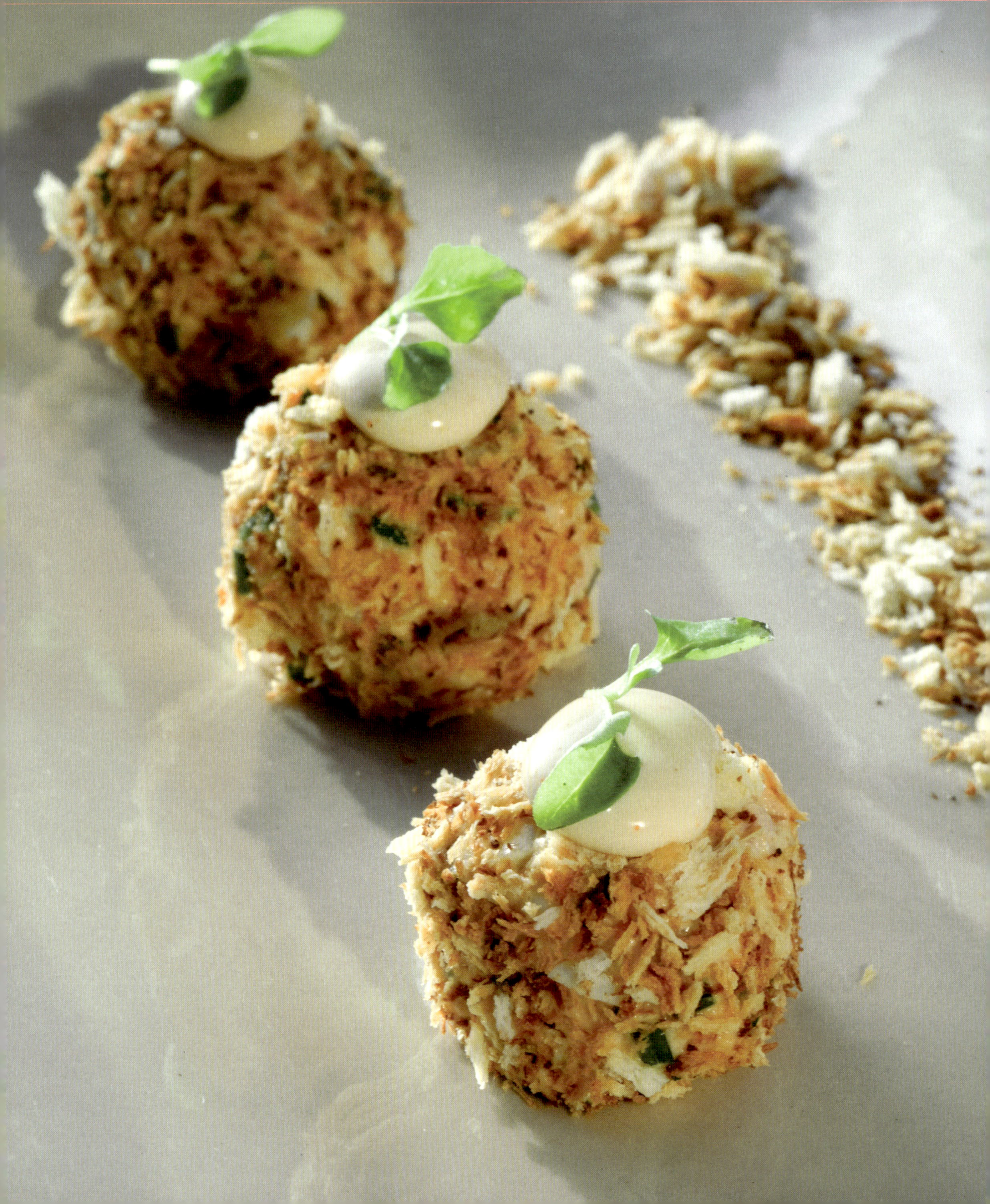

SMALL BALLS OF TUNA RILETTE WITH A MAYONNAISE OF VADOUVAN MASALA

WESTERN

FOR 4 PERSONS

200 g tuna fillet, 2.5 dl water, 2.5 dl dry white wine, 1 tablespoon sushi vinegar, pepper, salt, 2 pinches of sambhar masala, 2 tablespoons mayonnaise, 2 tablespoons cream, 1 lime, 1/4 bundle chives

MAYONNAISE *2 dl vegetable stock, 2 tablespoons vadouvan masala, 2 dl sushi vinegar, 1 dl old vintage sherry vinegar, 2.5 dl grape seed oil, 1 leaf gelatine*

CRUMBLE *100 g stale white bread, 50 g flaked almonds, a pinch sambhar masala, a pinch turmeric, 1/4 bundle chives*

PREPARATION

For the rillettes cut the tuna fillet into cubes. Bring the water with the wine and the vinegar to the boil and season with pepper, salt and sambhar masala. Poach the tuna cubes for 2 minutes and put them into a bowl. Allow them to drain and loosen the meat with a fork. Stir the mayonnaise, the cream, a few drops of lime juice and the finely cut chives into a smooth sauce. Mix the sauce under the tuna. Put the rilettes in the refrigerator.

For the vadouvan mayonnaise reduce the vegetable stock with the vadouvan masala by half the quantity. Add the sushi vinegar, the sherry vinegar and the grape seed oil.

Soak the gelatine, squeeze the liquid out well and mix the gelatine with the stock. Leave it to cool.

For the crumble rub the bread to a coarse crumb.

Roast the almonds under the grill and halfway through the process of browning add the bread crumbs. Season with sambhar masala and turmeric.

Cut the chives finely and mix them with the rest of the crumble. Shape the tuna into small balls and roll them through the crumble. Put a little vadouvan mayonnaise and a tuft of green herbs on each little ball.

TIP

The little balls stay nicely crisp if you roll them through the crumble only just before serving.

If desired, add some finely cut smoked halibut to the rillettes for a more subtle taste.

AVIAL OF ROOT VEGETABLES
WITH SQUID AND SALMON

WESTERN

An avial is a traditional stew of (root) vegetables, yoghurt and coconut, brought to taste with curry leaves and coconut oil. In India this is a striktly vegetarian preparation, but for this recipe we have added squid and salmon to it.

FOR 4 PERSONS

200 g carrots, 200 g sweet potatoes, 200 g French beans,
5 cm ginger root, 2 small green chilli peppers, 50 g coconut, grated,
2 tablespoons cummin seed, roasted, 1 tablespoon vadouvan masala,
4 dl full-cream (Greek) yoghurt, salt, turmeric, 10 curry leaves,
3 tablespoons coconut oil, 4 medium squid arms,
4 salmon medallions each 120 g

PREPARATION

Peel the carrots and the sweet potatoes and cut them into sticks 3 cm long and 0.5 cm wide. Cut the French beans to a length of 3 cm. Peel the ginger root and grate it. Chop the chilli pepper fine and mix it in the blender with the grated coconut and the ginger. Add 1 tablespoon cummin seed, the vadouvan masala and the yoghurt to this.
Bring 1 litre water with salt and a pinch of turmeric to the boil. Boil the carrots for 5 minutes and then add the French beans and the sweet potato. Cook the vegetables *al dente*.
Pour half the cooking liquid away and add the spiced yoghurt mix to the rest. Leave to simmer for 2 minutes.
Fry the curry leaves in a little coconut oil and put them with the vegetables.
Clean the squid and cut it into thick rings. Heat the oil with a pinch of cummin seed and a pinch of turmeric. Fry the squid rings a golden yellow, deglaze them with a little water and slowly let them cook till done. Remove the squid from the liquid and put it with the avial. Season the salmon with a little vadouvan masala and roasted cummin seed. Sear it crisp in hot oil and leave to simmer on a low heat till done. Serve the avial with the salmon.

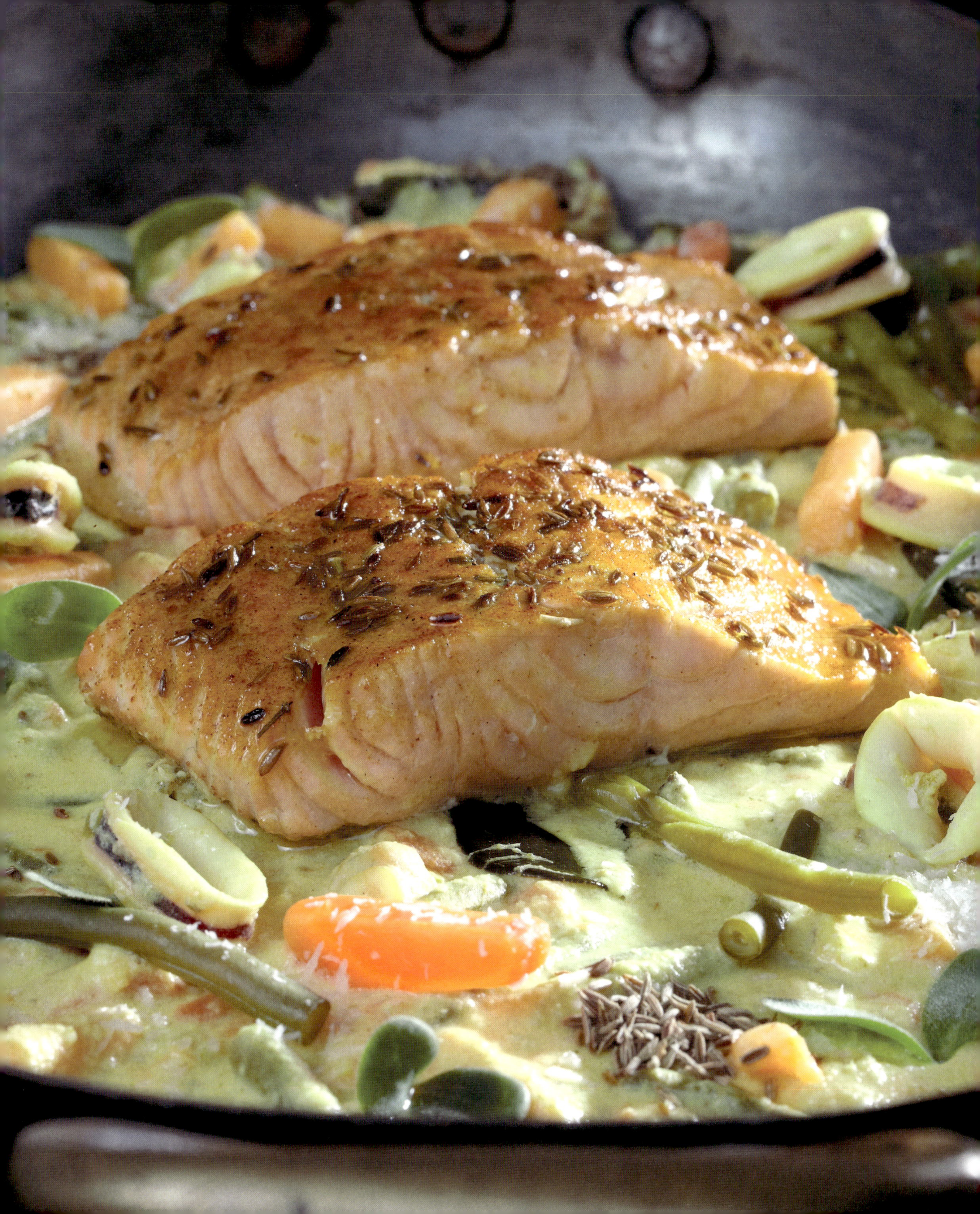

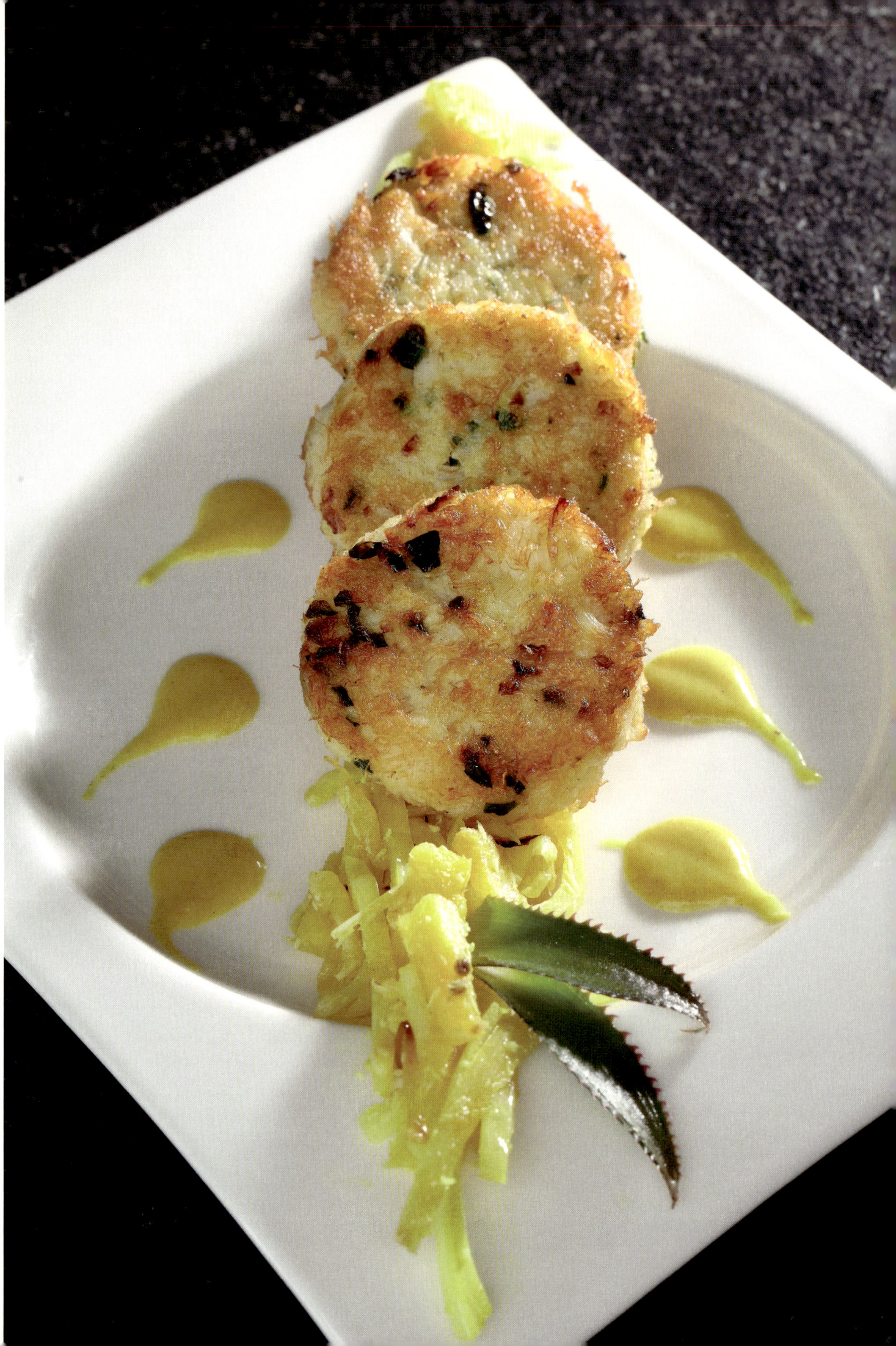

THORAN OF PINEAPPLE AND WHITE CABBAGE WITH FISHBURGERS FROM COCHIN

WESTERN

At Cochin station fishburgers are served as a light midday snack or tiffin. They are a tasty variant on the vadai which is made of lentils. Here two classical recipes are combined: the tasty burgers with a dry thoran of vegetables.

FOR 4 PERSONS

THORAN, 1/4 white cabbage, 1 large onion, ½ fresh and not too ripe pineapple, 1 small green chilli pepper, oil, 20 mustard seeds, a pinch of turmeric, 20 g coconut, grated – **FISHBURGERS,** 750 g white fish fillet, juice of 1 lime, 1 egg, pepper, salt, 50 g chickpea flour (or besan), 3 small green chilli peppers, 1 large onion, 4 tablespoons breadcrumbs, oil for frying – **SAUCE,** 2 dl fish stock, pepper, salt, a pinch of vadouvan masala, 100 g salted butter

PREPARATION

Chop the cabbage fine and cut the onion in thin strips. Peel the pineapple and cut the flesh in sticks. Cut the chilli pepper open lengthways, remove the seeds and chop it finely.

Heat the oil in a pan with non-stick coating and crisp the mustard seeds. Add the onion, the cabbage, the chilli peppers and the pineapple and season with turmeric. Add the grated coconut.

For the burgers put the fish in a ovenproof dish and pour a little water and lime juice over it. Put the dish in a preheated oven at 180 °C for 15 minutes.

Beat the egg loose with pepper and salt. Sieve the chickpea flour into it and stir it to a smooth batter.

Cut the chilli peppers open, remove the seeds and chop the peppers fine. Peel the onion and cut it fine.

Remove the fish from the liquid, pull it apart with a fork and mix it with the chilli peppers, the onion and the breadcrumbs. Add the batter to the fish and stir it all well. Form 8 burgers and fry them in oil on both sides to a golden brown.

For the sauce bring the fish stock tot the boil. Season with pepper, salt, and vadouvan masala. Remove from the heat and beat in the ice-cold pieces of butter.

ALAIN VANDEN ABEELE

Alain has been chef and manager of Catering Events Rustenburg in Bruges for twenty years. He is a single-minded and inquiring man, always looking for pioneering challenges. He was captivated by India, a country which in the last few years he has learnt to get to know well. His interest in the traditions and local customs obviously also included culinary matters. Alain took up the challenge to combine Indian elements with traditional dishes from his own country.

BIJU VARGHESE

Biju has for years been the executive chef of Malabar House in Cochin, Southern India. He is an expert at the traditional Indian dishes, a young chef with a passion for spices and products of his native soil. Yet he also manages to bridge the gap between the Indian, Keralan and Western cuisine. It made his encounter with Alain even more interesting for him.

CHRISTOPHE LAMBERT

Christophe has been working since 1992 as a freelance journalist and photographer. He writes articles for various magazines. The field of his activities is mainly concentrated on Asia and more specifically on India. Since 1998 he has published several art books through Lannoo Publishers. In 1998 he founded, together with some Indian partners, a humanitarian project in Uthani, Tamil Nadu, Southern India. In *Masala* his short descriptions of the local atmosphere and his colourful photographs introduce the reader to the scene in between the recipes.

SAM PARET

Sam graduated as a journalist and has worked with Christophe since 2002. He has been one of the driving forces of the project in Uthani and co-founder of the non-profit organization Vanakam vzw. In the space of ten years the project has grown into a orphanage from which some hundred girls find their way to school every day, and to a hospital which offers care to people from some twenty villages. *Masala* is Sam's third book with Lannoo Publishers. With fitting explanatory texts he has added useful background information on Southern India for the reader.

MICHÈLE FRANCKEN

Michèle Francken represents the third generation of Francken photographers in Ghent. She shares a studio in Sint-Martens-Latem with her son. She specializes in photographs on lifestyle and fashion. Michèle also exhibits her work regularly and has won several prizes. *Masala* was a wonderful challenge for her as the Indian cuisine is well-known for its explosion of colours.

STEVEN THEUNIS

Steven manages the design bureau Armée de Verre. He is a graphic designer specialised in books and packaging for cd and dvd and has worked for years for various publishers, among them Lannoo Publishers. This is how he met Christophe Lambert and Sam Paret. *Masala* is their fifth book together.

OLIVIER MONBAILLIU

Olivier is chef and owner of Restaurant La Tache in Bruges. Olivier's culinary skills clearly show a penchant for the French and Mediterranean cuisine. The aromatic, spicy-sweet mix of our masalas opened up an entirely new world of unknown aromas and tastes for him. In the future they will also spice up the La Tache cuisine.

JONAS VANDEN ABEELE

Jonas has recently graduated from the hotel school Ter Duinen in Koksijde. As Alain's son he grew up with cooking, testing and tasting from a very young age. He has seen how the Indian aromas have gradually wafted through the Rustenburg kitchens and how they coloured the catering dishes. Just like his father, Jonas became fascinated by the Indian cuisine. Hence he was pleased to take on the task of testing most of the recipes in this book thoroughly before they were given a place in it.

**TXUKU IRIARTE
& JOERG DRECHSEL**

Txuku and Joerg have succeeded in just over a decade in opening a number of stylish resorts, where in a unique environment guests can enjoy the breathtaking beauty of Kerala. They started with Malabar House in Cochin. Now they have also Serenity in the hills, Purity and Privacy on Vembanad Lake, Trinity in Cochin. The whole group bears the quality label of Relais & Châteaux. The Malabar Group and its chefs have also been present at the cradle of the book *Masala*.

SPICES BOARD INDIA

Spices Board India is the most important authority for herbs and spices in India and is based in Cochin. Messrs Thampi and Kurian made it possible for us to get a better insight into the world of masalas. Their expertise and their contribution to this book have been extremely valuable.

MANY THANKS TO OUR SPONSORS

VANAKAM FUND

4CCONSULTING · VAL SAINT LAMBERT · Allied · JET AIRWAYS · EXCELEASE · Ab · vlassenroot Group

SPECIAL PARTNERS

Rustenburg · LA TÂCHE · THE CINNAMON CLUB · Malabar escapes · RELAIS & CHÂTEAUX · hotelschool koksijde 'TER DUINEN'

CULINARY PARTNERS

Unilever · unizo VERSTERKT ONDERNEMERS · WEBA · BEERNAERT · NOVOTEL

WWW.LANNOO.COM

Register your name on our website and we will regularly send you
our newsletter with information on new books
and interesting, exclusive offers.

TEXT Alain Vanden Abeele, Christophe Lambert, Sam Paret
RECIPES Alain Vanden Abeele
TRANSLATION Alastair & Cora Weir
PHOTOGRAPHY Christophe Lambert, Michèle Francken
COVER PHOTOGRAPH Christophe Lambert
LAYOUT Steven Theunis & Olu Vandenbussche, www.armeedeverre.be
PROJECT COORDINATION Bram De Vos & Elsie Fernagut, Lannoo Publishers nv

If you have any comments or questions you can contact our editors:
redactielifestyle@lannoo.com

© Lannoo Publishers, Tielt, 2011
D/2011/45/333 – NUR 440
ISBN 978 90 209 9824 5

All rights reserved. No part of this publication may be reproduced,
stored in an automated database and/or be published in any form,
be it electronic, mechanic or in any other way, without the prior
written permission of the publisher.

Vanakam

The net proceeds of the book *Masala* will go to the non-profitmaking organization Vanakam. For more information go to www.vanakam.be